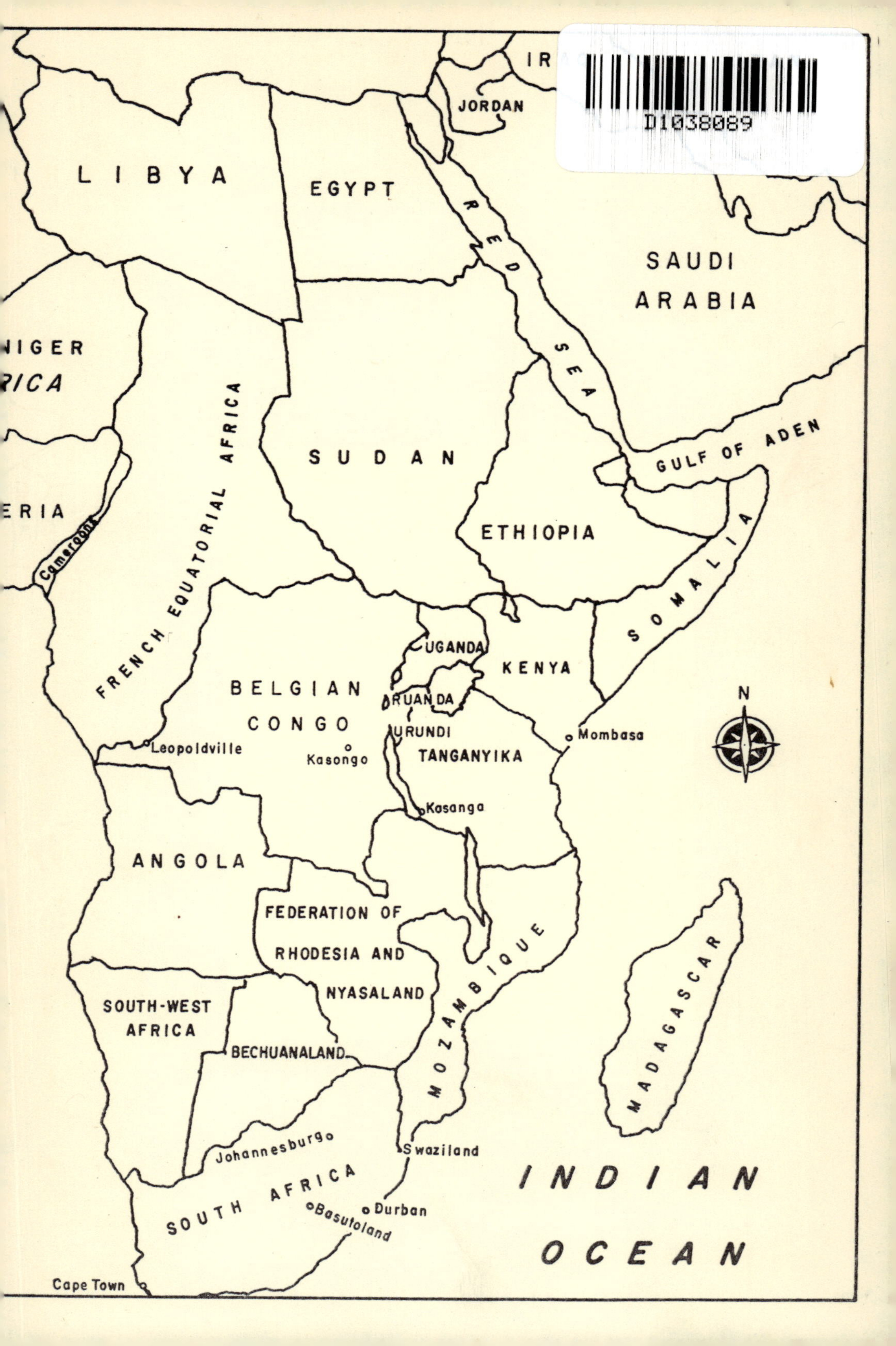

LIBYA
EGYPT
JORDAN
RED SEA
SAUDI ARABIA
SUDAN
GULF OF ADEN
ETHIOPIA
FRENCH EQUATORIAL AFRICA
Cameroons
SOMALIA
UGANDA
KENYA
BELGIAN CONGO
RUANDA
URUNDI
N
Mombasa
Leopoldville
Kasongo
TANGANYIKA
Kasanga
ANGOLA
FEDERATION OF
RHODESIA AND
NYASALAND
MOZAMBIQUE
MADAGASCAR
SOUTH-WEST AFRICA
BECHUANALAND
Johannesburg
Swaziland
SOUTH AFRICA
Basutoland
Durban
Cape Town
INDIAN
OCEAN

I Belong Where I'm Needed

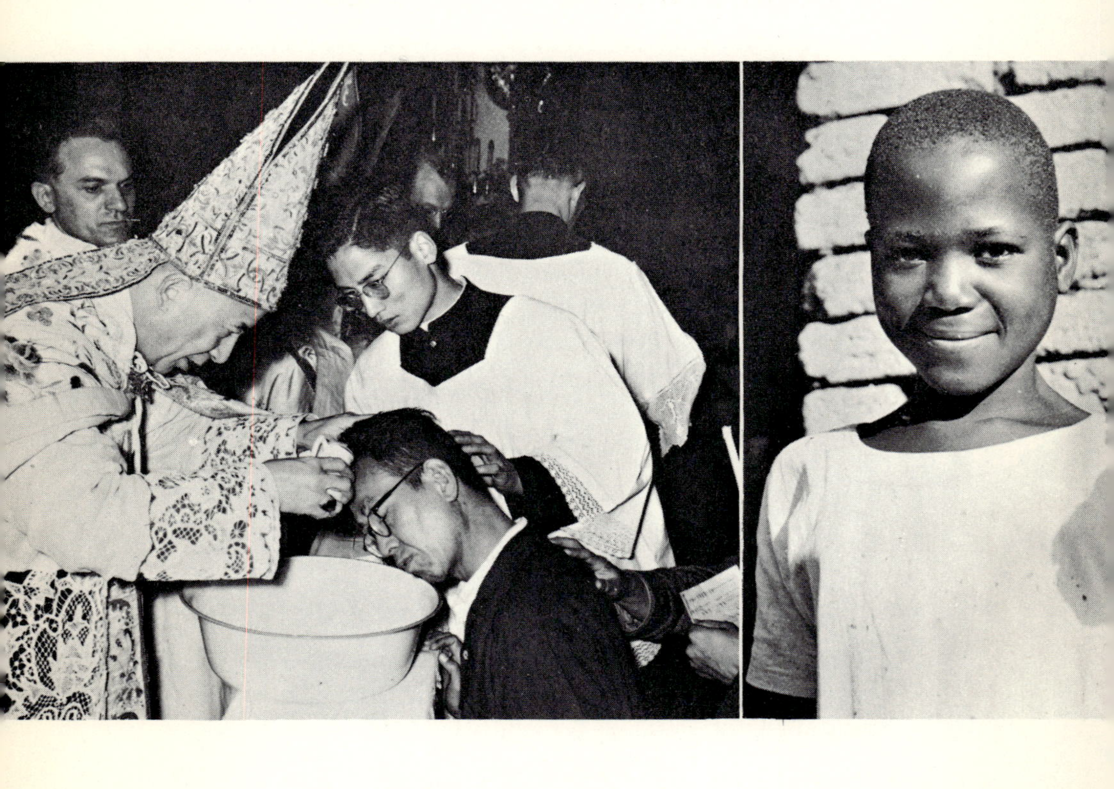

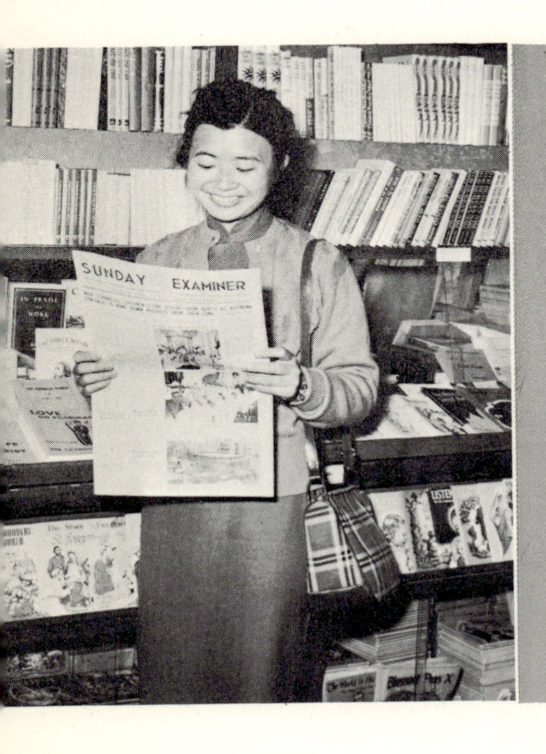

I Belong Where I'm Needed

BY ELIZABETH REID

NP

The Newman Press
Westminster, Maryland
1961

Nihil obstat: Edward A. Cerny, S.S., S.T.D.
Censor Librorum

Imprimatur: Francis P. Keough, D.D.
Archbishop of Baltimore

September 25, 1961

The *Nihil obstat* and *Imprimatur* are official declarations that a book or a pamphlet is free of doctrinal and moral error. No implication is contained therein that those who have granted the *Nihil obstat* and *Imprimatur* agree with the opinions expressed.

Library of Congress Catalog Card Number: 61-16570
Printed in the United States of America

Foreword

To say that this is an unusual book would be to make use of a trite phrase which, in this case, falls far short of accuracy. This is a book that every Catholic will read with interest and astonishment. It will stir up in its readers the impulses of charity that are born and nurtured in faith. It is a book that will move its readers —and in particular the young women to whom it is especially directed—to soul-searching reflection on the opportunities for saving souls that God places in their way as members of the Mystical Body of Christ. It is a book that brings to light the frightful reality of human misery that people who live in privileged areas could never imagine. It is a book, finally, that opens up both terrifying and challenging aspects of the missionary problem of the Church in our own day and age.

The work of the Grail Movement, under whose auspices this book is published, was inaugurated about thirty years ago in Holland under the direction of a zealous Jesuit, Father James van Ginneken. It anticipated by many years the need of the Church for the services of lay people in the work of the apostolate. Today, over one hundred and fifty women have sought and found in the Grail the means of dedicating themselves to the work of the Church overseas in a dozen missionary areas. Thousands of other Grail members are at work in various phases of the lay apostolate in America and Europe. They are not religious or members of secular institutes. Some of them are married and are fulfilling their responsibilities to their families as they grow in the spirit of the lay apostolate. All of them are on fire with the divine love which they hope to enkindle in the souls of their fellow human beings.

At Grailville (in Loveland, near Cincinnati, Ohio), the national center of the Grail Movement in the United States has been firmly established and has branched out into a number of other centers throughout North America. Grailville is a training center for women who are eager to live and work as lay apostles in family and community, in the professions and the arts, in education and business, at home and abroad. The training for overseas work is directed particularly toward areas in which the survival or the expansion of the Church are at stake.

"I belong where I'm needed"—the title of this book presents a challenge to the Catholic world. The Church can be saved only if hundreds of thousands of dedicated lay people are willing to offer their services for the cause of charity and social justice. If the world needs a "peace corps," it has even greater need of a similar group who will become missionaries of charity. For only in supernatural charity can peace be born and sustained. There must be a peace corps for Christ as well as a peace corps for freedom and international justice.

Thousands of young women who read this book will be inspired by its message. I pray that there may be many more Elizabeth Reids who will offer themselves for the tremendous work which the author of this book has so brilliantly and penetratingly brought to our attention.

✠ RICHARD CARDINAL CUSHING
Archbishop of Boston

Acknowledgments

THE AUTHOR and The Newman Press wish to thank the following publishers for their kind permission to reprint poems from the works listed below:

The Oxford University Press, Inc., for "Showdown," by Christopher Fry, from *Sleep of Prisoners.*

Alfred A. Knopf, Inc., for "Africa," by Langston Hughes, from *Selected Poems of Langston Hughes.*

PHOTO CREDITS

Indonesian Information Service: p. 107
Catholic Press Bureau: p. 119
Josephine Drabek: pp. 134, 143, 148, 153, 156, 166, 176, 188, 196, 245
Elsa Chaney: p. 198
Leo Rosenthal: p. 139
Edward Lettau: pp. 230, 240
Ghana Information Service: pp. 251, 271

All other photos by the author. The author wishes to thank Miss Mildred Francis of Tonawanda, New York, for her work in the typing of the manuscript.

Contents

PART TWO • AFRICA

PART THREE • SHOWDOWN

Introduction

When Father James van Ginneken, S.J., noted scholar and great-hearted apostle, spoke of a lay mission movement back in 1920, he was regarded as a visionary dreaming improbable dreams. But this did not stop him from making a daring prophecy: "I see in our own times an apostolic laity going forward *en masse* to the mission fields. . . . It will be a characteristic of the twentieth century that Catholic missionary bishops from all over the world will invite lay people to mission countries, and in this way the harvest will be reaped in great abundance. . . ."

Today his prophecy has found substantial realization. In the great upsurge of the lay apostolate which marks the Church in the twentieth century, a vigorous current is moving missionward. In Africa, in Asia, in Latin America, young lay men and women, and married couples as well, are at work on the frontiers of the Church, fired by an apostolic ideal, contributing their energies and skills to the conversion of the world.

Complete statistics are not available as yet, but a recent survey indicates that there are now some twenty-two lay mission groups with more than two thousand members working in seventy-five countries around the globe. These movements vary widely in scope, numbers, experience, extent of work. Some are exclusively for women; some are made up of lay men; others open their membership to married couples as well as to single men and women. Several restrict themselves to medical work; others embrace a wide variety of professions and skills—agriculture, medicine, education, social work, journalism. Some require a life-time dedication; the majority offer their members the opportunity for a limited period of service. But all are alike in that they recruit Europeans and Americans, give them an apostolic formation, and place them overseas.

The lay mission movement first gathered strength in Europe, which was to be expected, for the general lay apostolate had its first development there. Oldest of the lay mission organizations is the *Missionsärtzliches Institute* of Würzburg, Germany, founded in 1921. In 1932, the French laity formed *Ad Lucem,* which has sent over three hundred professional men and women overseas. Succeeding years saw the development of AFI (*Auxilaires Féminines Internationales*) in Belgium, ALMA (*Academische Leken Missie Actie*) and the Mission Training Center of the Grail [1] in Holland, and other active groups in Italy, Spain, Switzerland, Canada, and the United States.

At the first World Congress of the Lay Apostolate, held in Rome in 1950, the various lay mission movements formed a federation which sponsors international congresses and publications and generally fosters the lay mission movement at an international level. To facilitate contact with the specialized agencies of the United Nations, the federation has organized UFER [2] which has consultative status with ECOSOC,[3] UNESCO,[4] and

[1] In the case of the Grail, the mission program is only one aspect of a broadly conceived lay movement, international in scope, striving to develop the contribution of women to the apostolate of the Church in all spheres of modern life—the family and the community, education and the arts, business and the professions. Out of this universal concern has grown the program of overseas training and service, in which women from Europe and America work together with the women of the newly developing countries for the building of Christ's Kingdom.

[2] International Movement for the Fraternal Union of All Races and Peoples.

[3] Economic and Social Council.

[4] United Nations Educational, Scientific, and Cultural Organization.

UNICEF [5] and accordingly maintains permanent representatives in New York, Paris, and Geneva.

The work of lay missionaries has already won warm approbation from the Vicars of Christ. In his encyclical, *Fidei Donum,* May, 1957, Pope Pius XII wrote:

> Help to missionary dioceses assumes a form nowadays which gives joy to our heart. . . . We refer to the effective task which lay apostles, acting principally within the framework of national and international Catholic movements, accept in performing a service to the young Christian communities . . . how precious is the help brought in that manner to those dioceses which must face new and urgent apostolic duties!
>
> These lay apostles offer to new dioceses the advantage of a long experience of Catholic and social action, as well as of all the other forms of specialized apostolate. . . . We felicitate them with all our heart for their zeal in the service of the Church.

And Pope John XXIII in his first encyclical on the missions, *Princeps Pastorum,* is equally encouraging:

> We know what has been done and is being done by lay missionaries who have chosen, either temporarily or permanently, to leave their own countries in order to contribute by various activities to the social and religious life of mission countries. We ardently pray to the Lord to multiply the ranks of these generous persons and that He support them in the difficulties and labors which they meet with apostolic spirit.

Here in the United States the lay mission movement, despite a rather late start, has enjoyed a rapid growth both in acceptance of the idea and in the development of organizational structures. In 1946, when Mary Louise Tully left Grailville to prepare the way for a Grail team in Hong Kong, the idea that Catholic lay people might play a part in building the Church overseas was outside the purview of the lay apostolate. In 1950, when Grailville began the first formal lay mission training to be offered in the United States, the theoretic possibility of a lay contribution

[5] United Nations Children's Fund.

was occasionally discussed, but only as an experiment that had still to prove itself.

In one brief decade, remarkable changes have taken place. In 1950 the Grail was the only lay mission group in this country. Today there are seven lay mission organizations in the United States, with a total of two hundred and eighty-three people overseas or completing final preparations for mission assignments. Among them, AFI and the Grail offer opportunities for lay women; AID, for lay men and couples; the Lay Mission Helpers of Los Angeles, for men and women, married and single; the Regis College Lay Apostolate, for women teachers volunteering a year or more of service. The YCW have sent some of their American members overseas, and the Women Volunteers Association sent their first team to Africa in 1960. Several other groups are in the process of formation. A national co-ordinating agency, the Committee on the International Lay Apostolate, which grew out of the Mission Secretariat, has inaugurated an Annual National Conference on Lay Mission Work. The Christian Family Movement adopted "International Life" as its theme for a year's study and discussion. In the Catholic press, stories and articles on the work of lay missioners are numerous. For example, a recent issue of the Cincinnati *Telegraph-Register* carried three stories: an airplane pilot and his wife serving in New Guinea; three Regis College graduates to teach in Bolivia; an AID couple and their five childern embarking for Chile, where the father's engineering skills will be put to use in planning a housing cooperative. And all this is reported no longer as a startling innovation but rather as a normal acceptance of responsibility by twentieth-century Christians.

A major development is PAVLA, the nation-wide program of the American hierarchy to recruit lay volunteers for Latin America. Among the first to answer the bishops' call were twenty-two young men and women from Kansas, who set out in June of 1961 for a three- to five-year tour of duty in Central and South

America. "The New Boom in Lay Missionaries" proclaimed by Douglas Roche in *Sign* Magazine may be a pardonable overstatement, but there is no doubt that a wave of enthusiastic response to mission service is sweeping over the American laity.

The enthusiasm for actual mission service is one sign, a most significant sign, of maturity in the lay apostolate in Europe and America. The apostolate of the laity grows out of a deepening awareness of the mystery of the Church as the Mystical Body of Christ; it is rooted in a more profound understanding of baptism and confirmation as incorporating the Christian into Christ and bestowing a share in His priesthood. The laity have become increasingly conscious, in Pope Pius XII's memorable phrase, "not only of belonging to the Church, but of *being* the Church." It is impossible to be a conscious member of the Body and not to be concerned about the growth of the whole. Stirred by the vision of the Church as the people of God on the march toward the heavenly Jerusalem, more and more lay people seek an active share in her mission of bringing "all tongues and tribes and peoples and nations" into the unity of God's family.

Along with this fuller realization of lay responsibility, the twentieth-century theology of the laity is developing a more precise definition of the layman's specific role. Too often the laity have been regarded simply as substitutes for clergy and religious, filling a gap until more priests and nuns can be found. This attitude overlooks the distinctive role and contribution of the laity. As Reverend John J. Considine, M.M., points out, "At least half of the unfinished task of the Catholic Church in the world cannot be carried out by pope or bishop or priest or Sister or Brother. It must be the direct responsibility of the laity, working in cooperation with Church authorities." And Emmanuel Cardinal Suhard writes in *Priests among Men:* "The laity have an irreplaceable work to do. They have their own witness to bear. . . . The Church intends to confide to the laity the full responsibility for human society." The layman's role is the sanctification of the temporal order. He is citizen of both the city of man and the city of God, and he bears witness to Christ through the "consecratio mundi," the development and sanctification of the properly human values.

Fundamentally the lay role is the same whether it is performed at home or overseas, but the layman's task in the missions takes on special emphases, partly because the missioner is working in a culture not his own and partly because of the bewildering variety of social changes in most mission lands today. To the lay missioner, the Church entrusts a fourfold task:

1) TO GIVE AN EXAMPLE OF CATHOLICISM IN LAY LIFE

Perhaps the first responsibility of the layman is to give witness to Christ by his example of Catholicism fully lived in a lay pattern. Clearly this is a task which neither priest nor religious can perform. Pioneering in Hong Kong as editor of the Catholic paper, Mary Louise Tully had this to say about her role: "My real work as a lay apostle consists in trying to live according to Christian principles a truly God-centered life in all the daily relationships, jobs and responsibilities; at the office or hostel, at picnics, at recreation; in dealing with printers, missionaries, celebrities, coolies, table companions, fellow workers."

This example of Christianity in the market place is often needed in areas where the conduct of colonial officials and business men has led the local people to associate the "Christian" West with materialism and religious indifference.

The new Christian communities tend to develop the secularist mentality which regards the vigorous practice of the Faith as the exclusive province of priests and nuns. "In the mind of my new converts," one missioner writes, "the living of the Faith is not associated enough with the life of the lay person. That the layman lives his religion profoundly, that the Holy Sacrifice of the Mass is the center of his life, that Christian ideas and customs leaven all his activities—all this is a revelation to the newly-converted people in the missions," a revelation which can be most effectively made by the example of lay people in their midst.

2) TO PUT PROFESSIONAL SKILLS AT THE SERVICE OF THE CHURCH

Here is a second crucial function of the lay worker. The planting and development of the Church in the rapidly evolving societies of Asia and Africa is a vastly more complex undertaking today than it was fifty years ago. The Church must have at her command a great variety of skills in agriculture, engineering, public health, medicine, education, communication, social work, community development.

Let one field serve as an illustration: education. Among the millions of newly independent peoples in Africa and Asia, a tremendous aspiration for education is astir, and Catholic educators are needed at every level from elementary schools to teachers' training colleges and universities if a Christian spirit is to penetrate the new educational systems.

Journalists, radio and television program directors, doctors, university professors, social workers—clearly it is not possible for the clergy and religious alone to provide the technical competence needed in these many different spheres. The laity, whose vocation takes them into the professions, have their special contribution to make in the missions.

3) TO TRAIN LOCAL LAITY FOR APOSTOLIC LEADERSHIP

A major responsibility of the lay missioner is to help to prepare an indigenous elite, local lay men and women who are ready for responsible Catholic leadership among their own people. In this respect, the vocation of the lay missioner is like that of every missionary: to make himself dispensable. The goal of the priest missionary is to plant the Church, with all the organs necessary for her life, and he cannot consider his task accomplished until he has trained a local clergy to take his place. Similarly, the goal of the lay missioner, under the direction of the hierarchy, of course, is to work for the full development of the lay apostolate, with local lay leaders taking over the entire responsibility. The lay missioner can help the local laity to understand their specific role in the Church and to develop a sense of personal responsibility for the conversion of their people.

Perhaps most important of all, it is by working side by side in apostolic endeavors that the lay missioner can best help the local leaders. In this close collaboration, the one can contribute his experience of Christian life and apostolate together with an objective view of the local problems; the other brings his intimate understanding of the people, their mentality, their language, their needs and aspirations. Out of this collaboration will come the necessary adaptation of apostolic training to local needs, as well as the most fruitful approaches to the twofold apostolic task: the conversion of individuals and the Christianization of institutions.

4) TO CHRISTIANIZE THE CULTURE AND THE SOCIAL ORDER

This latter goal—the Christianization of the social institutions—is so complex that it deserves special discussion. To penetrate the temporal order with a Christian spirit, to build a Christian culture, to foster social institutions and an environment which help rather than hinder man in his search for God—all this is the specific responsibility of the lay apostle wherever he works, but the changing cultures of mission lands offer special problems and opportunities.

Under the impact of Western industrialized urban civilization, the feudal societies of Asia, the tribal societies of Africa, even the traditional Catholic cultures of Latin America have been thrown into profound upheaval. The lives of millions of people are undergoing drastic changes: from the personal processes of hand-production to mechanization and industrialization; from the warmth and security of family and tribal life to the anonymity and isolation of the individual lost in the urban masses; from the leisurely tempo of the village to the tension and pressures of the modern city; from education as the privilege of the few to mass literacy; from age-old traditions to dizzy change. And all this takes place in the context of a political evolution from colonialism to self-government and independence. Old traditions crumble; the individual torn by conflicting currents is often confused, unsure.

The fact that these societies are in flux opens special opportunities for the apostolate. New patterns must be found. If Christians can bring the light of faith to bear upon the issues, they can exercise a far-reaching influence in economic, political, and social life. Take, for example, the major social change now taking place in the position of women. The women of Asia and Africa, emerging from a more or less inferior status, are grasping eagerly for education and for the freedoms enjoyed by women in the West. The desire for freedom can carry them to an extreme, which disrupts family life. Or it may be possible to give a Christian direction to this powerful current, provided a nucleus of leaders can be formed who will find a balance between personal freedom and the demands of family life, and who will set a Christian pattern.

I have tried to outline briefly some of the major principles on which the lay mission movement is built. The purpose of the present book is to bring the theory to life through an account of what is actually being done by some lay people in Asia and Africa today. Most of the examples are drawn from the work of the Grail, the movement which Elizabeth Reid knows best.

The Grail Movement originated in the Netherlands in the 1920's with a group of young women at the Catholic University, under the inspiration of Father James van Ginneken, S.J. From the beginning the Grail was conceived in a global dimension, its seed an unshakable confidence in the contribution which a world-wide union of lay women could make to a spiritual renewal. Keynotes in this concept are lay, women, world:

Lay—The Grail is one of the new instruments which have developed from the abundance of the Church's life in response to the needs of the modern world.

Women—Central is the vision of woman: her role in Redemption; her spiritual and psychological capacities for love, for dedication and self-giving; the opportunities open to her through her entry into economic, social, and political life.

World—With the enthusiasm of youth, but with a courage born of faith and sound theology as well, the first group of Grail leaders formulated as their goal nothing less than "the conversion of the world." This goal in turn was viewed under various aspects.

It meant, of course, the unconverted world within each of us—hence the emphasis on spiritual deepening through the liturgy, personal prayer, and sincere striving to live the spirit of the Gospels. I can remember an early Grail campaign with the succinct title, "Convert the world—begin with yourself."

It meant, too, the unconverted world around us: how to bring Christian values into the patterns of life and the social institutions—into family and community, education, work, recreation, into attitudes on race and social justice and international affairs—how to unite the energies and talents of young women to form a leaven of Christian influence in our own environment.

The goal embraced, too, our relations to non-Catholic Christians. As theologians have pointed out, the scandal of disunity perhaps more than any other single factor stands in the way of the Church's mission in the world. We wanted to reach out to our separated brethren, to help to break down prejudice and build up sympathy and understanding. Father van Ginneken was famous for his retreats for non-Catholics, and one of the activities of the first Grail members was to collaborate in these efforts. That experience opened the possibilities of a contribution to "dialogue" through woman's gifts of tact and sensitivity and love.

Finally, we wanted to work with the women in mission lands, show them the Christian concept of woman's role, and help them to take their place in the Christian evolution of their countries.

It was this last aspect of the goal that first captivated our hearts, and the first concrete project of the Grail was to start a university for the women of Java. But the bishop who had approved the plan died, and his successor requested the little group to turn their energies to the factory girls in Holland. The year was 1929; Dutch women and girls had just begun to enter the factories and offices in considerable numbers, with grave effects on their moral and religious life. Into the factories, shops, and offices the first Grail leaders went, working side by side with the young women, forming "circles of action," and soon the Grail as a youth movement had come into being. Banners, uniforms, mass demonstrations and plays with thousands of participants, national campaigns, groups for press and film—through all these means we endeavored to intensify the spirit of the young women and to influence the country at large. Time was ripe then for this kind of organized youth movement—by 1932, there were thirty-five houses and twenty thousand members in Holland alone, and the Grail had been invited to Germany, Britain, and Australia. The move to the United States was made in 1940, and Grailville was established as the main U.S. center in 1944 at the invitation of Archbishop McNicholas of Cincinnati.

With World War II and the occupation of Holland, the Grail on the continent was forced underground. But immediately after the war, it became possible to carry on with the missionary goal and, in 1947, the Grail Mission Training Center was opened at Ubbergen, Holland. In 1950, the Grail Lay Mission School was begun at Grailville, and in 1956, the American mission training program was expanded through the Institute for

Overseas Service in Brooklyn. By 1960, Grail Centers had been established on all six continents, and Grail teams were at work in twenty-two countries, under the guidance of forty-two members of the hierarchy.

The concrete works of the Movement are exceedingly varied, which testifies to a concern to respond to local needs and possibilities. To indicate a few: a professor-student team at Pius XII University in Basutoland, a hospital and chain of dispensaries in Uganda, an international student center in New York, a guest and retreat house for non-Catholics in Holland, a bookstore and cultural center in Surinam.

Beneath the variety of works is the underlying ideal: to develop to the full woman's capacities for dedication and self-giving, and to express this dedication in concrete services. In the United States at present the Grail is concentrating on the following fields as spheres in which women have a special contribution to make:

Family and Community: marriage preparation, emergency assistance to families, adult education for Christian family living, youth leadership training, neighborhood projects to develop a sense of community in urban and suburban areas.

Religious Education: training young women to instruct children and teen-agers according to modern approaches, experimenting with new materials on primary and secondary levels.

Service Careers: bringing Christian values into the professions, giving vocational guidance to students preparing for service careers.

Christian Culture: emphasizing daily living as the basis of culture, encouraging creative talents, producing valid contemporary works for home and church, carrying on cultural education through bookstores, lectures, exhibits, concerts, drama and other means of linking artist and public.

World Community: giving hospitality and apostolic orientation to international students, training and sending American girls overseas, maintaining representatives at the UN and other international organizations, offering general educational programs on the theme of world unity.

The Grail Movement comprises thousands of young women in all walks of life, of many races and nations, bound together both by their commitment to an apostolic ideal of life and by their acceptance of specific apostolic tasks. At the heart of the movement is a core of permanent lay leaders who, living in total dedication to Christ, assure the continuity of whatever work the Grail undertakes. Ready to go to any part of the world in which they are needed, serving in whatever field they can best contribute, these young women provide the basis of unity and a guarantee of spiritual strength for the entire Movement.

For all aspects of the lay apostolate, preparation is needed; hence, the emphasis in the Grail on centers of formation and periods of intensive training aimed at developing mature Christians who know how to nourish themselves at the primary sources of the Christian spirit: the Mass, the sacraments, the prayer of the Church, Holy Scripture; who have developed the art of prayer and made it part of their daily lives; who have learned to find the Cross in the small events of daily routine, as well as in the greater issues of life. Intellectually, the mature Christian needs systematic study of the theology of the lay apostolate and the special spheres of lay responsibility.

For those who are going to serve in a land and culture not their own, special orientation and study are necessary. For the most part, the mission lands are the areas where colonial empires ruled until recently; they are also the less developed areas and the areas inhabited by peoples of the black, brown, and yellow races. Nationalism, racial feeling, distrust of the West, a tendency to identify Christianity with the West and with colonialism—all these attitudes combine to make the task of the Christian witness difficult and delicate. Hence it is not enough to proclaim the fundamental equality of all men in Christ or to state the principles of self-determination and respect for every people and culture. These principles must be translated into attitudes, action, genuine human contact.

Even vocabularies are changing as a new awareness of other peoples develops. Words like "native" and "heathen" no longer have a place in our lexicon. Even the word "mission" to the awakened sensitivities of this mid-twentieth century carries overtones which make it preferable to speak of "international apostolate." Nor is this just a question of verbal niceties. Fundamental values and attitudes are involved—the approach of understanding, respect, mutual exchange, and helpfulness.

The apostle going overseas must make strenuous efforts to orient himself toward another people, toward a mentality, customs, culture which are strange to him. He must be prepared to enter with sympathy and understanding into the new environment, to avoid passing judgment, above all to avoid making comparisons with the life he has left. He must rise above ethnocentrism in all its forms to achieve a real love of his adopted country, for the whole strength of his apostolate depends on his oneness with the people, his ability to stand beside, to work with, to serve. A member of *Ad Lucem* writing from Africa gives a glimpse of the tact, the humility, the profound stripping of self which genuine adaptation demands: "Either we are Western teachers, that is to say, we impose our views, our principles, our institutions, and for a time we have the illusion of making disciples who are one with us; but this soon leads to disillusionment, for a forced assimilation is quickly rejected. Or, on the other hand, we are willing simply to be catalysts, facilitating experiments, discreetly directing, encouraging, participating from within, but without imposing and quite willing not to be followed. . . ." Out of such self-stripping, we may hope that an authentic adaptation may be achieved and the way prepared for the growth of cultures and societies at once deeply Christian and truly Asian or African.

I Belong Where I'm Needed is an appropriate summing up

of Elizabeth Reid's life and work in the Grail. I first met Elizabeth in Australia in 1937, an enthusiastic girl, just out of school, eagerly responsive to the idea that she had a part to play in the conversion of the world. She was one of the pioneers in the Australian Grail who helped to build the Movement; she served on the staff of Tay Creggan, the main Grail training center, and edited the national Catholic girl's magazine. In 1948 came the call to join the Grail team in Hong Kong. Soon Hong Kong was all but submerged in the flood of refugees from Communist China. I can remember cabling Hong Kong in the early days of the Communist triumph, suggesting that Elizabeth and her teammates seek safety in the US, a suggestion which was politely but firmly rejected. Elizabeth wrote: "If we have a fear in our hearts, it is only that God might want us to leave China. For ourselves, we cannot tell you how much we want to stay. Here we belong. Here we are part of the wall that is the Church in China—funny, lopsided stones perhaps, but still a part. It is strange to say, but it is true—we belong here, we are part of the morale, and we can be faith, hope, and confidence for all the people who come to us."

Hard-pressed Hong Kong was full of needs, and Elizabeth rose to them with verve and energy and generosity: head of the Grail team and hostel, friend and counselor to refugee students, a one-woman relief service through her "wanted" column in the paper, on the reception committee to offer comfort and help to expelled missionaries, adopted mother to numbers of abandoned children, godmother to scores of converts. As a journalist, she has a gift for being where history is in the making: Korea during the exchange of prisoners, Vietnam at the fall of Hanoi, Indonesia for the Bandung Conference, the UN during the Suez crisis, Togoland on its Independence Day. With her warm heart and quick sympathies, she readily makes friends. To her first-hand experience in Southeast Asia and West and East Africa, she has added several years of contact with world currents as UFER representative at the UN in New York.

In the pages which follow, Elizabeth Reid speaks out of her own experience of the needs of the world and the way in which some young lay people are striving to respond to these needs. The examples she details make clear, I think, the tremendous possibilities for lay people today. It is her hope and mine that the world's needs will speak to the imagination and the generosity of young Americans. Time is short. The Holy Father has called for "great legions of apostles similar to those to which the Church knew at her dawn." May countless American lay men and women rise to the challenge of this hour of the world's history and give not only their goods but themselves for the building of the Body of Christ.

LYDWINE VAN KERSBERGEN, PH.D.
President of the Grail in America

Grailville, Loveland, Ohio
June 1961

I Belong Where I'm Needed

PART I *Asia*

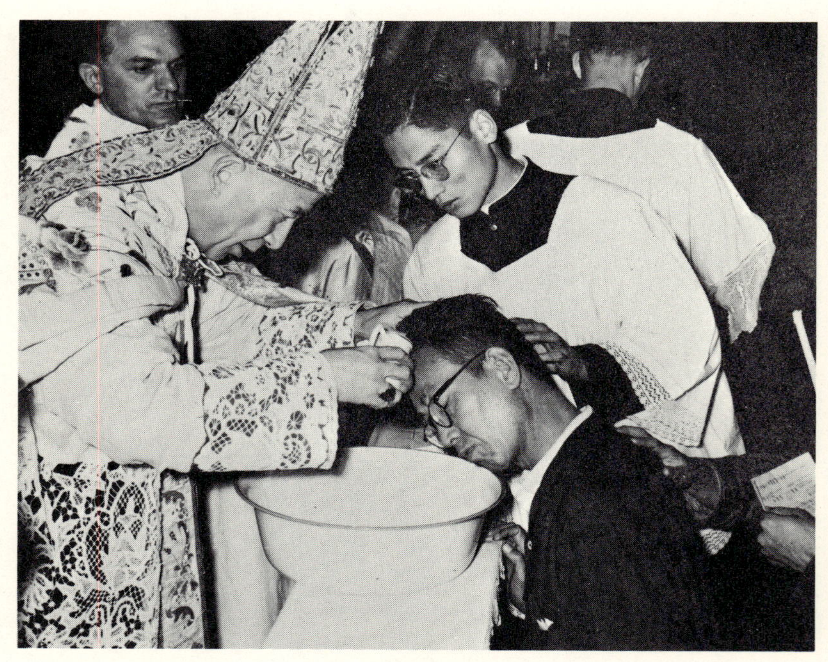

Easter Vigil: His Excellency, Bishop Joseph Yuen, exiled from Chumatien, baptizing one of Hong Kong's thousands of catechumens.

ASIA

"Is there a rice plant which sprouts
and does not flower?
Is there a rice plant
which flowers and does not bear fruit?"
The point is the seed,
the seed which dies in order to bring life . . .

—*Adapted from a Chinese proverb*

Chapter One

Assignment Hong Kong

EVERY TIME the prow of the freighter dipped, the blurred edge of the China mainland was spray-screened from sight.

Soaking wet, I peered out from the foredeck on that December morning in 1948. My sunny Australian homeland suddenly seemed very far away, and I began to wonder how on earth I had gotten myself into this situation. Easy enough to say in the Sydney Town Hall with five hundred other Grail members in a speaking chorus, "We will know ourselves God's messengers and ours the world to leaven and to win." I was just out of school then; now with eight years and half a dozen seas stretched behind me, my world was taking on new and unknown proportions. Now I began really to understand that the leaven has to be lost in the dough in order to function.

We plunged on towards the shore, and Hong Kong began to take shape: the peaked grey mountains jutting out of the troubled sea, teasing glimpses of sampans and junks tip-tossing on great breakers which pounded the rugged shore, and the barren hills around the city scarred by countless huts, homes of refugees.

For twenty-two days we had been on the water, first hugging the east coast of Australia, deserted shores for days on end, an occasional lighthouse, then a great expanse of water, the Tasman Sea. Across the Tropic of Capricorn we sailed into the Coral Sea, calm, blue, brilliant, and parted the waters inside the barrier reef. We moved alongside Papua with its jungles, dark, mysterious, touching the water's edge, into the Arafura Sea where we were startled by exotic flying fish skimming over the water. Threading our way past thousands of storybook palm-fringed islands, we entered the Banda Sea. For sun-drenched days we crept along the Moluccas, remembering Xavier on the same route four hundred years before, and crossed the equator with the Celebes on our port side and Borneo in the distance. Northward and westward into the Sulu Sea, the ship was buffeted by powerful headwinds, whipping up huge rollers. Storm-tossed days followed in the South China Sea, waves breaking over the bows, surging in reverse and falling in cataracts from the flared fo'c'sle head.

Now with the calm precision of the inevitable, we entered the harbor on which Hong Kong is built. We lay at anchor waiting for the customs and police to come aboard.

Perched on the doorstep of Communist China, Hong Kong, under the British flag, is the largest free port in the East, with its dockyards, banks, commercial houses, cotton and silk mills, glass, rubber and electrical factories. The tiny colony, only thirty-two square miles on the island (plus a piece of the China mainland which the British hold on a ninety-nine-year lease), trades with the world.

Down along the waterfront edged by tall office buildings, junks tie up to discharge pigs and chickens, rice and vegetables from the mainland. Immediately beyond, warships lie resting and waiting, grey giants, looking oddly out of place in the midst of myriad small craft crisscrossing the sparkling harbor waters. Around the island buses and jeeps, small English cars and ricksha pullers vie with each other to keep pace along the highways.

But the overwhelming impression Hong Kong gives is people —the kind of swarming, bursting life one finds when a stone is lifted in the heat and an ant hill is disturbed. At the end of World War II, there were only some 750,000 people in Hong Kong; today there are upwards of 3,000,000, for the most part refugees. People are everywhere, lanes and alleys so crowded that pedestrians jostle shoulder to shoulder along the footpaths.

This was Hong Kong, where I worked and lived for seven years between 1948 and 1956, going out from it with my notebook and camera to Macao, Taiwan, Korea, Japan, Vietnam, the Philippines, Malaya, Singapore and Indonesia to record stories of the Church present in her people through this eventful period of current history. During these years I met refugees and expelled missionaries, returned prisoners of war, celebrities and coolies, stranded students from the interior of China, unmarried mothers and beggar children from the streets, the sick, the discouraged, the hungry, the dying, all calling with a thousand voices for their stories to be told.

* * *

I think it is the fact that I have always liked stories so much, listening to them as well as telling them, that ultimately landed me in Hong Kong.

The first stories I remember were those told me by my father, as we tramped for miles in the bush with the dogs—a large, lumbering man, swinging a cherrywood walking stick, and myself, a small brown-skinned girl, tagging along, completely absorbed in the various triumphs and failures of the Reid clan.

I loved the tales of my Scottish forebears who roamed the highlands, that wild untamed country with always another mountain beyond. The snatches of Robbie Burns' poems which my father would break into stirred my imagination, and I would dart ahead with sudden bursts of energy, skimming after the dogs, ideas of faraway places and strange adventures beginning to take shape in my mind. I seemed to know my great-grandfather, who left the rocky crags and shaggy mountain sheep of his native Inverness to sail around the Cape of Good Hope and across the Indian Ocean to Australia. The next generation, which produced an explorer, a parson, a prime minister and a Poor Clare nun, had endlessly fascinating sidelights. As well, I was specially proud of the prime minister, Sir George Reid, who had whole books written about him and pictures taken at Buckingham Palace with King George V. These were wonderful trophies to show schoolmates fresh from England or Scotland when they put their plump pink arms beside my skinny brown ones and said, "Ya, you're only a native Australian, a colonial!"

My father, John Fergusson Reid, married my mother, Ann Catherine Phibbs, just before World War I. He was soon caught up in the war, and became an officer in the Australian Light Horse, those long lean men in the wide-brimmed hats with flowing emu feathers, who were, I think, the last men in history to *ride* away to war. He was one of that gallant company of Anzacs who fought at Gallipoli and later he saw action in Flanders. His stories of the broken cities and the hungry people haunted me. He told of giving food to children "with eyes as big as doorknobs" staring out of their tiny starved faces. Over and over again I made him tell what happened when he gave them the chocolate Mother had sent from Australia and they didn't know what it was; and how when they had tasted it, they smiled and smiled and their eyes didn't look so big any more. Mulling over these stories in the hammock slung between the jacaranda trees, I wanted nothing more than to grow up soon and give out truckloads of chocolate to hungry children.

In the following years, like millions of other Australians, I settled into an unbelievably peaceful existence on the remote island continent. Australia *is* off the beaten track, "down under" from the surging currents of world affairs. We lived outside the city of Brisbane in our family home high on a hill, with no near neighbors, and I attended the same school, Lourdes Hill Convent, all my life. My journalist father continued to be a delightful companion, and my mother who loved and cared for all of us

Victoria Huang of China shows Nan Johns of Australia some fine points of Chinese calligraphy at the Grail House in Hong Kong.

was always available. My father stood for Parliament in the federal elections for the district of Maranoa in South Queensland. I greatly admired his writing and speeches, and went to listen to him whenever I could. It was in these years that I determined to become a reporter and even imagined myself a member of Parliament! I began writing, and spent many hours reporting school activities and sending letters to the editors of local papers. In these latter, influenced by my father's ideas, I often held forth on the deep injustice of the "White Australia Policy" in regard to our Asian neighbors.

For the rest, swimming in the river, playing tennis or golf, grooming my dog, studying, going to picnics or parties, discussing books and Australian nationalism filled my days.

Then came the first inkling of a new stirring in the Church when one evening, just before World War II, Dr. Lydwine van Kersbergen showed a movie in Brisbane of 10,000 Dutch Grail members in a mass play. They were praying round a huge, brightly colored cross in the Olympic Stadium in Amsterdam, communicating their spirit and conviction to some 40,000 onlookers. The impact of that movie shattered me. Here was a staggering new idea—that the conversion of the whole world concerned me, and right here in Brisbane were five Dutch women who had left their own land and sailed across half a world to tell me so! I had a vague idea that the Cross and sacrifice were involved in it somewhere, but at eighteen the only tangible knowledge of sacrifice I had was to go without sweets during Lent.

A few weeks later a letter came in the post from the secretary of the Grail inviting me to take part in a summer school in Sydney, six hundred miles south of my home. And so "the journey of a thousand miles begins with a single step," as I heard years later from a Chinese philosopher in Taiwan. The idea of the lay apostolate, of one's personal responsibility for the growth of the Mystical Body, of the need for training to take one's place in the ranks of the Church—all this began to take shape. For the first time in my life I took part in a dialogue Mass, and it began to dawn on me that the sacrifice of Calvary is the focal point of history, and that the daily Mass in my parish church is Calvary projected into time. The Cross and sacrifice began to make sense. A whole new vision unfolded before my eyes: a vision of woman's talents, of her capacity for sacrifice and self-giving, a vision of

With the budding reporters of The Catholic Students' Press Group I plan an edition of the "Hong Kong Student."

the Cross as the deepest inspiration of a woman's heart and the climax of the message the people of God are called to bring.

The vision grew and deepened. I saw that working for the conversion of the world in this time could not be just a girl's dream, something to be gotten at a bargain price. It was a tremendous task, something for which to give one's whole life. I joined the Grail Movement, and in the training years that followed, preparing for lifetime dedication in the Grail, I began to discover how rich and full our life can be in Christ, this life we are called to share with all men everywhere. During the five years until 1948, I helped to build up the movement, giving courses in the major Australian cities of Sydney, Melbourne, Brisbane, Newcastle and Rockhampton. I was appointed editor of the National Catholic Girls' Magazine, *Torchlight,* and was a staff member of the Grail Adult Education Center, Tay Creggan, in Melbourne.

At the same time the Grail was expanding internationally. From the very beginning Father James van Ginnenken, S.J., had urged us to work among the women in mission lands, helping to build the young Church and to develop local lay leaders. By the end of World War II, time was ripe to carry out this cherished plan of sending Grail members to the missions. Grail teams began to leave from Amsterdam, Sydney and New York, from Edinburgh and Bonn, and to arrive in Hong Kong, Djakarta, Sao Paulo, Johannesburg, Kampala and Cairo. Nurses, doctors, teachers, social workers and journalists were on the move.

In Hong Kong, Bishop Henry Valtorta, P.I.M.E., wrote to the International President of the Grail, asking for a press and publicity team, and soon after I was sailing northwards. Already two Americans were there from Grailville, near Cincinnati, Ohio, Mary Louise Tully of LaGrange, Illinois, and Veronica Forbes of Detroit, Michigan.

What was our task to be? I could frame the theory for myself easily enough, as I stood on the boat deck looking out towards my new home.

We wanted to serve the Church through our professional skills—for me, that meant journalism. We had a special concern for these Chinese women, to help them prepare for lay leadership and to work hand-in-hand with them towards Christian solutions to the multitudinous problems on this doorstep of a swiftly changing China. And, at the deepest level, we wanted to be witnesses to Christ's life, simply to be present in the midst of the family of man in crowded Hong Kong, as seed is present in the earth, trusting that the Lord would bring the blossoming and the fruit. How many surprises the reality was to hold for us! And wonderful and strange were the forms in which these basic ideas gradually took shape.

I began work at once on the weekly diocesan paper, *The*

Sunday Examiner. It did not take long to discover that the *Examiner* was completely my affair. I was editor, layout man, photographer, advertising and sales manager. "It's all yours," said the bearded Italian missionary, Father Nicholas Maestrini, who at that moment was surely exercising the virtue of hope in a heroic degree to keep the paper alive. He called from the door at the end of our first interview—I still had to get my land legs after three weeks at sea—"We're so relieved that your ship arrived on time. The deadline is tomorrow at 5 p.m.!"

At the same time, I made preparations for the Hong Kong Students' Press Group, to train representatives from the local high schools in the apostolate of the press. It was just two weeks later that Wong Sau Ying made this famous statement. "I think no elf, ghost, angel, Christ, Catholic, and no God are in everywhere, but I still want to belong to your Catholic Students' Press Group," and with this shattering speech bright-eyed Sau Ying edged a bit closer to my desk. Desperately trying to take my visitor seriously, I managed not to laugh and took my first hurdle in making friends.

I wanted so much to do it properly right from the start. "Remember," said my friend, Father Gerry O'Collins, a Columban missionary I went to see before leaving Australia, "that your function in Hong Kong is to be a bridge. You will be serving the Church only if you prepare local people to take your place—and it shouldn't take too long! A bishop prepares young men for the native priesthood, and when there is a local-born bishop in charge of the diocese, he has done his work well. You must prepare the Chinese girls to play their parts in the apostolate of the Church, christianizing the various levels and structures of society."

So I ran the first pile down in my bridge by advertising that the Catholic Students' Press Group was about to be born. Soon I realized I had twins on my hands—the weekly *Sunday Examiner* and the *Hong Kong Student,* written and edited by the members of the Press Group. Strenuous days and nights followed, work-packed, but filled with laughter and fullness and color, with loving and being loved—with high moments when Wong Sau Ying dropped a note in my box: " . . . I have been a girl out of mischief. I always make fun of friends who believed in God, but now I wish baptism. This is a matter of mirth. You have prayed for me. You have enshrined and kept silence. . . . " No matter at this point that one had sweated week after week on the literary creations of these young journalists in the making—at least the first part of the "bridge" was being built, the group was beginning to take shape as a "Catholic" Students' Press Group. I had indeed "enshrined and kept silence." I could have torn those news items to shreds during the first months, had I come to Hong Kong for any other reason than to help establish a local lay apostolate!

I remember another afternoon when I was up to my ears in work, scissors and paste operating full speed, and, because I didn't have a third hand, a bunch of twelve-em news items in my teeth. There was a gentle knock at the door—just quiet enough to make me think perhaps I hadn't heard it at all. But it came again with a more insistent vibration.

I mumbled, "Who's there?"

And the door was pushed open. One of those rare, exotic Chinese girls stood in front of me. A flower dew-wet, a butterfly poised on a blossom—whatever figure you like to use—there she was, and I was covered with glue, and my mouth full of newsprint. We were both silent, both surprised, for different reasons. My usual visitors were refugees needing clothes or food, or students who for the most part were anything but flowerlike!

Then she spoke. "Could you tell me who made me?" Straight, plain, just like that. I said, "Please sit down," and forgot the deadline for the next hour. This was the story:

She had been walking along the street when she saw a crowd of people lined up. From their clothes one could see that they were obviously refugees. For the first time in her life she felt a sudden compassion for them. She spoke to a woman, and asked what she was waiting for. The woman replied that she was hoping for some milk powder to be given out.

"Who gives it to you?" the girl wanted to know.

"The foreign-one from the Lord of Heaven Religion" (literal translation of the Catholic Church), she was told.

"Who is the Lord of Heaven?" asked the girl.

"Why, the One who made me," said the refugee at once.

The girl was stunned. "That ragged refugee knows who made her, and I don't know where I come from or where I am going."

With a great sadness in her heart she continued walking along the street. Then she saw the same Chinese characters—"The Lord of Heaven Press Bureau" (Catholic Press Bureau). She walked up the steps, and saw the sign "Information" on the door of my office. As simple as that! The grace of faith came so swiftly after the movement of compassion—little miracles like that happen every day in Hong Kong. The "butterfly" began her instruction that afternoon; ten months later she was baptized and received the Christian name of Rachel. Rachel now knows well who made her and where she is going; she has brought seventeen other people into the Church. The "bridge" was on its way. Rachel does what I came to do. . . . And she is still there; the seed of the local lay apostolate is sown.

The apple lady, happy to be set up in business outside the Catholic Centre.

Chapter Two

Who Is a Refugee? Someone Like You

WHO ARE these people who stand in long lines waiting for food? Who are these refugees who have come as far as they can to get away from Communist domination in their homeland?

They are everyday people like any of us: students, teachers, mothers, children, soldiers, writers, artists, storekeepers, engineers and farmers.

Look at the blind soldier in the remnants of his Nationalist uniform as he taps his way along the city street. Watch him grope to find a place beside a pillar to spread out before him a paper on which all his miseries are written—with the expectant tin can beside him for alms.

Or follow the mother with her straggling children as they pick up cigarette butts from the street and stow them away in a paper bag. See them later in the day lay out the salvaged strands of tobacco in the sun to dry, to be resold for a cent or two to other refugees.

Watch the small boys scavenge in the rubbish tins or grab a bun from a hawker's basket like starveling birds. When you walk into the heart of the downtown area, your footsteps are dogged by dozens of beggar children, carrying younger brothers and sisters strapped on their backs, bent low with the load. Small insistent fingers clutch at your bag or pocket, thin voices bleat out: "No mama, no papa; give rice, give money."

Evenings in the heart of the business district street sleepers spread out old newspapers and odds and ends and settle down for the night. Whole families live in this way, unshielded from the flies and dust and heat in summer and whipped by the rain and wind in winter.

Poignant too are those refugee women, Italian, French and Dutch, who married overseas Chinese in their homelands, and having returned to China to visit their husbands' families, were caught in the Communist push, suddenly torn away from husband and family, uprooted and expelled. Some managed to get out with one or two of their children, forced to leave the others inside China and mourning them as completely lost. Deep and haunting is the suffering of these women with European faces and Chinese names who stay on in Hong Kong, waiting for the day they can return to China.

I had just finished talking with one of these women at the end of a steaming hot morning. Five interviews were stowed away in my reporter's notebook. I flipped back the pages a bit wearily—my heart seemed worn away. Always the open hand, always the mouths to be fed and shelter to be found, and those endlessly repeated stories from the expelled missionaries—house arrest, imprisonment, torture, brainwashing, People's Court, confession, expulsion.

Day after day, wave after wave they came, the Church continually on the receiving end of a kick. Phrases like "finger in the dyke," "back against the wall," jumped out of the typewriter.

Then came the little old Frenchwoman, a Franciscan Missionary of Mary. Determinedly pushing her way past my Korean secretary, Madeleine Kim, she stepped over stacks of papers, inkwet from the presses. With a vigorous rub at the black streak

I had just taken a picture of His Eminence, Francis Cardinal Spellman, arriving in Hong Kong, when someone photographed the photographer. Bishop Adolph Paschang, M.M., who had been released a few weeks before from a Communist prison, is looking on.

she had just collected on her habit, and a final grunt, she planted herself in the chair at my desk. She was out of breath and her black paper fan beat up and down with generous sweeps.

"Nice to see you, Mother," said I, "but I thought you were resting in Macao."

"I am not resting," she almost snorted with indignation, "and I want you to do something for me here before you go on leave. I need some desks, a table or two, a blackboard, and any other furnishings you can get. Just write a few hundred words with perhaps a little picture, and let the people know that I am building a school at Ma-On-Shan."

I could have hugged her on the spot. Ma-On-Shan is a few miles from the Communist border, and this little old nun, as provincial of a great missionary order in China, who had seen in the past five years of her life sixty-five foundations swept away by the Communist regime, had enough HOPE to build her sixty-sixth foundation within earshot of Communist China.

For a reporter, Hong Kong was an island of stories—a happening place. Coming out of the Press Bureau one day, I handed a bun to a woman begging on the step. She took it, broke it in half, and offered the remainder to me. I observed the courtesies as if we had been in her own front parlor. In fact, I had a distinct feeling of being on the receiving end of hospitality.

"It is a miserable day, grandmother. I am glad to sit and talk, if you have the time."

She moved over and made space on the stairs. She talked of her husband and how she had been the proud wife of a village elder; then how the "Land Reform" was announced, and how after that her life was changed.

We sat silently for a while, eating the bun.

"My husband was beaten and imprisoned because he could not pay the crippling taxes; our two sons were conscripted and sent to fight in Korea, with the army of the People's Republic. They didn't want to go—one morning the cadres came to the village, called everyone to a meeting. At first they just sang together, then they told everyone to get up in the trucks and they were driven away. I talked late that night with my two daughters-in-law and the older children. We decided to leave.

"The next week we began walking over the mountain into Hong Kong. Ah Mei, the younger one, died as her second child was born. We did not have enough food the first weeks we were in Hong Kong, and she didn't have the strength. Now I live with my other daughter-in-law and six of the grandchildren."

I still had time before the Press Bureau was opened for the afternoon, and we walked along together to the hut which they had made in the corner of a bombed-out warehouse. We became good friends. With money given by readers of the paper, after her picture and story had been published, I was able to set her up in business, selling newspapers and fruit at the entrance to the Catholic Center, and in a one-room home in a resettlement area.

In this way literally thousands of refugees were resettled with money contributed after editorials, feature stories and pictures showed the needs of individuals and families. The enormous social problems, as the refugees continued to flow from the mainland, were reflected in the columns of the paper, and the *Examiner* began to live! Week after week, I wrote about the people I'd talked with, the conditions I'd seen—being a voice for the voiceless ones challenged all one's capacity to reach out and be heard. And the readers responded. With their help, jobs were found, school fees paid, rice-tickets provided, funerals paid for, milk supplied for babies, blankets for street-sleepers, hospitalization for the destitute sick. We ran regular campaigns for funds to build housing for the refugees, and under the direction of Father Paul Duchesne, M.M., thousands of one-room waterproof homes began to replace the cardboard shacks.

Before long, beside the typewriters and the dictaphone and the scissors and paste were shelves of clothes and food and medicine for emergency calls. The office became the meeting place for those who had and those who had not: refugees and wealthy women, priests and sisters from resettlement areas with hundreds of daily requests to meet, government welfare workers, British soldiers and American sailors giving their funds and free time.

That a pressroom can be invaded by so many and so often may seem strange in America, but this office was in the heart of a city dubbed "the biggest D.P. camp in the world." It became simply part of the daily doing in Hong Kong for Christians, no matter what their race or social standing, to turn aside and listen and try to help the many calls to their hearts.

Preparing for Sunday Mass at the House of Joy: Noella Liu is writing the Gospel theme, "Unless the grain of wheat falling into the ground dies . . ."

Chapter Three

The House of Our Lady of Joy

WHEN I FIRST arrived in Hong Kong in 1948 I lived in a hostel for working girls run by the Canossian Sisters. This massive grey stone building, clinging to the hillside overlooking the mainland, housed half a dozen major Catholic works: a high school and grade school, an orphanage, a hospital, a poor school for street sleepers' children, a distribution center for CRS-NCWC,* and, on the top floor, two long dormitories for Chinese working girls and students.

These warmhearted Italian nuns made room for the Grail, just as in succeeding years they opened wide their doors to expelled missionaries from every diocese in China. Mary Louise Tully, the first American from the Grail to go to Asia, lived for two years at Canossa. I stayed there for six months, and then, by sheer chance, one Saturday afternoon on a ramble round the island, I found Taikoolau, a Catholic village surrounded on three sides by pagan villages. It lies on the far side of Hong Kong island, facing the South China Sea. It was from here that the young French missioner, Blessed Théophane Venard, set out in a fishing junk for Hanoi—a journey which ended in his martyrdom. The men of Taikoolau for the most part work at the

* Catholic Relief Services of the National Catholic Welfare Conference, the American bishops' agency for world relief.

printing press attached to the Paris Foreign Mission Society headquarters, a large rambling building which dominates the area. The women cultivate terraced gardens to add to the daily food supply for their families.

I think it was the exuberant fruitfulness of Taikoolau which first attracted me—there were children everywhere: darting in and out of the old grey stone buildings, popping up suddenly from behind a crumbling wall and registering no fear of the "foreign devil" at all, tugging at my coat and pointing to the camera, then darting away again and shouting back "T'ien Chiu bo-yau," "May the Lord of Heaven bless you," as I continued exploring my new find.

A bell began to clang, and I was caught up in a noisy chattering throng going into church. I was at home at once. The people began to pray with such vitality and strength in their loud sing-song that it still resounds in my ears as I sit here writing 12,000 miles from Taikoolau!

The sanctuary was festooned with paper flowers and great silk hangings—it was February 10th, the eve of the patronal feast of this village church dedicated to Our Lady of Lourdes. Coming out onto the steps, I met a tall, bearded French priest in a long silk gown. He was friendly, and interested to find out who I was, and soon a crowd began to gather as I answered his questions in stumbling Cantonese. I must have been making quite a few mistakes, because the crowd roared with laughter at everything I said, but somehow that only made me feel more like one of the family. It was the first time in many months I had felt so completely part of Hong Kong. That night I decided that I wanted nothing more than to live in Taikoolau.

After some discussion, Mary Louise Tully and I agreed that I would rent a room in the village and look around for a suitable piece of land on which to build the first Grail Center in Asia. With the help of Father Nicholas Maestrini, P.I.M.E., who had sponsored our work in Hong Kong, we were able to lease a tiny bit of land from the Paris Foreign Mission Society. Around October, when the wet season was over, it was time to build; and on December 3rd, the feast of St. Francis Xavier, twelve of us moved in. Some of the girls came from the Canossa hostel with us, others were university students from the interior stranded in Hong Kong, two were working in the *Examiner* office with Mary Louise and myself: all had been carefully selected for this adventure in Christian living; eight were newly baptized, two were still Buddhists.

In this small house overlooking the South China Sea, I lived and worked with American, Dutch, Chinese and Australian Grail members. It was built in Cantonese style, of mud bricks, whitewashed outside and in, with round rough hewn beams creosoted deep brown and covered by terra cotta tiles overhead. The cement floors were covered with plaited rice straw mats; an outside kitchen was set up on the same plan as that of all the other village houses in Taikoolau, with a series of little charcoal-burning stoves. We had no running water and no electricity in the first years—these came later, along with other village improvements we helped to introduce. On the main floor we had three rooms: two sleeping rooms, one on each side, and one gathering place for meals, study, and prayer together; on top, two cocklofts reached by a bamboo ladder, where four more of us slept.

I have lived in many Grail centers scattered across five continents: the stately Tudor mansion, Tay Creggan, in Melbourne, Australia, the Ohio farmhouse at Grailville in America, the grey stone town house in Edinburgh, the pink louvered-window bungalow in Ghana—but the little house dedicated to Our Lady Cause of Our Joy in Taikoolau is the one to which I turn with greatest nostalgia.

We were packed in like sardines—not only the twelve of us, but Ah Ying our faithful amah, and Po Luk the man-about-the-place, plus the children, Kau-tsai and Ah Wan, and the more than a dozen other small ones who lived with us sporadically in the interim between the street and adoption. Each morning we all went to Mass together in the parish church, and then we'd go off to work or to school, while Ah Ying and Po Luk held the fort. We were grateful to Ah Ying, a young widow in her early thirties, who turned up one day looking for work, and soon took over the cooking and cleaning and shared all our ups and downs.

Po Luk just happened to us. He had spastic paralysis, and had never been employed. A skinny boy, he came at first just to look; then he offered to feed the rabbits, and bit by bit he was in. He slept under a staircase in the village, ate with Ah Ying from our pots and continued to pick grass for the rabbits and water the plants. He grew and blossomed with us and for the first time in his miserable life found a rootplace where he belonged.

And Kau-tsai was my special pride and joy. He came to us on the Feast of St. Thomas Aquinas in 1950, a tiny three year old with tuberculosis and skin disease. Like Po Luk, he just happened to us, but I still think the Lord has His hand in a special way on this little boy. I had known him from the streets. Often I had seen him standing at the bus stop with his grandfather, selling a few shrivelled olives. When a sale was made, the little boy would salute and put out his hand for the money, and who could resist giving him a few extra coins. Sometimes I left a package of milk powder or a few warm things from the Thanksgiving clothing collection for the oddly assorted pair. Then they disappeared from the streets, as suddenly as they had come. It was Christmas Eve 1950, and with others from the House of Joy I was carolling in the big tuberculosis hospital run by the Irish Columban Sisters. In the children's ward, I was halted by the thin cry of a very sick child, and saw it was my small friend. Because of an irritating skin disease, his arms had been splinted and tied to the sides of the cot, and in the dim light, all I could see was this suffering child in the form of a cross. I was rooted to the spot, and more than an hour must have gone by as I stood with him and tried to help. It was three months later that I brought him home to Taikoolau to try to nurse him back to health.

He grew strong on American surplus foods, but no matter how many stories I wrote about him in the *Examiner,* we never managed to get him adopted. So Ah Ying added Kau to her own son Pei-duc, and another portion was added to our rice pot.

In 1956 I came to the United States, and during the course of a talk on Pentecost Sunday in Detroit, Michigan, spoke about the lost children of Hong Kong. A young couple came to me at the end of the evening and asked if they could bring Thomas Yip Kau-tsai to the United States. I didn't think they meant it at first, as I knew all the red tape involved in bringing a Chinese child here. However, Val and Gerry Jaroch were deeply sincere in their request and by Christmas 1956 Thomas arrived in Detroit to become the eldest in a family of six. Today, as a jolly teen-ager, Thomas Yip Jaroch serves Mass in his parish church at Roseville, Michigan, every morning, helps at home, and plays with his little American brothers and sisters. This sole survivor of a family of eight who crossed into Hong Kong in 1950 does not forget the House of Joy and Ah Ying who mothered him in those early years. Last Christmas when he came to visit me at Grailville, his face lit up when we sang Compline together in the barn. Recognizing the familiar song tunes he edged closer to me and asked, "When will Ah Ying and the others come here?"

Ah Ying with her shining black hair and blue, starched "saam-foo," who had come through so many disasters, and who could still give out love to us all, is one of the valued friends of my life. In those years we had a stock phrase, "We don't have much money, but we have a lot of fun!" Only half of us were earning anything, so we pooled our resources and gave the money to Ah Ying to buy food. She made the most of every penny, haggling endlessly in the market over the fish or vegetables she bought for our table.

Quite a variety of activities developed in our little house. Soon we were using it as a center of distribution for CRS-NCWC relief; as a medical clinic in the evenings and Sunday mornings when Dr. Patricia Yip, a young interne at the Queen Mary Hospital, came home from work; for instruction classes; for training weekends to help new Catholics in their responsibilities as godmothers; and for English lessons to help educated refugees get white collar jobs in the colony. It also became the stepping stone for many students from Taiwan and Macao on their way to the United States to study. They lived with us while papers were arranged and bookings made, and we helped in the meantime to introduce them to western ways of doing.

Soon we were an established fact in Taikoolau, accepted into the community, invited to weddings and feasts, called upon in an emergency to bail someone out from prison for hawking without a license, or to use our prestige as a "foreign one" to get a bed in the overcrowded Queen Mary Hospital, reserved mainly for those in British government employ.

Making up our household over the years at Taikoolau have been young daughters from the northern stretches of Ninghsai, Peking, Mukden, Shanghai and Canton, fleeing the tide of Communism. They managed to seep into Hong Kong by wading through the low border marshes which skirt the colony, or by slipping over the sides of sampans and swimming ashore, as well as by the regular way. They came from the shelter of decent homes to the swiftly moving cosmopolitan life of Hong Kong. We counted among us one whose father was killed by the Communists because he was a land owner; two sisters who had been forced to join the Young Pioneers League of the Communist Party and were smuggled over the border by an aged grandmother after months of hiding and hardships; dozens who saw their Catholic universities closed, their professors humiliated and imprisoned, and who, rather than submit to learning without truth, came destitute to Hong Kong. Often these young ones had gone through tremendous interior struggles. I remember Zing-Zing, for example.

One evening after supper I remarked: "There's a jolly good film on, shall we all go the day after tomorrow and see it?" It was a rare occasion, for few good films found their way to us. There was an enthusiastic response, with, however, one exception. Later on there was a knock on my door.

"Miss Reid," said one of the girls, "Zing-Zing can't go to the film."

"Oh, what a pity! Why can't she?"

"Because she made a vow."

"A vow?"

"Yes, a vow not to go to the movies." I was determined to ask the girl myself what it was all about.

"Well, Miss Reid," she said quite simply, "you know what a struggle I had with myself when I had to follow that indoctrination course in Shanghai, but the moment came when I knew that I wanted to remain faithful to God and that all this Communism was no good. Still, when we had a movie, there were often things which impressed me, and I was afraid that I might not be able to remain true to my baptism. So from then on I kept my eyes tightly shut at every film, and I used to sit there praying that God would help me. It was then that I made the vow that if ever I got out of the course and if my father succeeded in getting me to Hong Kong, I would not go to see any films for three years, even if they were good ones."

"And how did you make this vow, Zing-Zing?"

"Well, just there in the room with my eyes tightly closed, I said it to Our Lord."

Zing-Zing was then seventeen years old. Her parents, both Catholics, are still in Shanghai, but now are as poor as it is possible to be. "Father always warned me," she told me. "He was so afraid that I would lose the faith, so he wanted to get me out of Shanghai. And mother," she added then with great simplicity, "mother did penance for me that I might stay on the right path."

This was the fertile seed we were given to work with in Hong Kong.

What a household! And how our hearts burned within us at the stories we exchanged around the dining room table. From Shanghai came word of how the Communists had been trying to receive Holy Communion with the faithful in the churches to make a mock of the Eucharist. At first the students tried to head them off, but they got into trouble and were either arrested or came to blows. So they organized their small brothers and sisters, children no more than eight or nine years of age, to act as spotters. When the people gathered at the altar rail the children would run along behind and with dumb show indicate to the priest, over the heads of the communicants, who were Catholics and who were not. It is not easy to arrest such small ones and certainly face-losing for the Communist guards. When the Legion of Mary was banned and all active members were called up to the police station for interrogation, children just past the age of reason were called and threatened. Without exception in more than a hundred cases they stood firm and went to the police with little bundles ready for prison. One non-Catholic mother even remarked, "Soon my daughter will be fat enough to endure the rigors of prison life. We expect her to be taken at any time, so I am feeding her up!"

No wonder the Gospel lived for us. Every evening at supper, we read the text of the next day's Mass. There was an occasion when this caught up with me in a way I wasn't prepared for.

It was a cold, misty Saturday afternoon. We had just made the long journey home from the city to Taikoolau in a fisherman's open truck. The steaming rice bowls were already filled on the table, and food never looked better. Suddenly we heard a great hullabaloo and the clip-clop of clogs down the cement steps at the back of the house. Ah Ying with much shouting tried to stave off the crowd.

"Where is the foreign one? She will tell us what to do. We want to speak with her." No chance to duck away in a three-room house when more than a dozen excited village women were on the doorstep. Weary and cold and barely observing the usual courtesies for guests, I came out to the door and invited everyone in, watching out of the corner of my eye the last curl of steam from the rice. There's nothing colder than cold rice. But then my eye caught the object of the excitement, and the weariness dropped off in a jiffy. A scarcely breathing scrap of human-

Debora, conducting story hour with Ah Wan and Kau-tsai.

ity wrapped in newspaper was held under the jacket of one of the women. Everyone spoke at once, and when the story was unravelled, we found they had picked up the abandoned mite in a broken water pipe at the entrance to the village. At first no one wanted to take the child up, but then it was agreed that I would be the one to consult about this unwelcome discovery. Everyone was poor in our village—another mouth to feed, especially a baby girl who would need milk which was hardly procurable and expensive, was an impossible problem. I took the child, explaining that on Monday on my way to the office I'd stop off at the Sisters' orphanage and leave her with them. That weekend instead of writing the editorial to meet the deadline of the paper, I hovered over the baby with the rest.

On Monday morning with a sigh of relief, I picked my way off the bus and hurried up the hill to Ling Yuet Sin Orphanage. The Sisters there were my good friends. We'd often worked together—on three previous occasions babies had been left in the basket on my desk at the Catholic Press Bureau while I was out to lunch, and the Sisters, in spite of tremendous burdens to keep the place going, had always made room for one more.

But this morning I met my Waterloo. There was no more place. Sister had three babies to a cot already, she explained to me patiently; she just couldn't take another one. As soon as a child died, she would call me. It was humanly impossible now. I turned away from the desk clutching the baby and my brief case, thinking of the blank editorial column I had to fill by midday!

Once in the office, I called many of my friends in the Chinese Catholic Club and the Catholic Women's League, but they also had reached the saturation point as far as babies were concerned. With some warm milk from the tea room tucked into her and an open file drawer to sleep in, the baby's problem was solved for the moment. I turned to my editorial.

At home that evening around the supper table we held a family council. It was decided that Ah Ying and Po Luk would look after her in the daytime, and we made a roster to take turns looking after her at night. We spent hours deciding what we would call her. I had baptized her quickly the night before, but had given her no name. Now we settled on Christine for the Christian name because we were still in the octave of Christmas, and Ah Wan—Little Cloud—for her family name. We still had a large tin of powdered milk left from a Christmas parcel sent up from the Grail in Australia, and we prepared to carry on until Sister called from Ling Yuet Sin.

Two weeks later the call came. I thanked Sister warmly, but as I put the receiver back on the phone I had a sudden sinking feeling which persisted all day. Once again the fifteen of us gathered round our supper table—it was always the high point of our day, back home from the press bureau, the clinic, the Poor Boys and Girls Club, the university and high school—each from her separate ways. All of us knew what it was to be uprooted and away from our homeland, and we responded to the oneness we were consciously building up together. After a few minutes, I told about the phone call and the place ready for Ah Wan at the orphanage in the morning. There was complete silence. No one said anything. I pushed back my bowl and reached for the missal. Without looking to see which Gospel it was, I began reading: " . . . At that time the disciples came to Jesus saying, 'Who then is the greatest in the Kingdom of Heaven?' " I saw the sentences immediately following, but it was too late to stop. As I went on, I could feel all those dark eyes on me. I think I even blushed as the last sentence came out, "And whoever receives one such little child for my sake, receives me." I closed the book. No one said anything. Then two naughty voices in unison said, "Look here, people, let's not just *read* the Gospel; we must *live* it," in exactly my intonation, and with a strong Australian accent. Until that moment I hadn't noticed it had become a usual ending to our readings. Then we all began talking at once and discussing ways and means of keeping our Little Cloud. We decided it should indeed be our group responsibility and it was agreed that all twelve of us, non-Catholics as well as the others, would walk the extra stops on the bus route and the money saved would buy the milk each day. We had a grand celebration the day she was "weaned" ten months later, and we no longer had the expense of buying milk.

The fact that we had taken in Ah Wan had repercussions in the whole village. At first the people were puzzled as to why we should shoulder the responsibility, but as the months went by they got the point. Within a year a dozen families in the neighborhood had taken in these small extra ones, and the Gospel was indeed being lived—and for very many of these families at a heroic sacrifice.

Debora Schak with some of the young students who lived with us at the House of Joy in Hong Kong.

Chapter Four

Wanted—Godmothers

THE RED bus rattled around the corner and jerked to a stop. People bulged from the windows and doorways. But Debora and I, with half a dozen Taikoolau villagers, still had to get on. At last we established ourselves with a toe hold on the running board.

It was Debora's introduction to the masses of Asia, not just cold hard figures in a report—"2222 persons to an acre in the densest part of Hong Kong"—but living, pulsating people from the fishing junks in our neighborhood. The pungent smell of their trade hung in their clothes: tar and oil and fish. Their voices, sharp and clear with the peculiar cadence of Cantonese and its nine tones, lashed our consciousness. All our senses, bodies, eyes, ears, smell, were merged into a oneness with these people as we jerked around the island. For me it was a routine run—for six years I'd fought my way onto the early morning bus into the city, but for Debora, fresh from the States, it was a plunge into the unknown.

Debora Schak grew up in St. Paul, Minnesota. During her third year at St. Catherine's College there, she met Janet Kalven and two other Grail members who were speaking in the city. Debora, who excels in math, knew how to count—she added up the needs of the world which were presented to her and knew the only right answer was to throw her weight into the balance. Within a few months she was at Grailville beginning her training in the apostolate. Now, eight years later, she had come to join our Hong Kong team.

Debora is shy. As a child she had been too tall for her age, and so her natural reflex is to try to melt into a crowd, but she did not succeed in remaining inconspicuous that morning. Her hands and feet are of such generous proportions that they immediately became the topic of conversation for the whole bus: "Look at the hands of the foreign devil, they are as big as the octopus which fed twenty people." But when they looked up into Debora's eyes, they met such a warm, friendly response that one passenger even ventured to reach over and measure her hand with Debora's—amid waves of laughter which rippled over us all. Communication was begun, a link was forged, and I knew that Debora was accepted by our neighbors.

For Debora, as for all of us who go to share the life of people in other lands, there are adjustments to be made. The language has to be learned, customs and ways of doing understood and appreciated, friendships made which weld one into the local community. We are not rootless people because we have left our familiar places. Far from it. Our roots in the international Grail Movement are deep in the world community of the Church, which transcends nationalism, frontiers, language barriers, oceans, continents. Surely we were plunged into a strange civilization among the Chinese people in Hong Kong, but just as surely we were soon completely identified with each other as fellow members of the people of God, as *being* the Church in this particular spot on earth.

This fundamental identification very soon found expression in a variety of practical tasks. One of our specialities was to be godmothers, and our godchildren were many, with a bewildering range of backgrounds, occupations and ages. With every big feast in Hong Kong, hundreds of converts are baptized. The Catholic population leaped from 50,000 in 1950 to 131,000 in

1960, and Hong Kong became the fastest growing diocese in the world. There are so many newly baptized that the bulk of the Catholics are less than seven years in the Church, a fact which gives the role of the godparents a particular importance. For although these new Christians have the faith, there is still the task of learning how to live it. How to translate Christian ideas and ideals into the patterns of daily doing at home, at work, in courtship and marriage, in recreation, in the larger issues of economic and political life? Here the godparents have to lead the way, and in less time than it takes to write, we found ourselves plunged into this great surge of new life in the Church. I have thirty-eight godchildren and, I would dare to say, I have a deeper, more tangible relationship with most of them than with some of my own blood relations in Australia.

The Easter Vigil Mass with its thousands of baptisms is the crowning feast of the year. Our Grail team, Debora, myself, Thecla Schiphorst from Holland and Nan Johns from Australia, were intensely aware of our unity with the people of Hong Kong as we stood in the packed Cathedral of the Immaculate Conception, each with a hand on the shoulder of a godchild while the life-giving water was poured.

They had been prepared during Lent, these hundreds of catechumens, won over and helped by Christians who had themselves been baptized only a year, six months, or even three months before. Among them were seventy girls from the upper classes of convent high schools; forty students from a Chinese boys' college; whole families with four, five, eight children with gleaming eyes; many mothers with their babies slung on their backs. They filled the front half of the Cathedral, right and left, and beyond them were hundreds upon hundreds who had come to celebrate the Resurrection of the Lord, and also their own resurrection from sorrow and darkness and suffering. O, that great majestic candle with the pure burning flame—Lumen Christi, Light of Christ—carried by a confessor-bishop (Bishop Lawrence Bianchi, P.I.M.E., fresh from Communist hands across the

Two of the small lost ones—the misery one was helpless to relieve broke the heart.

border), entering slowly into the pitch-dark church. What an image, what a glorious unforgettable image of the Reality—Christ the true Light, the warming Light for all in darkness.

With the bishop were four priests, each one with an assistant, who stood in the sanctuary behind the altar rail and baptized. In five long rows the candidates moved up. Don't imagine it as a precise, well-ordered solemnity, symmetrically arranged and rehearsed six times over. It was a teeming and a humming, a waiting here, a rushing there, so that a remark I once heard suddenly flashed through my mind: "The Kingdom of God moves along by jolts and hitches."

There they came, by jolts and hitches indeed, white-veiled women and girls, and the young men like young men the world over, gawky, angular, awkward, and the tiny children who had first to be awakened by their mothers, and who, dazed with sleep, kept tumbling against the bystanders. Up they went to the altar, followed or accompanied by a proud godfather or godmother; there they knelt at the Communion table with their heads tilted slightly over to one side. The godparent handed the assistant a piece of paper on which was written the new Christian name. He called it out for the benefit of the priest and held the dish under the head of the person about to be baptized so that the water could flow into it. "Matthew, I baptize you. . . . " With beautiful calm face a sixteen-year-old Chinese boy, his eyes closed, waits to be reborn. "Mary, I baptize you. . . . " A simple woman, a little bit nervous, with her head bowed, pushes her hair back and smooths her veil for the last time, blinks her eyes—the water flows, and she is a new creature.

While the assistant wipes the water from her forehead with a cloth, she bows still more deeply. The baby tied on her back croons softly, "ah . . . sh . . . ," and he blinks his eyes as he looks in astonishment at the priest, at the water container, at the burning candles. He clutches with a tiny hand. "Thomas, I baptize you. . . . " "Ah . . . sh . . . " says Thomas much louder this time as the baptismal water flows over his forehead. It is already done. He is a child of God, this Thomas, who finds the way back into the bench on his mother's back. It is Mother Church who gives life. It is Christ who celebrates the Redemption. It is the people of China who become Christian.

An exiled American missioner crosses the border at Lowu. Hong Kong police in the foreground, Communist customs regulations on the sign board in the background; Communist police post overlooking the Hong Kong border can be seen on the top of the hill.

Chapter Five

The Border Bridge

THE SOFT-FOOTED house boy put the tea tray down on the rattan table between my friend, Lam Ti, and myself, and the conversation drifted to a recent excursion we had been on together to Shau-tau-kok. This outpost on the Sino-British border is mildly famous as the village which gave Vice President Nixon perhaps his greatest shock in Hong Kong, for it was at the police post half a mile back that he was given a pair of binoculars and told to observe the concrete blocks set in the middle of the main street.

"Yes," he said, "I see them. What are they?"

"Those," he was told, "form the border."

And, it was said, he was silent for quite two minutes before rallying strongly and asking whether he could "Go right on down there." But it shook him, this little village where they have an international border instead of a white line down the middle of the road.

Lam Ti and I laughed as we remembered, and went on sipping our tea. That's how it is in Hong Kong. The fact that this tiny British colony is an island of freedom set in a sea of Communism was something as ordinary to us local people as the fact for New Yorkers that you can cross a bridge to go from Brooklyn to Manhattan.

But the Sino-British border in Hong Kong is more than cement blocks down the middle of the road; more than a bridge across the river at Lowu; more than a man in a loose khaki uniform shouldering a glittering gun; more than the red flag with five yellow stars on one side, and the British Union Jack on the other. The border is a spot where every man is alone for a little minute with the beating of his heart.

It fascinated me the many days I spent there between 1950 and 1956 with the "Border Patrol" which operated from our office, organized so that there would be someone on hand every day from the Catholic Center to identify and receive the expelled missioners. Standing beside the narrow strip of no-man's-land, watching the travelers who passed over, one was aware that it was either the end or the beginning for them, a moment of shining hope or jagged despair. One saw men more complete after years of imprisonment, and others diminished and broken by suffering, faces which showed fulfillment or disenchantment—always just across the border.

So many faces crowd before me: men and women from every western nation, empty-handed now after years of giving in hospitals, schools, orphanages, clinics; stooped old priests with grubby bundles, walking with the slow steps of those who have left behind them a lifetime of work; unstarched nuns with joking words, nostalgic words on their lips, but never bitterness. With sunken eyes and skin stretched across their cheekbones, they leaned across the table, forgetting to drink the tea and eat the sandwiches we provided, while they said over and over again, "Our Christians are wonderful. Nothing can change them. They are not afraid. They will go to jail, they will die, but they will never follow the Communist line."

I can never forget the long look backwards of a bishop forced to leave his flock, and then the near transparent hand raised in blessing over China for the last time; or the three young laughing Irishmen, Columban missionaries, able to change a poignant moment into hilarious laughter as they gave a deep

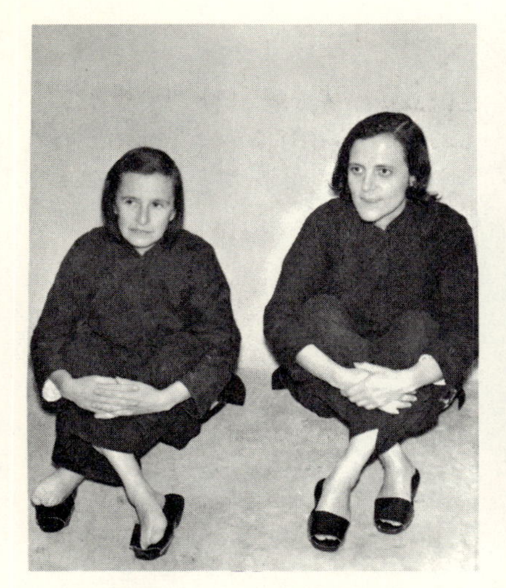

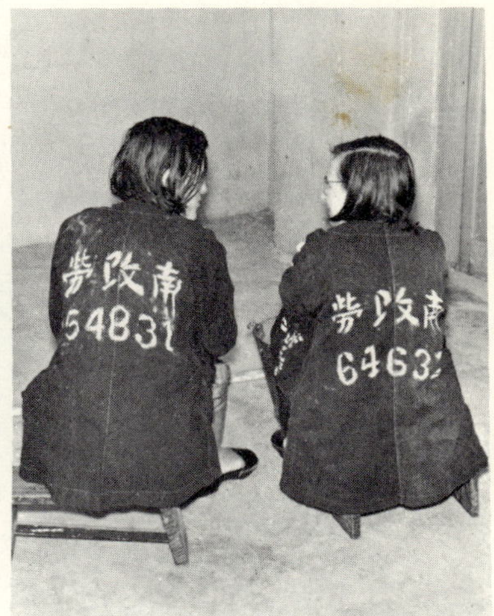

I took these photographs of two Canadian nuns on their arrival in Hong Kong, shortly after they had crossed the border, exhausted by the gruelling months of imprisonment.

solemn "honorable" bow to the British Union Jack, saying, "Just this once!" Or the Swiss priest who had for three years eked out a precarious existence as a carpenter, living and working in a cellar . . . and the old Canadian priest, who for five years had herded goats on the mountainside by day and cared for his Christians by night . . . and the French missioner, crossing the border after fifty-seven years in China, murmuring, "We shall return."

I think of the old Cantonese woman with the meagre bundle, who simply answered when questioned, "I came so that I could go to Mass. Our priest was taken away, and I am old and soon I'll die. I cannot face the Lord of Heaven and say I did not worship Him with the Holy Sacrifice of the Mass as we have been instructed by the Spiritual Father." She left everything, this ancient one, this witness of the faith that was in her, and lived on the streets of Hong Kong, so she could *do* just that!

And I think of the teen-age Korean girl whom I saw, standing alone and bewildered at the border, clutching her two cloth

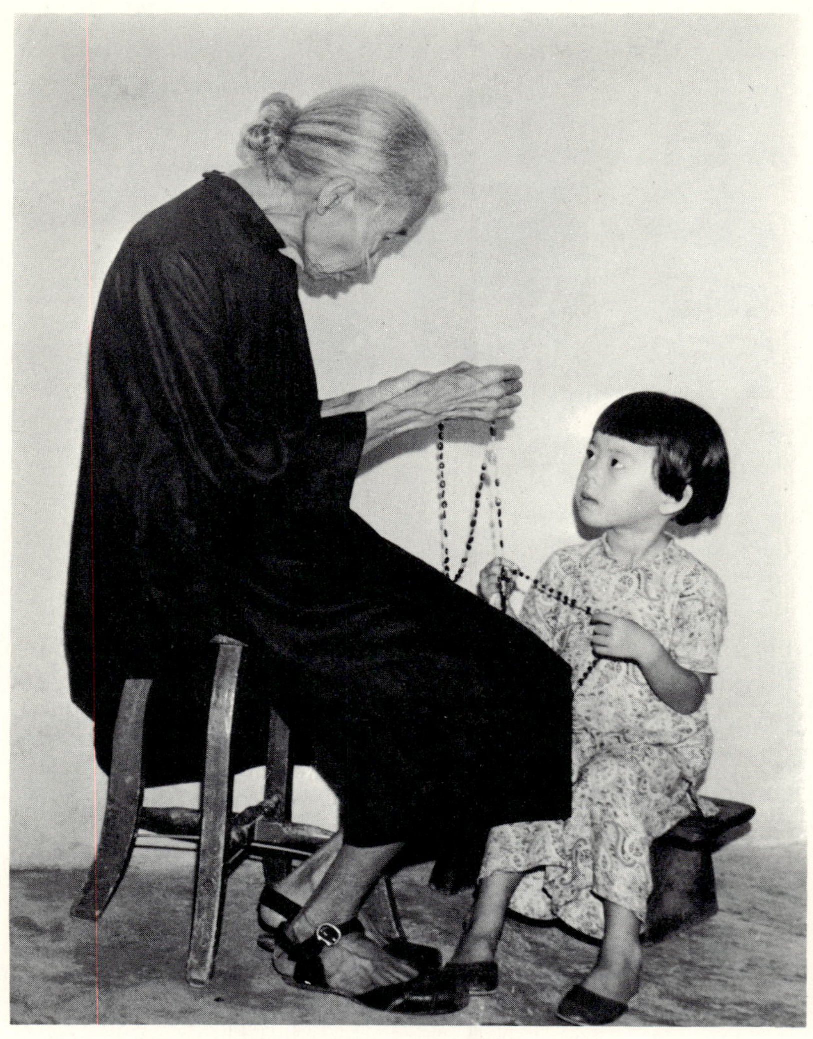

A refugee grandmother handing on the faith.

bundles, while tears streamed down her face. I asked if I could help. In a cascade of words, she poured out her story—the sudden arrest, the hours of questioning about her affiliation with the Legion of Mary, her refusal to "confess that the Legion is a tool of the imperialists," the order to get ready for a journey. She had no idea where she was being sent—she thought it was to an indoctrination school, but somehow she was placed with other non-Chinese refugees on the train for Hong Kong. This teenager was the first of many Legionaries who were expelled across the border after the Legion was outlawed in China.

In this way, thousands of Catholic people, men and women, boys and girls, even little children, left their cities and villages, and streamed across the border into Hong Kong. I see them still: parched faces, cracked by the wind; faces covered with boils; distended stomachs that told of worms and the swollen feet which announced beri-beri; little heads cropped by a dull razor, or with hair knotted and straggling; sunken cheeks and toothless gums, and sad eyes unused to tears.

Why did they come, these hundreds of thousands of Chinese people? Why did they crowd into tiny Hong Kong on its barren island? They came because they could not live under a Communist regime; they came because they knew by the most direct experience possible that there is no such thing as freedom of religion under Communism.

Some of Hong Kong's mothers call on me at the Centre.

Chapter Six

Panorama of Persecution

In 1949, on the eve of the great Communist push, the Catholic Church in China had 3 universities, 189 middle schools, 1,500 primary schools, 2,243 rural schools, with a total enrollment of 320,000 children. At the same time the Church was running 216 hospitals, 781 dispensaries, 5 leprosaria, 254 orphanages with 16,000 orphans, 29 printing presses, 55 reviews, an observatory, the largest library in Shanghai, 2 museums and an ethnological institute. Of all these, there now remains a *single* school, run by the Franciscan Missionaries of Mary in Peking for the children of foreign diplomats accredited to the Republic of China.

In 1948, when I first arrived in Hong Kong, there were 3,300,000 Catholics in China, living in 20 archdioceses, 85 dioceses, and 39 prefectures apostolic. There were 27 Chinese bishops and a Chinese cardinal; 5,788 priests of whom 2,698 were Chinese; 7,463 nuns of whom 5,112 were Chinese. In 1959, ten years after the Communist armies were let loose in China the visible organization of the Church, built up painfully through centuries of missionary effort, had for the most part disappeared. Foreign priests and religious have been killed or expelled; thousands of Chinese priests and nuns and laity have died in jails and slave prison camps; churches have been taken over, all activities suspended. There is no more public worship, no feasts, no sacraments; Sundays are no more. God is only spoken of in the secrecy of the family.

How did all this happen? In exactly the same way as in all the Communist dominated countries of Europe—the same pattern of infiltration, domination and persecution. In 1949 the Communist government quickly laid down its policy towards religion. Marxism is atheistic; it has nothing in common with religion, but will guide the people in their fight against imperialism. It will not allow the people to propagate their beliefs outside the churches. During the Land Reform all Church activities, whether in the churches or outside them, were to be suspended. Publications insulting the People's Democracy were to be suppressed and all such books were to be destroyed. All schools were to teach Communist political doctrine.

But after the completion of the Land Reform, services in rural areas were still suspended, and the Church properties were never given back. All the schools were lost—Communist doctrine cannot be taught in a Catholic school.

The Communist authorities then evolved as their principal weapon for the destruction of the Church a formula which has become known as the "Three Autonomies." Under the guise of self-rule, self-support and self-propagation, they demanded absolute separation of the Chinese churches from any alignment with foreign congregations. The same tactics had been followed in the Communist dominated countries of Europe. Setting up an "independent" church has always signified independence from all domination but that of the Communist government.

For Catholics, the matter touched on their fundamental beliefs. A national effort to explain the Catholic position was made in a pamphlet issued from Shanghai. This brought down the official wrath of Peking. The entire hierarchy and clergy were labeled "imperialists." According to the *People's Daily* the declaration of the Catholic position "afforded irrevocable proof of the attempt on the part of the imperialist elements of the Catholic Church to sabotage the Chinese Catholic Church's patriotic independence and reformation movements." Gruesome cartoons were published in all the dailies along with the accusations, so as to make sure those who could not read would also get an inkling of "the evils of the Catholic Church." One series entitled, "The Vatican, Servant of American Imperialism," purported to show the close alliance between the pope and the U. S. Secret Service. A cartoon depicting a group of priests with evil faces conferring with a leering Uncle Sam bore the caption, "The Vatican announced that it would train a group of priests as spies for Eastern Europe, and that American agents would undertake the work of their training."

Submission to the demands of the government to adopt the reformation movement, voiced by Chou En-lai himself to the assembled clergy in Peking, meant total surrender of the Church to the direction of Communism. Refusal brought about immediate reprisals.

Then the clear pattern of persecution began to emerge—attacks on the orphanages, the hospitals, the clinics, and espionage trials for foreign missioners. After farcical "trials" in People's Courts, they were sentenced, some to years of imprisonment, some to immediate expulsion from China.

Day after day we sat at our desks recording the systematic destruction of the Church in China, as told by the expellees who crowded in upon us. It wasn't easy to get their stories, they were not the talking kind; once the pedestrian facts had been stated, they always spoke about the Christians they had left behind. And they were right, the foreign missionary is primarily a bridge, and the Church in China today *is* the Chinese Christians left inside. How often in these interviews I was privileged to catch glimpses of heroism—of that same spirit of fortitude which flamed in the martyrs of the first Christian centuries.

It was an Irish priest who told me about a young Chinese girl, only fourteen years old, who had the courage to maneuver into position beneath a jail window in Kwantung Province. There she waited for a bamboo cylinder containing one hundred fifty consecrated hosts, which was attached to a string lowered by the priest from his cell on the second floor. The Catholics had found a means of supplying the priest with breads; he said Mass secretly lying on the floor, and slipped the bamboo "ciborium" out through the broken meshes of his wire window; so this young daughter of the Church was able to take the Bread of Life to her people.

Then there was the decent pagan soldier who had been hanging around an orphanage for over a month, watching the Sisters looking after the orphans. They had been embarrassed and worried by his persevering attendance. However, when they were being publicly tried for "maltreating" the children and when accusers had charged them with all kinds of torture, this brave man stood up before the judges and publicly shouted, "That's all a lie. I've been watching these women from the West for over a month, and they treat the orphans well." That act needed superhuman courage.

Can I ever put out of my heart the teen-age girl who slipped a note to a foreign priest in jail. It read: "Father, it is true that I am suffering a great deal (for the faith) and the suffering I shall undergo I cannot now see, but this is my first resolve. I shall never give up the One, Holy, Catholic and Apostolic Church until I die. Father, I plead and plead again for one thing—implore God to increase my courage. After we have found our way home to Christ, we shall rejoice together forever. . . ."

Then there were the courageous youngsters in the Salesian house in Peking, who for two hours squatted deliberately and defiantly around their superior, Father Paul Wong, to prevent the Red police from arresting him. The police had finally to call on Father Wong himself to quiet his "guardian angels." Only at his bidding would they allow him to be taken away. I do not know where Father Wong is now, or whether he is still alive, but I do know something about the fate of other Chinese priests. I quote at random from a list, prepared by Reverend Thomas Bauer, M.M., of 166 Chinese priests killed by the Communists:

Chang, Father Beda, S.J., Diocese of Shanghai; died in jail.

Ch'en, Father Ch'en Yueh-shih, Prefecture of Lintsing; beaten to death.

Hsia, Father Camille, Diocese of Jehol; dragged twice, shot.

Kung, Father Lawrence, Diocese of Kirin; burned, shot.

Liang, Father Andre, Diocese of Chengtu; jailed for Legion of Mary, shot.

Liu, Father Thaddee, Diocese of Pakhoi; beaten to death.

Shen, Father Joseph, Diocese of Hanyang; died in Shanghai jail.

Shih, Father Seraphin (Trappist), Yangkisoing; head crushed between stones.

Wu, Father Mathieu, Diocese of Chunking; beheaded.

Not since the first centuries of Christianity has there been so thorough and relentless an effort to wipe out the Church.

Early in the struggle the Catholic students distinguished themselves by their steadfast resistance. Typical of their spirit is the following report about the students of Aurora University in Shanghai, one of the three great Catholic universities in China. In the course of the "Three Autonomies" movement, the Communists decided to make Aurora the center of the Reformed Church, and sent thirty specially trained political commissars from Peking to "re-orient" the students' thinking. Months passed in preliminary skirmishes; the students refused to accuse their professors or to sign in favor of the Triple Reform. Peking sent a second, then a third team of commissars, who tried a different tack. Fifteen of the student leaders were invited to a tea party, where the atmosphere was made as friendly and seductive as possible. The chief commissars apologized for the lack of tact of their subordinates and promised that the students could speak their minds openly.

One of the students replied: "Thank you very much. I will speak my mind. A young girl is offered a ring by a sympathetic man. Is it of gold inset with diamonds or merely of copper? No

Rachel chooses some reading matter from the bookshop at the Catholic Centre.

matter. If she is honest, she will want to find out the intention of the donor. If he wishes to seduce her, she will refuse even the gold ring. But if he is sincere of heart, she will joyfully accept the copper ring. I am like the young girl. I am not interested in what you have to offer, but in your intentions." Frozen silence.

Another student: "Can you honestly say that the Internuncio (Archbishop Riberi) was expelled at the request of the Catholics?"

Another: "I dare you to assert that the Legion of Mary is a reactionary political organization."

". . . And when they bring you before the authorities, do

not be anxious what you shall say, for the Holy Spirit will teach you in that very hour what you will say."

Their campaign a failure, the Communists finally ordered the students of Aurora to be dispersed to other universities. One final incident preceded the dispersal. Right at the beginning of the campaign against the University, three student leaders had been arrested, one of them a girl. News seeping out of the prison testified to their heroic fortitude. Over and over in the meetings together during the months which followed, the knowledge of the three suffering in the nearby prison had given the whole group strength. Then suddenly, right at the end, the girl was released. Brought before the last assembly of students, before they were dispersed to the other universities, she accused the priests and her professors and proclaimed loyalty to the regime.

A stunned silence followed her words. Tears flowed freely. Taken out, she was guarded closely, but the Catholics, gathering together the individual beads of her rosary which had been divided among them on her imprisonment, managed to return the assembled rosary to her—delicate, exquisite appeal of fraternal charity.

At a meeting which followed one of the students remarked that the group had been too much shaken by her defection. This was how he was answered: "They have taken from us the heart of our sister, and we suffer. In entreating Christ from the bottom of our wounded hearts, we have discovered our own weakness. After resisting for more than a year in absolute isolation, our sister has broken. In this terrific struggle against the darkness, we are all together; if one has fallen and is broken, it is because the others have not helped enough.

"God alone is able to save us; if we should attribute to ourselves the merit of having resisted during the recent battle, we are near to losing the divine grace which alone can hold us up."

Words spoken spontaneously, not by a doctor of the Church during the heroic apostolic period, but in the mid-twentieth century by a young member of a race we so often think of as pagan.

Where are they now, these students of Aurora? Not much news of the Chinese Christians seeps through the bamboo curtain. But from the bits and pieces—a letter here, a reading between the lines of a Communist news report, from the very efforts which the Communists must make to set up their puppet church—one can gather testimony that the heroic constancy of the Chinese Catholics still goes on.

One final incident, perhaps the most poignant of all, was told me by a Chinese nun who had witnessed it. We were sitting outside the Grail Center in Taikoolau, in the solemn stillness of the evening, the sounds of the villagers muted in the dusk.

He lived in Kunming, this young Chinese priest. After a long and bitter imprisonment he was being led away to execution. Near the Catholic cemetery, he fell from weakness. The guards beat him fiercely. Lifting his head to try to pull himself up, he saw a great cross at the entrance. He gathered his strength in a mighty effort and dashed towards the cross. When the Communist guards saw his destination, they shot him. We sat quiet for a long time that evening looking out over the South China Sea, where from out the stillness as the sun went down a shaft of red shot out over the water, and our hearts were urged to burn as red, to shine, to be consumed.

* * *

Across the border in Hong Kong the life of the Church goes on. It was still and cold one Pentecost morning in the tiny mission church on top of the mountain at Wong Tau Ying.

A tiny boy in a faded padded jacket, with a pink woolen cap unravelling over his ear, danced delightedly up and down in a patch of red sunlight thrown from a high window onto the wooden floor below. His bare toes wriggled with satisfaction as they were transformed in the dazzling glow.

The tall Chinese Bishop Joseph Yuen, exiled from Chumatien, resplendent in cope and mitre, turned around and faced the congregation. All eyes were glued on him, and a shimmer of expectation ran through the people. The paper flower festoons swung sideways in the breeze, and one was aware of an immense surge of life. A straggling line of boys and girls formed up against the wall.

The bishop stretched out his hands over them. He called down the Almighty, everlasting God to send forth the sevenfold Holy Spirit, the Paraclete from Heaven, on the boy who tended the buffalo, on the boy who threw the welcoming firecrackers, on the timid bird-like little girls with the flowered cotton head-scarves tied under their chins, on the older roundfaced girls whose passionless voices lilted the ballad of the Comforter, "Veni, Sancte Spiritus." The bishop called on the Spirit of Wisdom and Understanding, on the Spirit of Counsel and Fortitude, on the Spirit of Knowledge and Piety . . . and the little boy went on dancing in the sunbeam, watching his grimy toes transformed in the dazzling light . . . the bishop's hands were still outstretched as he prayed the Almighty, everlasting God to fill these little ones with the Spirit of Holy Fear, and then he signed them with the sign of the Cross. They couldn't see their souls and what had happened to them as the bishop prayed.

Nor can we see the Holy Spirit at work on the China mainland, but we can HOPE for a radiant transformation, as the people of China are signed with the Cross.

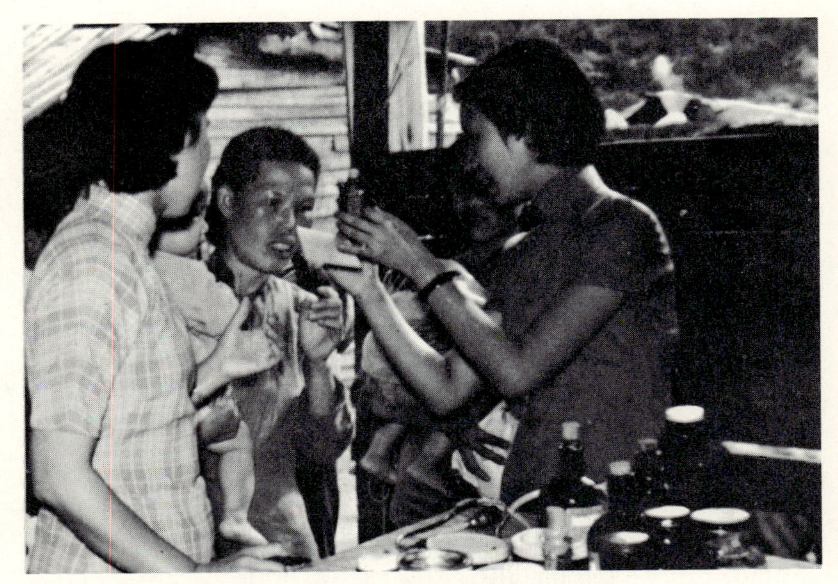

Dr. Patricia Yip holds clinic in Taikoolau village.

Chapter Seven

Fifty Thousand Korean Children Ask: Where Is Home?

WEEK AFTER week the *Sunday Examiner* came out, fresh refugee students came to Taikoolau, the Hong Kong Students' Press Group continued to draw keen senior boys and girls who kept me on my toes. But much was happening outside Hong Kong, and I wanted firsthand stories for the press bureau to keep the Hong Kong Catholics in touch with the reality of the situation in which they lived, so close to the Communist-dominated masses.

Father Paul Duchesne, M.M., Director of CRS-NCWC, arranged for me to fly up to Japan and Korea in April, 1953, to gather copy for the *Examiner,* as well as to take pictures and write human interest stories of women and children refugees in Korea for Catholic Relief Services, who were preparing for their Thanksgiving clothing drive in the States.

I flew up to Tokyo, thinking it would be comparatively simple to get my papers for entry into Korea as an accredited press corrsepondent, but I hadn't reckoned with Army red tape. After a lot of footslogging, I found myself—Australian accent and all—wearing an American issued uniform and classified in a neat card file marked "General Mark Clark's special staff," as holding the rank of "Major through Colonel," U. S. Army.

In the months which followed I came to respect the American G.I. and those generous human qualities often forgotten by people who have been at the receiving end. It is not easy to be a citizen of a "have" nation in a world of "have nots." I remember the red-headed boy from Oklahoma, just out of high school, who drove my jeep, and confided his fears and confusion at being thrust into a major scale war without a clue to what it was all about. He did the only thing he knew in the face of all this chaos. In off-duty times, he went out into the streets and collected swarms of kids around him as he fed them popcorn and cokes from the PX store. Then there was the freckle-faced UNKRRA * girl from a small town in upstate Ohio who gave up the luxury of leave to Tokyo in order to help out the Korean Sisters of St. Paul of Chartres when a new bunch of lost children appeared on their doorstep. I got to know hundreds of Americans like these.

It was mid-April when I flew into Seoul. I drove in a jeep from the air base to the correspondents' billet, and the impact on a newcomer was shattering. Gaunt skeletons of bombed-out buildings cast long shadows as the sun went down. People huddled in the rubble at their base, preparing some kind of evening meal over tiny fires. Women in dusty white flowing garments carried bundles on their heads. Children darted in and out of the constant stream of military trucks, jeeps and staff cars —ragged waifs clutching shoeshine outfits or banded together in disorderly hordes, small demons fighting and scratching.

Hardly a whole building had survived the bombardment. Water, power, sewer and transportation systems were in ruins; no telephones worked; there was no food; no hospitals were operative.

Seoul, Korea's capital city before that fateful day in June of 1950 when the Communists crossed the parallel, had a popu-

* United Nations Korean Relief and Rehabilitation Association.

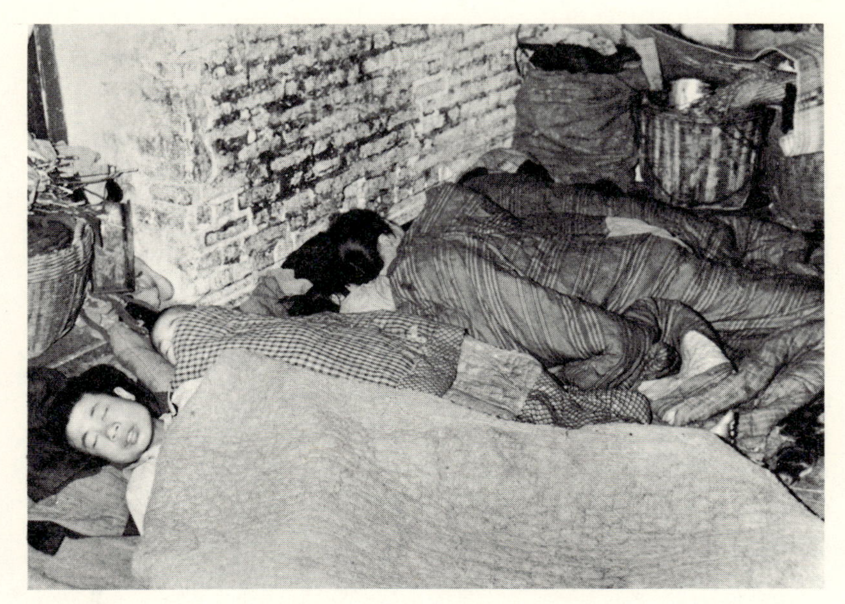

The Wong family, bedded down for the night on the streets of Hong Kong.

lation of 2,000,000. It was the site of almost all Korea's important colleges, hospitals and institutions. It was the rail hub and the center of the country's richest farming lands. It was the home of the apostolic delegate, and See city of the bishop. Twice Seoul fell—twice it was retaken: four times raked over by all the might of modern warfare. The last liberation by the United Nations troops found only 175,000 people living there.

To get all this misery in perspective we need to go back to the turn of the century, when the Japanese, seeking expansion, reached out across the sea to the "Land of the Morning Calm." For the next forty years the Japanese invaders taught the Koreans "to follow, not to know." This state of affairs led to inevitable chaos when in 1945 the Japanese control was ended, and Korea was given back to the Korean people to govern themselves. Hardly had they begun to find their way in the family of sovereign nations when on June 25th, 1950, the Communists violated the agreement they had made with the Western powers, crossed the 38th parallel and touched off what was first called a "police action," but which ended in a major scale war.

No need to write for Americans the immense losses suffered by so many thousands of the young people of your land; you can read it all in the back files of newspapers in any city. For the Korean people themselves it has been a story written in unsurpassed suffering, in the fears and tears of millions. 2,000,000 Koreans lost their lives either in direct conflict or by starvation and exposure brought on by the fighting; 3,000,000 Koreans left their ancestral homes and villages in the north and fled southward to become refugees and to join the growing ranks of the uprooted people on the roads of the world; 50,000 children became lost children, small wild creatures wandering over the countryside; 60,000 homes were destroyed, and 70 percent of all industry in the south was wiped out. The war finally terminated on July 27th, 1953, but on the people of the "Land of the Morning Calm" a great rough wound had been inflicted.

Let me translate these figures into a few concrete experiences.

One of the first fact-finding trips I made in Seoul was to the broken Cathedral of the Immaculate Conception and the orphanage of the Sisters of St. Paul of Chartres attached to it. Half the building of the original orphanage was in ruins, and the number of homeless children had more than doubled. Under the care of an all-Korean group of Sisters, the children were the happiest of all the little lost ones I saw scattered over southern Korea. Perfectly at home with visitors, some half dozen tagged along behind the Sisters as they showed me the makeshift arrangements to house, feed and clothe the children. Most of them had come from North Korea. They had either been picked up by United Nations soldiers in the front lines or had been found wandering in the streets of Seoul, separated from their families and friends. The average age of the children seemed to be from six to eight years. The reason for this was that during the dreadful Korean winter, when swarms of refugees clogged the roads leading south, children too big to be carried and too small to keep up with the fleeing families were left straggling behind.

As Sister gave this information in Korean, through an interpreter, the small girl clinging to my hand broke out into uncontrollable sobbing. Sister took the little one and held her close; the child had remembered, said the nun, how she had been separated from her own family, but she could not recall the name of her village. Other children who had memorized their complete address could not be returned to their families, as whole villages had sometimes disappeared in the destruction of war.

During a several weeks stay in the dusty, rubble-strewn capital of South Korea, I came to know many of these children whose few brief years of life held more suffering than dozens of average adult lives in America or Australia put together. But of all the Korean people I talked with, there is one woman I shall never forget, Mrs. Tu-koo-Yoon. Every line in her face, every inflection in her voice are as vivid to me now as when she first told me her experience, an experience that centers for us the tragedy of the 30,000 widows and the 50,000 lost children of Korea.

The iron hand of war first struck the Yoon family in July 1950, when millions of South Koreans were uprooted by the unprovoked attack of the North Korean Communists. During the first Communist push through Seoul, the father of the family disappeared. His fate is still unknown. Mrs. Yoon, who was pregnant at the time, kept herself and her two-year-old son, Ki-hak, alive by selling their furniture and personal belongings and begging for food. When the situation in Seoul became worse, she left the city with thousands of other refugees.

After the famous Inchon landing in September of 1950 and the recapture of Seoul by United Nations troops, Mrs. Yoon made her way back to the war-torn capital, hoping that her husband might also have been able to return.

Instead, her weary march led her to jail. Her husband had been mistakenly reported to the police as a deserter to North

Korean Forces. In the chaos which existed, records could not be checked. So Mrs. Yoon and her son were placed under detention. Some months later police authorities advised her to place Ki-hak, who by then was suffering from malnutrition, with an orphanage to ensure better care while her case was pending. So great was the confusion at the time, however, that Mrs. Yoon was left forgotten in jail.

A year later she was released, but once again the fortunes of war were against her. Seoul was again besieged by the Communists, and all the orphanages had been evacuated to the south. Her Ki-hak was lost in the shuffle. No trace of the child could be found. The young mother found shelter with friends for herself and her young baby, who had been born in the prison. A few weeks later she too joined the stream of refugees moving southward. Eventually she reached her parents' home in Chengtu. Once more she began her search for Ki-hak. Parents, parents-in-law and other relatives contributed what little money they could spare. Telegrams were sent to all receiving stations for children in South Korea. Newspaper advertisements were run in every area containing an orphanage evacuated from Seoul.

Three years of fruitless search went by, and then the mother received one last ray of hope. As Mrs. Yoon came to this part of the story, her tired eyes began to sparkle and she reached out and held my hand. The young Korean student who was interpreting the story for me said she could not find "smiling enough words in English for the next part"!

Through a chance conversation she heard of a former Seoul orphanage relocated on the island of Cheju Do, approximately two hundred miles southeast of Pusan and four hundred miles from her home. A few weeks after receiving the information, Mrs. Yoon made her way to the island.

More than four years had elapsed since mother and son were separated in Seoul. All that remained by which to identify the six-year-old youngster was a picture taken when he was two. Four days of searching among the many war-orphaned small

Mrs. Yoon with her newly found Ki-hak.

fry on Cheju Do produced three small boys resembling the worn snapshot, but none bore the name of Ki-hak Yoon. One, however, had a small scar on the side of his face. Upon the mother's insistence that this was her child, records were checked thoroughly. It was proven beyond a doubt that an error had been made in name registration. The six-year-old boy with the scar was definitely Ki-hak Yoon, entered in the Seoul orphanage four years before.

But for so many of the 50,000 other "lost" children of Korea, there is no such happy ending. It is good to recall the story of Ki-hak, but what of the dirty, sick and diseased beggar boys, growing up unloving and unloved, snatching a little sleep on the pavement, begging food and scavenging for an existence? What of the two little girls I saw living in a wretched railway carriage, trying to put a home together with a few rags and rusty tin dishes? They weren't "playing house"—this *was* home for them. What of the small bundle of misery I saw crouched on an old temple floor with staring eyes and rigid limbs, shocked into immobility by the horrors of war? And what of the 30,000 widows? And the maimed men of Korea? Korea—that little Asian nation, still divided and longing for unity—continues to suffer even though the guns have ceased to rain destruction.

The years following the war have been characterized by mass poverty, insecurity, hunger, sickness and struggle for survival. And in Korea today for the most part these same conditions prevail. Although much effort has been made to rebuild, it is almost a superhuman task. Old temples have been converted into temporary quarters for the children; orphanages have been set up, as have schools, hospitals and clinics. Some Korean children have been adopted into American homes. A Catholic university is in its initial stage. Seoul is gradually rebuilding. Newly completed power projects provide electricity for the city, and coal is available for cooking and at least some heating. Cement, fertilizer and glass plants are operating, but all this is still a drop in the bucket. Recent political upheavals have added to the insecurity of the people, but although the "growing pains" are sharp, South Korea is struggling gallantly on to rebuild and to develop the natural and human resources of the "Land of the Morning Calm."

Father Aloysius Schwartz, a priest from the Washington, D.C. archdiocese who volunteered for the Korean vicariate of

Pusan, has recently been speaking in the United States to recruit personnel and to raise funds for Korea, and I would like to pass on some of the things which he has said.

"In Korea, the average daily calorie intake is 1,900, whereas the required daily minimum is 2,600 and the average calorie intake in the U.S.A. is 3,100.

"At the NCWC Relief Services feeding station, 200,000 persons line up every day to receive what is often their only substantial meal—a bowl of hot gruel made of cornmeal, flour and milk. Forty percent of the working population in the cities is unemployed. The average net income in Korea is $35.00 a year (in the U.S.A. the average net income is about $2,100). Tuberculosis, dysentery, typhoid, worms, and skin diseases are widespread. Hundreds of thousands of families in Seoul, Taejon, Taegu, and Pusan live in one-room tents, shacks, and squatter huts located along the rivers, under the bridges, on the mountain slopes and even on the city dumps."

A Korean friend of Father Schwartz expressed well the contrast between life in his country and life in the United States when he said, "In America you ask: How can I make my body thin? In Korea, we ask ourselves: How can I make my body fat? In America you wake up in the morning and ask: How can I make my life more enjoyable today? In Korea we ask ourselves when we wake up in the morning: How can I stay alive today?"

Yet out of all this suffering has come an immense flowering of the Faith. The chief preoccupation of the Church in South Korea today is to train and support enough catechists for the wave of converts which threatens to slow up merely because there are not sufficient missioners.

Ten years ago there were less than 150,000 Catholics among the 23,000,000 people who live in South Korea. Today there are more than 320,000 Catholics. It is a moment in history in Korea and a place where American lay Catholics would be more than welcome. Teachers, doctors, nurses, social workers could be used to enormous advantage.

Kau-tsai shares his rice with Ah Wan in the garden of the Grail house in Hong Kong.

When I discussed the possibility of sending Grail teams to Korea with Madeleine Kim, our first Korean Grail member, who lived with me in Hong Kong and is currently getting her university degree in Vienna, her round face glowed with delight. We talked for hours on end about our hopes and plans for her homeland. Just in case I might forget about Korea as I speak of the needs of the Church in the wide land of America, she sent me this Korean legend, asking me to find some Americans who will share chopsticks with her.

The legend tells of a Korean warrior who died and went to heaven. Coming to the portals he said to the gatekeeper, "Before I enter the celestial gates, I'd like to see hell to appreciate more fully my happiness here." The request was granted.

Taken to hell he saw a large and exquisite room in the center of which was a great table richly piled with life's choicest things. But to his horror the people milling around the table were anguished and starving. Harsh words came from their grim faces. "Why?" he asked.

The guide explained: "Everyone who comes to hell is given a pair of chopsticks that are five feet long. They must be held at the end. With these each person is to secure his food. But you can see that though they can pick up the food they cannot get it to their mouths. It always goes past their shoulders." The warrior was glad to return to heaven.

On entering paradise, to his complete consternation, he found himself in the same room. There was a similar table laden with life's good things, but here the people were happy. Here was joy and laughter and peace. Here all were healthy and well fed. He stammered to the guide: "How does this happen? The rules must be different here."

"Oh, no," the guide replied. "The rules are the same. The chopsticks are of the same length. They must be held at the end. But you see, these people have learned that if every man feeds his neighbor, all will be abundantly fed."

Young daughters of Asia join together in song at a Grail training course in Hong Kong.

Chapter Eight

Vietnam—in the Red Dragon's Path

MY NEXT assignment out of Hong Kong was to Vietnam in March 1954. When the cease-fire was called in Korea, hundreds of correspondents descended on our island, but failing to find anything at that point to make headlines in the world press, they soon made their way south, to the other Asian shooting war in Vietnam. It seemed a good time for me to go too, and gather a series of stories for the *Sunday Examiner* and a picture story for the *Mission Bulletin*. So I flew into Hanoi, the capital of North Vietnam, on March 12, 1954.

Those were tense days in Hanoi as news of the civil war reached us. The struggle had originated in the troubled days immediately following World War II. Japanese occupation of Indochina had ended in 1945. The leading resistance group during the occupation had been the Vietminh, a coalition of various forces working against the Japanese for independence, and drawing a major share of support from the Indochinese Communist party. In 1946, the Vietminh endeavored to set up a Communist-dominated Republic of Vietnam; the French countered by backing the rival government of Bao Dai, and a full scale civil war ensued. For eight years the fighting had dragged on.

That spring of '54, Dien Bien Phu, a small village northwest of Hanoi, was beginning to break into the headlines. The French and Vietnamese troops had taken up positions there in underground bunkers. On March 12th the Communist Vietminh began the siege of Dien Bien Phu which forty-six days later was to bring the war in Indochina to its tragic yet heroic end.

But first some background on this nation which was an obscure and little known part of southeast Asia before war forced it into newspaper headlines.

Vietnam is the most important of the three states of Indochina, the other two being Laos and Cambodia. Its surface occupies approximately one half of the total area, about 287,000 square miles, and its population of 20,000,000 far surpasses that of Cambodia (3,000,000) and Laos (1,000,000). The People's Republic of China lies to the north, Burma and Thailand to the west, and for the rest it is bordered by the South China Sea. The people have many of the racial characteristics of their Chinese neighbors, although traces of various aboriginal tribal strains can be noticed. As the former name of the country, Indochina, suggests, they are the offspring of both India and China. Earliest Aryan migrants came from India, amalgamated with the indigenous peoples as well as with the Chinese, who came into Vietnam both as invaders and as traders.

For more than a thousand years the Vietnamese were subject to the Chinese emperor and it was not until the tenth century, A.D., that they were able to establish an independent dynasty. The kingdom of Vietnam came into contact with the West in the sixteenth century through the Portuguese who came to exchange arms and European cloth for tea, silk, rare woods and spices. In the seventeenth century came the Dutch, then the English and the French. Together with the merchants came the missionaries. In 1625 the Gospel was preached for the first time in Vietnam by Father Alexander of Rhodes to whom Vietnam owes a written alphabet of Latin letters, the *quoc-ngu,* universally used throughout the country today. Catholicism, well received at the outset,

Mrs. Dai, my hostess in Saigon.

was subsequently persecuted. French intervention in Vietnam began in 1862 in the south, and in 1884 a treaty established the French protectorate over the entire country. Now this last period of French control was coming to an end with the siege of Dien Bien Phu.

In Hanoi I stayed in the home of the Dai family, one of whose daughters had lived with us in Hong Kong the year before.

It was a well-to-do old Catholic family with several members in the priesthood and religious orders. An incident which took place in their home will always remain with me. I was waiting to get word about transportation to Haiphong one afternoon. We were all sitting around stiffly in blackwood chairs inlaid with little squares of marble, talking without stopping to cover up our anxiety. The day was hot and sticky, and the red tile floor was moist from the humidity. Suddenly the door from the courtyard opened.

Framed there in silhouette against the brilliant Vietnamese skies was an aged bishop, one hand on his cross, looking at us with arresting dark eyes. His face was shrunken and line chiselled. A drift of white hair wreathed his parchment-like skin and a white waterfall beard flowed over the purple buttons of his dusty cassock.

His entrance was so swift and quiet that he seemed like someone from another world, dropped among the Vietnamese people on this sunny afternoon. He was Bishop Louis de Comman of the Paris Foreign Mission Society, Vicar Apostolic of Thanh-hoa. It was the end of a five-day journey for him, on foot and boat from his vicariate in the Vietminh zone to Hanoi. For the past eight years he had not been able to move from his mission. Now at last the Reds had let this man of almost eighty years go free, with the words of expulsion ringing in his ears, that he could never return to his flock.

Unsteady from weariness and age, the bishop slumped into a chair that was offered. He unravelled for us the pattern of the eight year struggle—the restrictions, the accusations, the death of many of his Vietnamese priests, imprisonment, hunger and distress unmeasured.

It was a commonplace story of our time, heard everywhere in Red Asia—the Church at grips with Communism. I did not know it then, but the bishop's entrance into that room, and the other events of that day, were the prelude to an heroic witness to the Faith.

All through the afternoon and evening, as we had been listening to Bishop de Comman, history was being enacted close by. It was May 7th, 1954, the day of the fall of Dien Bien Phu. In Hanoi the news passed quietly through the night that the fort had fallen, and men wept openly in the streets.

On May 10th, Giap, the Communist general, issued his victory communique: "The Vietminh People's Forces have completely defeated the enemy on the Dien Bien Phu battlefront. 21 enemy battalions and 10 companies, numbering over 16,000 crack troops, and all the French Commands, including one brigadier general, 16 colonels, 1,759 officers and non-commissioned officers were killed, injured or made prisoners in the offensive."

And in Geneva, Mendes-France with one stroke of his pen signed the agreement which was to give Vietnam, north of the 17th parallel, to the Communists.

Denis Warner, an Australian correspondent, wrote shortly after: "The moral tragedy of it all was that only in the north (the part given to the Communists) was there any real resistance to Communism. Nearly a million and quarter devout Catholics formed a hard core of resistance there. It was not courage which the non-Communist Vietnamese lacked, but leadership and the proper appreciation of the tactics and methods of the enemy. And now at one stroke those who had fought best, and who believed and trusted in the West's capacity to defend them, were obliged to decide between flight and Communism."

Eighty-six percent of the people of the Tonkin River delta area were Catholics, and when this choice was presented to them, 900,000 chose freedom, and the long trek south.

The Vietnamese people were so little known to the American public in general that the poignant exodus—within the short interval of ninety-two days—hardly made a one column headline in the daily press in the United States; yet this small nation has a great deal of significance in the Communist bid for power in Asia's divided countries.

I came to love and deeply respect the Vietnamese people,

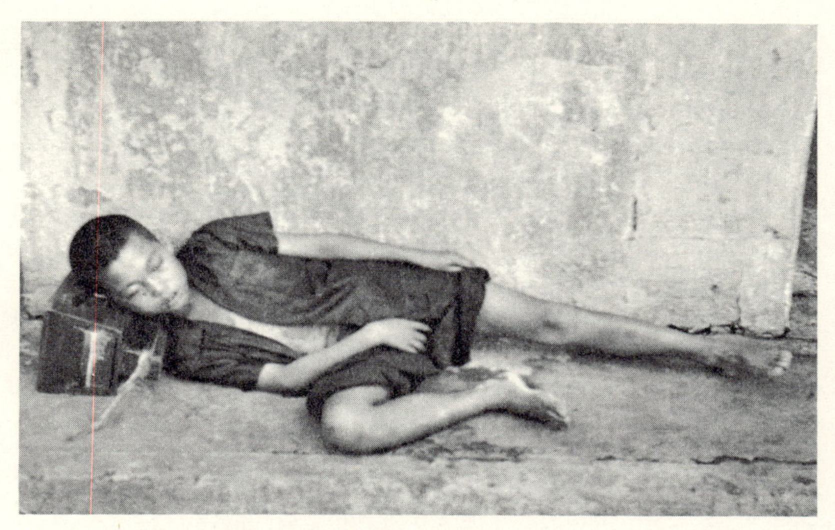

A lone waif, shining shoes by day, without even a quilt to cushion his slumber on the pavement at night.

and during the years in America since then, their faith and fortitude have been a constant inspiration for me. To listen to the Vietnamese at prayer is like hearing the buzz of a swarming beehive—vibrant, alive, virile. My friends, the Dais, with whom I stayed in Hanoi for so many weeks, held family prayer each evening for upwards of two hours, and many times the assembled household drowned out the rumble of war as French tanks ground their way to the front outside our courtyard.

But now the streets in Hanoi were silent, no more rumble of war; and the people who had prayed so long and so intensely were heading south to Saigon 1,100 miles away. On foot, by junk or sampan or flimsy rafts, they streamed southward. Some were airlifted by the French and the Americans and thousands were packed into warships, clinging to every available space.

All means, including murder and torture, were used to prevent the exodus. But still they left, these sturdy people of the Tonkin delta, clutching just what they could carry in their hands, with many times a crucifix or a large picture of Our Lady of

Perpetual Succor selected as one of the most precious possessions to carry on the flight.

I had planned to go back to Hanoi from Haiphong where I had been taking pictures of the evacuation, but it was suddenly too late—the area was sealed and I could get no word through to the Dais, so I followed the refugees south to Saigon. There I sought out a French nun, Soeur Françoise of the Sisters of Charity of St. Vincent de Paul, who had known the Dais in the north. She told me they had arrived a few days before, and she thought they were located in a camp outside the city. We set out in her battered jeep to find them.

It took a good hour to get out of the city. The roads were packed with all kinds of motor vehicles, carts, and people walking with bundles of brushwood on their backs. Saigon, the "Paris of the Orient," looked a bit the worse for wear. Suddenly on top of a hill we lurched to a stop, as this Sister of Charity, with her white-winged headdress limp with dust and heat, jammed her foot on the brake.

We got out and stood looking for a moment, then with a wide sweep of her hand, she indicated as far as eye could see, the camps of the refugees. The little people of North Vietnam who had left their rice fields, their compact thatched houses, their one pig or two buffalo, were living piled up in tents on this dustblown tract of land outside the city of Saigon.

"The camps are a temporary arrangement," said Soeur Françoise, "until the refugees can be resettled elsewhere." But the machinery for the shift had barely begun to turn. Meanwhile, squalor and malnutrition made the refugees an easy prey to disease.

Beyond the tents for mile after mile stretched huts made from saplings. Here I found my friends, already installed in a house beside the priest, helping to administer relief goods brought in by CRS-NCWC. I thought of their lovely old villa with the enclosed courtyard, the teakwood chairs and the well-stocked kitchen, and learned that the old ones had stayed behind, but the young ones had left at their mother's insistence. We walked around together and they showed me with pride the church built to look like the familiar one back home. It was a crude edifice with bamboo joints and flimsy wood façade, and I wept when I saw the cardboard clock with the hands placed at the time of the takeover by the Vietminh a few weeks before. It *did* look like the parish church in Hanoi, this mute reminder of how much it cost these people to abandon home and countryside for the faith. And within the people were praying—a continuous chant which haunted me as we walked for four hours through the camp, visiting the people, and waiting while Soeur Françoise arranged for treatment for the sick.

A closer look at the camp revealed the appalling conditions under which these people were living. It was a common sight to see thirty or forty men, women and children crammed into a ten by twenty foot space. Clothing looked as though it hadn't been washed or even removed for weeks. The typical garment is a loose shirt-like top of coarse brown cotton, worn with a pair of wide-legged black calico pants. Plaited straw coolie hats keep off the broiling sun. All wore rosaries and medals around their necks, many had embroidered scapulars.

Every drop of water had to be counted twice. At the edge of the Ba-Long camp, which I visited, a small stream ran out of the ground into the bottom of a crumbling, weed-overgrown reservoir, the only water supply for the two thousand inhabitants of the camp. All day long the women flocked to the spring with pots of rice, dirty crockery, bits of clothing, or children to wash. They pushed and shoved to get at the single source of water—no one's turn lasted long. A shrivelled old woman peeled off to the waist for what merely approximated a bath. Squatting on a stone ledge, a girl washed her clothes, then dumped the water over her head to make sure it served a double purpose. A stagnant, scum-covered pool had collected in the reservoir bottom, and many used this to wash in. In some of the camps, the refugees have dug by hand wells seventy or eighty feet deep into the rock-hard earth, but the water table lies too deep to get more than a dribble.

"Sometimes we can fill two barrels a day from the well," remarked an old priest as I questioned him about his people. There were twenty wells in this camp, and 6,400 refugees.

Idleness prevailed in the camps; there wasn't much alternative at that time. The same old priest explained to me: "We can't grow rice here as the earth is so dry, and we have no water. We can't fish," and he pointed to a pile of fishing nets, carefully brought on the long pilgrimage south, "for we have no boats, and no river to fish in. So my people sit here each day and do nothing."

Some of the refugees were more fortunate. Those from Buichu Province lived in a camp not far from a forest. "My people go to the forest each day and gather firewood to sell for rice and clothing," their pastor told me. "And some of the men scrape together a few piastres (35 piastres in those days equalled $1.00 in U. S. money) a day working on nearby plantations." But where a handful had found work, thousands remained idle.

A voice from the loudspeaker broke the hot afternoon calm that had settled over the Ba-Long camp. The words were interrupted every few seconds by a Vietnamese ballad, sung to the twanging of a guitar. A crowd gradually formed around the speaker-equipped jeep, probably attracted more by the music than by the voice which announced, "The government will soon get you new homes. The farmers will have good soil to grow their crops, and the fishermen will be able to fill their nets in the rivers. Living will become easier for you. . . ."

I stood in their midst as the message was repeated over and over again, and no one seemed tired of hearing it. The speaker was an agent from the Commission of Refugees in Saigon, sent around to the camps to inform them of the government's plan for resettlement.

Across from the camp, another crowd of refugees were getting action in the form of medical relief dispensed by a team of

Filipino doctors and nurses. Part of "Operation Brotherhood," it is a hopeful sign when one Asian nation comes to the aid of another.

This medical team was something tangible, something whose results the refugees could see and feel. It offered them immediate relief from suffering and at the same time a new hope that they could find a better life in the south under a free government.

Monsignor Joseph Harnett and his staff were giving out milk powder from CRS-NCWC. Again I saw the familiar barrels which I have photographed in the numberless refugee camps which stretched down Asia, from Korea, Japan, Taiwan, the Philippines, to Hong Kong and Macao, and now to Vietnam.

A Vietnamese priest who had come south with his parishioners (sixty-four percent of the priests came with the people, and an estimated sixty-five percent of the Catholic population of North Vietnam made the trek south) stood by watching a Filipino nurse shoot streptomycin into the hip of a young victim of tuberculosis.

"When my people come to Mass, they leave with a new look of hope on their faces," he said. "I see something of the same look on their faces as they leave this clinic. What these medical teams are doing is helping to keep their faith alive."

"To keep their faith alive"—that is what spurred these predominantly Christian people to uproot themselves from home, village, and countryside, from patches of fields they had tilled for generations, from churches where their relatives had suffered martyrdom for the faith, from all the familiar things men hold dear. They left everything because they knew that life under the Communist Vietminh regime would mean no freedom to think and act and speak as they wished; it would mean a godless education for their children; a life without priests to administer the sacraments and to offer the Holy Sacrifice of the Mass. On the arid, sun-parched ground of their camp sites around Saigon, they gathered under the shadow of their crosses, a people magnificent in their poverty, splendid in their faith.

The heroic trek of these 900,000 has not been in vain. Their leader in the south, President Ngo Dinh Diem, is a member of an old Catholic family converted by the early missionaries in the seventeenth century. He was actually called from retirement in a monastery in Belgium to take over the reins of government, no easy task in the chaotic situation which existed when the treaty was signed at Geneva. In the period since 1954 he has managed to restore order to a considerable degree and has enabled South Vietnam, an area of perhaps 10,000,000 inhabitants, to absorb 900,000 refugees from the North together with 165,000 southerners whose lives were shattered by the war.

Says Monsignor Joseph Harnett, Far East Director of Catholic Relief Services-NCWC, "There is not a country in the world capable of absorbing ten percent of its own population in a five-year period without more than the residual problems that would arise from such an effort. Thanks, however, to the able leadership of the government of Vietnam, and the generally wisely-administered Economic Aid Program of the United States Government through its Foreign Operations Mission, Vietnam has gone a long way toward doing exactly that."

Resettled in some three hundred villages, the great majority of refugees have achieved at least a minimum degree of normalcy. By and large they have been adequately housed and are able to take care of their basic needs. They have found employment in farming, in fishing, as laborers in the cities, and many of the more enterprising have established themselves in the crafts or in village commerce. According to Father Paul J. Duchesne, M.M., of CRS-NCWC in Saigon, the present status of refugees in South Vietnam, five years after the exodus, is far better than that of the refugees in Hong Kong, Macao, Korea, India or Pakistan. Of course this does not mean that they do not have many unfulfilled needs. It would be a serious mistake to understand "adequacy" in western terms. In a newly independent country in southeast Asia, "adequate" village housing, for instance, means a one-room thatch and bamboo hut with an earth floor. Village

Family supper at the House of Joy in Taikoolau. How we all looked forward to this time together, a time to exchange the experiences of the day at school or office, to discuss and plan for the diverse activities which mushroomed around our little house, or just to relax and enjoy each other.

schools are usually in the same style, only larger, and may enjoy the dignity of wooden walls, while dispensaries usually have cement floors and plank walls. Mechanization means bicycles, small water pumps for the wells, simple devices for moving water from one rice paddy to another.

In brief, in 1960 the Vietnamese refugees were out of the woods, but their needs have increased proportionately with the rest of the world. Having come in contact with more developed standards, these courageous, hard-working people are not satisfied with marginal living. They are determined to develop social welfare institutions, provide more and better education, eliminate drudgery by simple mechanization, supply medical care as needed. In a true sense Vietnam is undergoing a social and economic as well as a political revolution. There is a great push for construction of schools and hospitals with the goal to have all school-age children of South Vietnam in classrooms by 1962.

Fullest encouragement has been given to the missionary priests and sisters. There is a movement towards the Church, both in the large cities and among the mountain tribes. Never has there been a more encouraging mission field, and never and nowhere have missioners been more sorely needed.

Much of the resettlement in Vietnam has been due to the willingness of President Diem to work with all the nations and agencies who offered to help his country: the governments of the United States, the Netherlands, the Philippines, and France; various Catholic groups in Germany and Ireland; CRS-NCWC and other voluntary agencies in America.

The shining courage of the men who fought at Dien Bien Phu, the resultant "pilgrimage of grace" of those hundreds of thousands of Asian Catholics who stood for freedom and faith, the compassion and ready charity of the nations who came to their aid—all this has given us a high moment in the history of the human family—God *does* write straight with crooked lines!

Since those months in 1954, Vietnam has been a constant reminder to expect the most from people. Sometimes, speaking across the United States, I felt hesitant to ask something hard from high schoolers, from comfortable nurses in well-equipped hospitals. But then I would remember Vietnam, and the trek south, and the old woman by the side of the road who said to me as I took her picture, "God gave me the strength to walk with pain." So when I received a letter from Father Duchesne, postmarked Vietnam, asking me to find a doctor for the leprosarium in Kontum, I went to Dr. Pat Smith with full confidence.

Pat had first of all wanted to be a reporter, and she entered

Seattle University in Washington with that in mind. During her years of study she read an article written by a Hungarian physician, Dr. Ignaz Philippe Semmelweis, which fired her with the idea of serving humanity in the field of medicine. So she switched to pre-med studies, and in 1951 entered medical school at the University of Washington.

After graduation Pat interned in a Cincinnati hospital, and the following year signed up for a period of work among Kentucky coal miners in the drab little town of McDowell. It was at this point, when Pat was preparing to go into private practice, that she met the Grail.

It was the summer of 1958, and the courses at Grailville were in full swing. A red convertible drove around the main house and came to a sudden stop. A tall, rangy girl with a lighted cigarette in her hand, and a shy smile, got out. She walked over to me. "I'm Doctor Pat Smith from Kentucky. I read about your courses on careers of service at home and abroad, and have come to stay for a week."

Pat never wastes words or time, and soon we were unloading her car and walking towards the converted barn where the summer students were living. I had a room in the same building, and had left my door wide open. There was a Chinese scroll over my desk with the text written in Chinese characters, "In so many different ways the most beautiful of tasks is the sowing of the seed." Pat saw it and asked me about it. . . . Within ten minutes of her arrival, we were deep in stories of Asia and the people there and my reason for being in America.

By the end of the week, Pat had decided to give up the idea of private practice in the States for a while, and to go to the Grail Institute for Overseas Service in Brooklyn when the classes resumed in October.

It was the following January when I received the letter from Father Duchesne. Pat said at once, "If you think I can be a help, of course I'll go." Immediately she plunged into preparations, gathering experience about Hansen's disease (the clinical name for leprosy) at the leprosarium run by the Sisters of Charity of St. Vincent de Paul outside New Orleans, Louisiana; assembling equipment, taking time to pray and think and read. Then she sold her red convertible to help pay her expenses. By June, Pat was on her way. She flew out of Seattle, via Tokyo and Hong Kong, and landed in Saigon just a year after she had come to Grailville to find out what these service careers abroad were all about.

Soon letters began coming back to the States from Dr. Pat. "Have you a nurse at the Institute who would be willing to come and help out here?" Actually we had. In the summer of 1959, the week Pat left for Saigon, another one hundred and fifty young Americans were gathered at Grailville, among them two sisters from Wisconsin, Mary Agnes and Joan Blonien. Mary Agnes is an executive at the Cardijn Center in Milwaukee, and Joan is a nurse with an impressive experience in public health and rehabilitation work. Hearing Dr. Pat's first letter back to us on her arrival in Saigon, which was read to the group at supper, Joan was instantly interested. Mary Agnes backed up her younger sister and soon Joan was at the Institute in Brooklyn, preparing to join Pat in Kontum. Letters began to go between the two, and Joan had the advantage of hearing at firsthand just what she was in for. Pat wrote:

Mission Catholique
Kontum, Vietnam

DEAR JOAN:

Mighty glad to get your letter! Sounds like we'll get on fine together, and I'm really counting the days until you get here. You'll have more than enough work to do, but if you were here just to talk to, it would be wonderful!

To begin to answer a few of your questions, and give you some idea of what life is like here—to begin with, you might just as well anticipate that things are about as primitive as you can get. As far as present plans go, you'll live with me here in the house "in town." It's built of earth with wood doors and a brick floor—the walls are calcimined, so it's not bad looking at all, and the earth construction makes it cooler than houses built of wood or cement. We have a well with some running water—when someone pumps the hand pump. During the rainy season, though, we'll always have plenty of running water, since the reservoir is an open one! No electricity here as yet, but there's a possibility we may be getting it in a few months.

Our food is limited somewhat by the fact that we don't have a stove—cooking is done on a concrete deal with holes in it under which one burns wood or charcoal . . . Beef and pork are quite plentiful on the local market, with fish sometimes (no Friday abstinence in Kontum!), but no other meats available. Mostly, I eat in a kind of modified French style, though we have some Vietnamese dishes from time to time. . . . One item we badly need in our "installation" in Kontum is a refrigerator—a small kerosene-operated one.

We can use almost anything in the way of medical or surgical equipment here. Almost anything else you can think of that normally a dispensary has, we don't have. All drugs can be used but the biggest lack we always have is that of antibiotics—especially oral ones and more especially preparations for children.

The kinds of diseases we must treat here? A little bit of everything and oodles of some things! Almost everyone has malaria . . . the leprosy rate approaches ten percent in some villages, pneumonia and bronchitis are common, tuberculosis is rampant—but no one knows the actual figure since there is no x-ray here; fungus diseases are common, worms, of course, and amoebae . . . just about everything, in fact.

I got some midwife kits from CARE when I was in Saigon, and will take two or three Montagnard girls from the Sisters' school here with me on my calls to the villages to help with deliveries. This is the only way we can start until we are able to build a small maternity clinic for Montagnards here. The teaching will be on a very elementary level—but we hope eventually to develop a full scale program for Montagnard girls, giving them also a little knowledge of child care. . . .

Not much in the way of diversional activities here. . . . The work itself is pretty diversified . . . when one has to hike to a Montagnard village anyway, it's easy to consider it "hiking for fun" as I used to do in my college days.

This letter just got interrupted by a most delightful and

totally unexpected occurrence—one of the men who works with an American building concern here just stopped in, bearing with him, of all things, a beautiful little portable tape recorder. We have just been playing with it—he thoughtfully recorded some excerpts from "My Fair Lady" and some jazz before bringing it over. It's going to be a most useful gift, since this way I can record Montagnard music and songs out in the villages.

I hope I've answered some of your questions. Your background sounds more than adequate for the job here—just be prepared to do anything and everything you've ever done, plus many things you haven't, and you'll do fine. Do write soon.

Love in Christ,

PAT SMITH

Joan left Milwaukee to fly to Vietnam on June 29th, 1960. Jeanne Platz, another Milwaukee nurse, boarded the plane for Kontum in February, 1961. I'm wondering who the Americans will be to follow them.

Young Asia, thirsting for knowledge.

Chapter Nine

Land of Eternal Summer

It was March 1955, and I was off to Djakarta to visit our Grail teams at work in Indonesia and to get a picture story for the *Mission Bulletin*. We left Kai-tak airport—a narrow strip between the mountains and the sea on the edge of the China mainland in Kowloon—in the early morning rush hour.

All the carriers fix their departures to take advantage of daylight flying over the South China Sea and the sky that morning was was thick with aluminum snouts. The control tower seethed with calls—TWA, BOAC, QANTAS, CAT, PAN-AM were all aclamor for a ration of air space.

Our big DC-4 nosed its way out, climbing and dodging the rugged mountains that encircle Hong Kong. For the next six hours we were high over the sea. The fifty or so passengers dozed on in their seats: the international business executive from Standard Oil with a hand in the affairs of a dozen different nations from the Persian Gulf to the China sea, beside him the British colonial official in well laundered linens and cambric shirt en route to Singapore. They spoke the same language, these two men, the language of debits and credits. Both knew years of strenuous work grappling with social changes they scarcely understood, yet both were more at ease on the rim of the world than in their native Kansas and Devon.

Behind them dozed a newspaper correspondent, his lean lined face reflecting the endless stories of wars and revolutions which had been his to record during years vibrant with radical change. A honey-haired teen-age girl from Minneapolis, travelling on a Ford Foundation scholarship, sang snatches of song with an Indian girl with a red caste mark on her forehead. Both were taking enormous delight in knowing the same songs. A pedestrian journey for them, born as they are into a growing world community, but for their grandparents an unthinkable experience.

Most of the passengers were awake by this time, and beginning to stand and stretch and yawn. A tow-haired young man, a CRS-NCWC representative, who a few months before had been a student at Fordham University in New York, was checking lists of surplus supplies and bills of lading, to be forwarded to Seoul at the first stopping place.

Across the way from him was Li-Li-wa, the beautiful Chinese film star, on her way to Taiwan to make a movie for circulation among ten million dispersed Chinese in Southeast Asia. She was travelling with her amah, whose shining black pigtail hung listlessly over the arm of the seat. After one fearful shuddering look as the plane took off, she had remained glued to the spot ever since, a pathetic figure, pinpointing the harsh changes in the lives of millions of Asians who are experiencing the conflict between ancient traditional social customs and modern ways of living and communication. Now the great sleeping dragon of Asia is waking. For generations millions of women like this amah have considered a trek across the neighboring mountain to the next village a major undertaking. Now their social patterns are shaking and shifting at their very roots.

Soon the great silver craft began to lose altitude in a steep, rapid descent towards the grey-green island rising out of the sea, and a few minutes later we touched down in the blistering heat of Singapore. In the heart of southeast Asia, this tiny island at the tip of the Malay peninsula harbors a million and a half people—eighty percent Chinese, and the rest Malay, Indian, European and Eurasian. The city was glued up with a Communist-inspired strike, and I got a blow-by-blow description of a student riot the night before from a group of correspondents who had come down from Saigon for a rest. Like many visitors to Singapore, they had been impressed on arrival with the cleanliness and the big new buildings, including the Communist Bank of China, which here as in Hong Kong dominates the Hong Kong and Shanghai Bank Building. These men, used to seeing the story behind the externals, had comprehended that here on this green little island a distillation of the whole complex struggle between East and West was fermenting.

In 1958 our first Asian Grail team to return to the home continent was assigned to Singapore—Clara Sun, a graduate of Marquette University in Milwaukee, Wisconsin, and Mary Wong, a graduate of Our Lady of Cincinnati College, in Ohio. Clara and Mary met at the Grail in America and after some years of apostolic work in the States wanted very much to throw in their lot with their own people. Singapore with all its complexities and opportunities was chosen for their work, which is now beginning to develop and blossom.

I didn't spend any time in Singapore this visit—the air was incredibly heavy. "We expect rain at any time," said the airways official, tapping his pencil on the weather chart. The crew called us together and hurried to get us into the air before the rain hit. Soon we could see it moving in, a tropical squall which caught us as we rolled down the runway. At 8,000 feet the plane was cool again—palm-fringed beaches, a strip of fierce blue sea, then Djakarta below.

Djakarta is the capital of Indonesia, a sprawling city of closely packed red roofs, tangled city streets, endless traffic knots and unexpected splashes of beauty from wide flowering trees.

Java, on which Djakarta is situated, is an island with varied and beautiful gifts—mountains veiled in mist, softly terraced sah-wahs, and 54,000,000 of the 80,000,000 Indonesian people.

But it is blessed with a generous rainfall and tropical sunshine and an abundance of rice which grows tall and luxuriant. It is a land of eternal summer, and new rice shoots are planted immediately after the harvest.

Indonesia is a hauntingly beautiful archipelago of more than three thousand islands stretched along the equator. Wedged between Australia and the rest of Asia, it is a strategic link between East and West. A country of great potential wealth, it has petrol, rubber and tin in abundance. For three hundred years it was a colony of the Dutch known as the Netherlands East Indies; in 1949 the Republic of Indonesia was proclaimed and it became a sovereign nation. Ninety percent of its people are Moslem, 0.6 percent are Catholic. There are three Indonesian bishops; the rest are foreigners from the various religious orders who have missions on the islands.

I untangled myself from various customs officials at the airport and looked round hopefully for someone to meet me. There was a fairhaired Westerner with her back to me, talking in rapid Bahasa-Indonesian, the national language, to a couple of musicians who were squatting behind an instrument made of bamboo cylinders—it looked like a portable pipe organ to me. They began to play, and as I walked closer I saw the girl jotting down music notes on the back of an envelope. I sat down on my duffel bag and relaxed to take in the scene fully.

This thin, fairheaded girl was surely Francine Wickes, enjoying herself while she waited for my plane to come in. Soon she was humming along with the musicians, and I figured it was time for me to say hello. It *was* Francine, and the glimpse I stole of her that afternoon in the midst of the Indonesian people is typical of her interest and thoroughness in making herself one with the people in this land of her adoption. This first impression intensified as the weeks went by, and I saw how she had plunged herself into a culture so different from her own, rarely speaking English, playing a gamelan instead of a violin or piano, singing strange plaintive melodies, eating with relish raw turtle eggs and spiced foods.

The Kodak city in New York State is a far cry from Java, where Francine now has her roots. She was born in Rochester and grew up there. Her father is a lawyer and Harvard man, and her mother, small and vivacious, hails from Belgium. Her parents met after World War I, when the young American, a member of Herbert Hoover's welfare program, was billeted in the large family home of his future wife. The great and holy Irish monk, Abbot Marmion of Maredsous, blessed the marriage. At home in Rochester the language spoken was French, so Francine, already bilingual, mastered Bahasa-Indonesian without much difficulty.

Greetings exchanged, we scrambled into an incredible bus which seemed to be held together with bits of wire and string, and set off for Sukabumi. I was all ears and eyes, looking and listening to our fellow passengers, and catching glimpses of the kampongs as we rattled past, when abruptly the bus staggered to a stop. We were just seventeen miles north of Djakarta, and it had taken us longer to cover this distance by road than to fly from Singapore. We tumbled out onto the grassy slope by the roadside to wait for repairs and began exchanging experiences. Francine told me how she had first met the Grail and how she had come to be assigned to Indonesia. "It all began with Mariette, my elder sister," she explained. "She had been at Grailville for a few years, and the summer I turned sixteen I went to visit her. I had planned to be there ten days but I stayed all summer.

"But of course a lot of other things went into it. Funny how we can see a pattern clearly in our life five or ten years later." I agreed. How often "yes" instead of "no" in seemingly small decisions brings about undreamed-of chances for adventures in the conversion of the world!

It might be worth noting that many of the steps that went into Francine's presence today in Indonesia go back to her school days. For eleven years, from first grade up, she attended Nazareth Academy conducted by the Sisters of St. Joseph. In high school she was taught by Sister M. Florentine, one of those nuns who have the capacity to spark their students with an apostolic spirit and love for the missions. Following the year at Grailville, she went to Europe for travel and further study, and had the opportunity to attend the Institute Jacques Dalcroze for Music and Eurhythmics.

"Even when I was little," Francine told me, "I loved dancing and music. A childhood friend of my mother, Dom Ermin Vitry, used to visit us for weeks on end. He would play the piano or chant parts of the liturgy and I would dance. It was only later, when I was in the Grail, that I saw how this could be useful for the apostolate."

After the year in Europe, Francine returned to Grailville for further study, specializing in the fields of music, drama, eurhythmics and later taking part in the Overseas Service program. This last period was the second step to Indonesia—the first was made in her high school mission group. In the meantime, her musical education continued. In 1951 she was assistant to Dom Vitry at the Summer School of Liturgy at Notre Dame University, teaching the adaptation of rhythmic movement to Gregorian chant, especially for children. In the fall of 1952, Francine enrolled in the Cincinnati College of Music in order to earn a music degree to equip herself more fully for her future task in Indonesia. Because of her previous studies at Grailville, she was allowed to take an accelerated course and graduated *cum laude*.

In the meantime, there were new stirrings in the Grail internationally. Bishop N. Geise, O.F.M., had been urgently requesting the international Grail president, Rachel Donders, to send a team to the prefecture of Sukabumi; and the staff in Surabaia, East Java, also needed expanding. Young Americans were ready to shoulder their responsibility internationally, and very soon Francine and Mary Helena Fong were sailing from New York to Indonesia.

Mary Helena hails from Helena, Montana—of Chinese parentage, she is an American citizen. Caught in Hong Kong where she had been sent to study during the eventful years of the Japanese occupation, she had found the faith there through Father Nicholas Maestrini, P.I.M.E. At war's end she came back to America to be trained in the lay apostolate at Grailville, so it was with a deep sense of fulfillment that this Asian-American apostle went to her task in Surabaia. There we help to staff a Home Economics Teachers Training College which fills an urgent need by providing teachers for the community development programs in Java. Mary Helena joined a Dutch Grail member on the staff, taking over the management of the school shortly after her arrival.

Francine's first destination was Sukabumi in West Java, and as soon as our bus was tied together again, we were on our way to this fascinating provincial city set at the foot of a volcano.

I loved Java right from the start. It is a photographer's paradise. The people are as colorful as the countryside. The women are especially striking, with glossy, fine black hair knotted on the nape of the neck, multicolored batik sarongs gracefully draped around them, and jolly, well-fed babies in slings on their hips.

Sidewalk restaurants are set up under cotton umbrellas, and for a few rupees a quick meal can be tucked away. How often, as I've waited in New York or Sydney for an order to be taken, have I remembered the speed and ease with which one could get a meal in Java!

With Francine in Sukabumi was Maria Malone, with whom I'd worked for years in the Grail in Australia. Maria was born in New York of Irish parents but crossed the Pacific as a child and has an Australian accent as broad as the rest of us! Between these two I got a thorough indoctrination in the area—there is nothing like living with people who are a little bit mad about their work to catch their enthusiasm.

"The people," Maria informed me, "are of two distinct groups here—the Javanese, who are from the central and eastern part of the island, and the Sudanese, in this western part where Sukabumi is located."

They did not look very unlike to the casual observer, but my two friends spent hours differentiating the language, customs, traditions, food, expressions of culture of each.

"As far as religion is concerned," Maria went on to explain, "the Sudanese on the whole are much stronger Moslems than the Javanese. For this reason, although the Church in the eastern part and particularly in central Java counts many converts, in the west, in Pasundam, as it is called, there are very few local Catholics. In the prefecture of Sukabumi, which includes a good portion of West Java, there are 2,800,000 people. Only 1,244 are Catholics, almost all of them 'foreigners,' Japanese, Chinese, Eurasians, and Europeans.

"But the future looks hopeful," Francine assured me, her blue eyes looking serenely over the huge white mosque which dominates downtown Sukabumi, "for in the many Catholic schools which have been established, the first Sudanese are beginning to enter the Church—the first steps are being made, and the walls of prejudice and ignorance of Catholicism are beginning to crumble."

During the ensuing weeks I discovered for myself that Central Java presents quite a different aspect of the apostolate from the other southeast Asian countries where I had worked. Here, with fertile volcanic soil and abundant water, the people live quite well. Although the farmers subsist simply, there are no extremes of poverty, of which I had seen so much in Hong Kong, Macao, Vietnam and Korea, except perhaps for sections of the larger cities.

In Sukabumi, the bulk of the population are Moslems, and so the first task there is to be Christ *present* in the midst of this particular group of the family of man who have such a rock-like faith in God.

"Allah-Allah-Allah," over and over, God's name was invoked by the beggar who reached into the bus window when we

At the Grail Center in Sukabumi, Java, music makes a bond between young women of many nations. Francine Wickes of Rochester, New York, plays for Benedicte Milcent of France, Mary Helena Fong of Hong Kong, Maria Malone of Australia, and their Indonesian friends.

stopped for gas; "Allah-Allah-Allah," wafting out from the tiny mosques in the hundreds of compounds I walked through; "Allah-Allah-Allah," from the lips of diplomats gathered for the Asian-African Conference in Bandung. One is aware of a recognition of God in Java—far more tangible than in Chicago or Montreal, for example. But so few of these people know Christ and His teaching—much breaking of ground has to be done even before the sowing of the seed. And this means making friends, genuinely sharing the life of the people day in and day out, year after year. Primarily an assignment for those who understand the virtue of hope!

One way to cement friendships is to give English lessons. Even in this city high in the mountains there is great demand for

English, and the lessons help the team to earn its living as well. As pupils become more proficient in English, discussion highlights the lesson. Through this there is an interchange of ideas about a variety of subjects—the proper education of children, the real meaning of independence, birth control, the role of woman in private and public life. Alongside giving these private lessons, Francine teaches singing and theory of music in the Normal School, which trains teachers for elementary schools.

A second aspect of the work is directed towards the handful of Catholics. The first organized effort was a Mass campaign. This is a "natural" for the Grail the world over. We began with it in Hong Kong. I remember it was my first public relations job in Australia to stir up interest in such a campaign. The Grail—the symbol of our Movement—the Chalice of the Grail Legend, Cup of the Last Supper, Cup that caught the blood of Christ on the Cross, has become a universal symbol. It is the symbol of man's quest for enduring peace and happiness, a quest worthy of every heroic striving, sign of Christ's redeeming sacrifice and of the Christlife flowing from Calvary to be communicated by His Church to mankind; image of man's receptivity before God, open, waiting, longing to be filled. Behind the Chalice stands the Cross, poignant reminder that new life comes through death, that Christian unity and peace can be reached only through sacrifice. Of course we started with a Mass campaign in this seedplace in Indonesia!

The first objective was a deeper understanding of the Mass, an understanding which we hoped would lead to full participation. With the enthusiastic leadership of the pastor, the campaign proceeded for an entire month. There were sermons and demonstrations of the Mass, explanations of the vestments and sacred vessels; and, since very few people had even a translation of the Ordinary of the Mass, Francine and Maria mimeographed a small booklet of this part of the liturgy.

At the close of the campaign, there was an exhibition of drawings which the people had been encouraged to make with the Mass as their theme. The finest one showed a group of Indonesian people bringing symbols of their work to be offered with the bread and wine. Done by one of the young men of the parish, it was completely local in design. This drawing has been used for an attractive Dialogue Mass Book, just off the printing presses.

One last glimpse at "Operation Hope" in this Moslem stronghold in Asia. A letter from Francine: " . . . We have just had a week-end here at the Center attended by twenty-three Moslem girls, most of them from Sukabumi or from Mardi Juana. They were really interested in what they heard, so much so that after the bishop's talk on 'Why was I created,' the discussion continued for two hours. Bishop Geise is an exceptional person who speaks both the national and the regional language fluently and knows and loves the people thoroughly. Very distinguished, yet simple. Yesterday he came to our house, one mile up a steep hill from his, on his bicycle, with our new gardener riding behind!"

The bishop pedalling uphill on his bicycle; Francine bending over the street musicians; Maria groping to make personal bonds through the fog of a strange language; tiny glimpses, insignificant circumstances, as small as the mustard seed and the lost groat Christ told about, but perhaps opening out a new understanding of what it is *to be* the Church, Christ present in the human family; Christ dying in His members, that the people of Java may live.

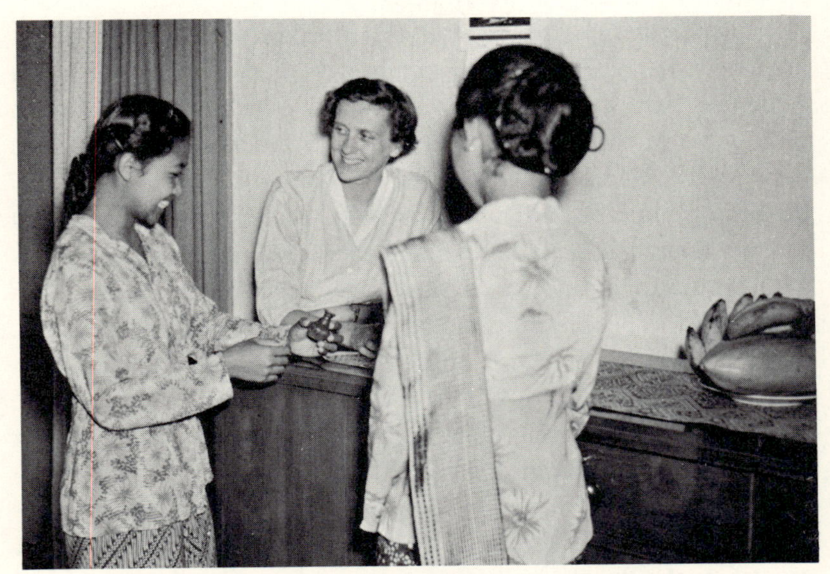

Francine Wickes chats with Indonesian friends in Sukabumi.

Chapter Ten

The Bridge Builder

ON THE surface, the Grail in Indonesia looks like just a handful of people—French, American, Chinese, Dutch, Australian—building face to face relations with the people of Indonesia: in the university and schools where they teach, in the existing organizations on a parish and civic level, over countless cups of tea in the homes of the wealthy and well educated, as well as in those of the people of the newly evolving industrial communities. Dig below the surface a little, and you will find a pattern in the work there that goes right back to the first days of the Grail.

Thirty years ago the idea of lay people going to the missions was not apparent in the mind of the Church. Today the Holy Father has spoken—he desires it—urges it, and the mission bishops and priests are clamoring for trained lay workers who can help to make the "total Church" present everywhere.

For Elisabeth Allard, who paved the way for the Grail in Indonesia, it was quite a different story—in the beginning. Sitting in her tiny office in Bogor, almost opposite President Sukarno's palace, she took time out from her teaching and research work to tell me a story behind the story of the Grail in Indonesia, a story which goes back to an afternoon in the bishop's residence in the diocese of Haarlem, Holland, in the year 1928.

"Your missions are at home." Kindly, gently, firmly, the bishop had spoken, and the interview was over.

They were dismissed. How was it that their words had not moved him? If only there was some way to reopen the discussion they had prepared so carefully, to pour out their story once again so he would understand. There was nothing to do now but bow themselves out.

Elisabeth Allard bent over the new bishop's hand. Never before had she realized the full significance of kissing the episcopal ring. Now she knew it was no archaic formality. It meant submission, surrender, obedience—it meant the cross they so often talked about.

She stood behind and watched the other four, Marguerite van Gilse, Lydwine van Kersbergen, Louise Veldhuis, and Mia van der Kallen, wondering if they were thinking the same thing. Swiftly the polite murmurings of the departure were over, and they were ushered down the wide steps of the bishop's house and into the evening dusk of Haarlem. No one said a word.

Their thoughts raced back over the years the four of them had spent together at the University of Nijmegen, years of intensive study and preparation. Their plan had been a bold one, but they had been so sure it was what God wanted. They would go to the missions of Indonesia to establish a university for Javanese women, based on the life and culture of that country. They had taken their degrees with this goal in mind, in history and sociology, Sanscrit language and literature, philology and art. It was a daring idea with all the verve and shine of youth—when we remember it was before World War II and the government was just beginning higher education for the Indonesian people.

At the University of Nijmegen, the great Jesuit scholar, Professor James van Ginneken, had begun to work with their small group, firing them with the spirit of the apostolate, preparing them for the task ahead. The former bishop of Haarlem had fully approved of their project and given his encouragement.

True, others had not understood. But the five young students knew that the fundamental principle on which the whole missionary venture hinged would not readily be accepted by many. For the vocation to the missions which had drawn them together, which colored all their plans for their future life in Java, was not a vocation to the religious life. They were not connected with any religious order—they did not intend to begin one. They saw their work as a participation in a movement whose very name was strange thirty years ago—the lay apostolate in the stream of life of the Church.

But now the dream was over. The bishop had spoken. He had asked them to begin, not in Java where they had lived in spirit during the years of preparation, but in their own backyard—among the girls and women of Haarlem and Amsterdam and the other cities of Holland.

Two courses were open. They could admit failure and abandon their plans. Or they could accept the mandate of their bishop wholeheartedly, strike out boldly in a new direction, begin a lay apostolic movement in Holland as the bishop had suggested. They could accept the cross.

As the little group made their decision that night, the Grail Movement was born. Three years later, in 1931, the Grail put on its first mass demonstration in the Olympic Stadium in Amsterdam, an interpretation of "The Royal Road of the Cross" performed by 3,000 girls before 50,000 spectators. A Pentecost play with 10,000 girls followed in 1932, and the Grail set out to use every modern means for the apostolate—radio, a widely recognized film group, the publication of books and periodicals, exhibitions of modern art, interpretative dance, and mass demonstrations.

Marguerite van Gilse was now the overall leader, and the movement spread rapidly to Germany, England, Scotland, Australia and America. Building the Grail Movement meant more than setting up a Grail Center in each country; it meant working out again and again in each new situation a pattern of dynamic, integrated Catholic life; it meant training new leaders from the local area and moving on. But these first ones never put aside their plans for a lay mission movement. Often separated, each with her duties in a different country, the missions were a frequent subject of their correspondence and their prayer.

From the beginning their goals in the lay apostolate were clear. The Grail would first of all work at home in the various countries, developing apostles to exert a Christian impact in their own environment; secondly, it would initiate an apostolate to non-Catholics. But there would surely come a time when the third goal of the Grail would materialize—when the very best from each country could be prepared specifically for the missions, with particular emphasis on working among the educated women of the land.

And this third goal has materialized. In 1951, after Marguerite van Gilse had handed on the international leadership to Rachel Donders, she herself set out for Africa and steered the Grail there through its first formative years; Dr. Louise Veldhuis at the Grail Mission Center in Ubbergen has trained European professional women who are currently at work on three continents; Dr. Lydwine van Kersbergen, who has headed the Grail Movement in England and Australia and was chosen to bring it to the United States, has had for the past ten years the deep satisfaction of sending off dozens of American girls to Asia, Africa and Latin America. Dr. Mia van der Kallen, after ten years of valiant apostolic work in Holland and Germany, died of a sudden illness. In reality she gave her life in the constant struggle and responsibility of the first beginnings of the Grail.

And what of Dr. Elisabeth Allard, our bridge person in Asia? With two doctorates to her credit, one in linguistics (including Sanskrit and Javanese) and the other in cultural anthropology, she has spent fruitful years caught up in the midst of the educational ferment in Java. In a country where schools are rising out of the ground like the proverbial toadstool, she has served first as lecturer in the temporary university, then as Conservatrice of the Institute of Linguistics and Cultural Research, then as professor of cultural anthropology at the University of Indonesia. To all her encounters with the eagerly questing minds of young Indonesians she has brought her grasp of Western culture, her faith, her deep concern to understand Javanese traditions and her warm appreciation of Javanese culture.

When we said good-bye at the gate of her apartment in Bogor, I remarked laughingly that with her brown eyes and tranquil expression she was beginning to look like the Indonesian women she admires so much.

"I think it would be untruthful," she said seriously, "to pretend that I am Javanese when I am a big Dutch woman. People would smile and say it is poor taste to try to look like one. But I will never rest in my efforts to know this people better and to appreciate more fully their culture and traditions."

As bridge-builder, Elisabeth has opened the way for the Grail teams in Java, who carry on in the same spirit of openness and appreciation for the rich cultural background and the strong aspirations of this new nation. She herself is back now at the other end of the bridge—serving as professor at the Catholic University in the Netherlands, sharing with young Europeans the insights born of her years in Indonesia—quietly, patiently working to build a surer, deeper understanding between peoples of different cultures.

Benedicte Milcent and Mary Helena Fong go shopping in Djakarta.

Chapter Eleven

Where the Centuries Run Side by Side

THE MAIN railway station in Djakarta is a cross between a market before a public holiday and the entrance to the cricket field at the beginning of a Test Match series in Melbourne. It takes all one's ingenuity and energy to carve out a way to the ticket office. I had arrived there at the crack of dawn to catch a train for Semarang, some ten hours' ride up the island of Java, where I would meet Benedicte Milcent, one of our French international Grail people.

Sticky and hot in a third class compartment, I was nevertheless completely enchanted hour after hour, watching from the window. It was like a never-ending picnic to see the chattering groups of women in gaily colored kabaya and sarong, faces shaded by wide straw hats, cutting rice by hand.

Towards evening, I watched the slowly moving processions of peasants along the roads, rice sheaves slung over their shoulders, some jogging along in little carts pulled by horses. I expected any moment to see the minute animals dangling in mid-air, lifted by the weight of drivers and rice sheaves.

At journey's end, Benedicte was there, cool as a cucumber in a white linen dress, with a car borrowed for the occasion. We lost no time in getting to know each other, as we piled the typewriter and the cameras onto the seat, and began crazily to weave our way in and out of the traffic of the evening rush hour.

Benedicte comes from Pau in France, a charming town in the Pyrenees close to Lourdes. She was president of Père Jean Daniélou's Cercle de St. Jean Baptiste in Paris, a group of students and young professional women with a profound concern for the mission of the Church. Through lectures and discussions, through the monthly *Bulletin* of Le Cercle with its penetrating studies of the role of the Church in newly evolving societies, through contact with the international students in Paris, Benedicte's missionary vision deepened, and she felt increasingly drawn towards work in an Islamic culture.

After a time of preparation at the Grail International Center in Holland, Benedicte left for Indonesia, to take a position on the staff of the French Embassy in Djakarta in the department of cultural relations. When her contract expired, she moved to Semarang, capital of central Java, a city of 500,000 people, largely Moslem. Here she is instructor in French at a teachers' college and works with the Indonesian women and girls in a variety of ways—in fact, she does everything from organizing liturgical celebrations with the Catholics to acting as advisor to the women's section of a workers' union.

Benedicte is deep, warm, and original in her approach to the apostolate; it was a tremendous lift for me to talk over events with her from a wider, deeper angle than the usual natter around pressrooms in Hong Kong and Saigon. It is so easy to become glib, and to "have all the answers" to the needs of our time from a purely political or economic viewpoint.

We had just finished our evening meal and a long, hot night stretched before us. Benedicte and I were outside under a widespreading flamboyant tree, the grass beneath carpeted with fallen red blossoms. The conversation got around to what was uppermost in our minds—the people, the apostolate, the position of the Indonesian women, ways and means of bringing Christian

Like good housewives everywhere, these Indonesian shoppers look closely before they buy. Baby rides happily along in the customary sling, resting against mother's hip. I found the Indonesian women particularly attractive, with their glossy black hair, gracefully draped sarongs, and charming manner. Today, despite centuries in purdah, they are taking their places readily in public life.

values into the local social structure and institutions; how we could forge bonds of unity across continents, oceans, frontiers.

"Already after this brief acquaintance," I remarked, "I find the Indonesian people irresistible, charming, and so open and ready for new developments. I guess part of the fascination is that these people are rich in centuries of religious and cultural history. Today, as I watched Mrs. Sastromoeljono organizing the batik workers in her home, I could hardly wrench myself away."

"Enfin . . . " Benedicte responded warmly, "three years in Indonesia is more than long enough for me to love these people as I love my own brother, and to make me aware of the great privilege of being able to share the life of this nation young in its independence and political life.

"Today the world knows that although the many wounds on the personality of the Indonesian people will take time to heal, their spirit is healthy and original. As well it is quickly recovering its freedom. Of course, mistakes are made but this is a revolutionary nation, a nation which began its independent existence only in 1950. There is great push for modernization, and an amazing growth and development in fields like education, social welfare, health. This country is in a hurry because the world has no intention of standing still while Indonesia catches up. The people have to cram the experiences of centuries into one generation, and it is important that the revolutionary spirit of self-sacrifice and solidarity be maintained—that is the driving force which will bind the nation together.

"And of course the Church cannot remain static in all this—we have so much to give by applying the Church's social principles. This is why with our work here, I seem to have so many fingers in different pies."

We lapsed into silence and I sat watching the steady stream of traffic going past our gate—rattling jeeps, streamlined American cars, sweating young men pedalling passengers in "bedjaks," students in blue and white uniforms with books heaped on bicycle handlebars, a long dray stacked with firewood drawn by a yoke of buffalo—old and new Asia, where the centuries do not follow each other but run side by side.

The people of Indonesia are lively, spirited and remarkably intelligent. The basic stock is Malayan, with an overlay of Indian, Chinese and Arabian blood. I was delighted especially by the women, their grace and charm, and the deep-water quality of their round brown eyes. I was never tired of looking at them. Benedicte told me some fascinating discoveries she had made regarding the education of the Javanese women, which we both agreed could be the reason for the tranquil facial expression of so many.

When the young girl reaches adolescence, around thirteen or fourteen years, she is shown by her mother or perhaps her grandmother, the art of sacrifice. She is taught to reduce her hours of sleep to perhaps five hours a night, to go without food, and to fast three days a week outside the usual Moslem fasting period. She is taught to restrain her taste by eating only rice on one day, a certain quantity of bananas on another, or perhaps food without any spices or salt on certain days. In all these exercises, the Javanese girl surrenders her judgment to that of her mother or grandmother and remains pliable and confident in the older woman's hands. Sometimes she may even be asked to sleep outside on the ground, and this training in sacrifice goes on until her marriage, according to the traditions in each family. In these days some of the customs are tending to disappear, but many remain.

I asked Benedicte how her friends explained the reason for this education, and if there was a similar training for the young men. The answer she gave me was simple: "Women are made to suffer and to endure hardship. This idea is deep in the heart of the Javanese woman." And I understood then how it is that this daughter of France is so at home with her Indonesian sisters. "They have to be strong to suffer," she continued, "and to know how to control their feelings and needs." For a Catholic, this explanation seems unsatisfactory compared to the Christian concept of penance as redeeming-with-Christ, making up for our own sins and those of others. "But," Benedicte assured me, "for the Javanese girl it is enough to believe that Allah will bless the woman who has lived the years of her youth in a controlled and sacrificial pattern. Often after the girl is married, she will go on fasting one or two days a week, when she wants to obtain something for those she loves."

As for the boys, Benedicte told me she had never heard of a similar training. This may explain why foreign visitors to Indonesia have remarked quite frequently that Indonesian women have more personality than the men. And the fact is that they take their places easily in public life, in spite of centuries in purdah. The Press and Public Relations Officer of the Indonesian Delegation to the United Nations is a woman, charming Miss Rochmuljati Wirjohatmodjo, who is also a second secretary at the Embassy. There are women in the government ministries, in the health and education departments, in film censorship, and in prison control. In fact, seven percent of the major government functionaries are women, a higher percentage than in many western lands.

I have not seen Benedicte for some time but although we are not physically working side by side, we are in communication. A letter with the Semarang postmark is on my desk now, and our conversations continue across oceans and continents.

Semarang
Java, Indonesia

. . . in these six months all the plants in our small pavilion have grown a lot, and the fence between Mrs. Su's yard and ours is all green. You will understand what this means, when you remember how the yard used to be filled with stones and old bricks. Flowers are still very slow in coming, but they will come. Roses and melati are starting to bud, one by one—and this is true, too, for the work! A lot of green has spread out, and flowers may be slow in coming—but longed for. . . .

Our small family, Francesca, Rinastutti, Juliana, are still here, and now Francine has joined us. The cement of love and unity is growing through living together, and singing every evening in sincere oneness "Dalam tangan Mu Tuhan": "Into thy hands, O Lord, I commend my spirit." I have just been very busy correcting exams. It has been a good experience and an opportunity to tighten the link with the teachers of the SMA Negeri [the government secondary school] where I am asked to teach again next year. With my pupils at the teachers' college who are young adults I begin to have some friendly contact, and many like to drop in.

We have a good and free contact with our parish. The parish priest is Father J. Dijkstra, S.J., who has been the soul of the "Pantja Sila" * here and works hand in hand with many of the young Indonesian priests. I started translating some French pamphlets on the Mass and liturgy into Bahasa-Indonesia for the parish bulletin. Then I was asked to work out the liturgical calendar for each month, and to fill in some short explanation on the main aspects of the Mass as it should be lived by lay people. It works! For August we have a plan for Dialogue Mass, and I have to work out the booklet—taking inspiration and some translations from Sukabumi's effort. Our parish priest is so deeply sensitive to the urgent need for the renewal of life and real, concrete social charity that it is a great asset for all of us.

Francine and I are very busy with the "Seksi Wanita," the women's section of the national workers' union. With Francesca and another girl, we went round the different groups of women workers; most of them are servants in the various boarding houses of the city, but eighty percent go home every evening to their quarters. Our aim is to work out a womanly approach to the problems of the women members. The directing committee of men are very pleased with this, because they have already experienced that as men they were often unable to have real contact with the women who come frequently to the cooperative, more often, in fact, than the men.

Through literacy courses and sewing courses we hope to develop more contact between young teachers and office workers and the servant women. We have contacted the various Sodalities and other groups, to stimulate a social consciousness among

* A social action movement based on five principles: belief in one omnipotent Being, humanism, nationalism, sovereignty of the people, social justice.

their members. Almost as soon as we began, difficulties cropped up. Teaching adults is quite a different cup of tea from teaching children! We are now using the methods of the "Pendidikan Masjarakat" (which is the social education program here) and which has had sound experience on an adult level. I now have thirty-five girls packing our little pavilion who will become teachers for the literacy courses. What I am aiming at is that there will be *real* contact between the teachers and the members of the "Pantja Sila," through the courses, but also through home visits, services, personal contact. This is just in the beginning stage—it will be a work of love and patience. You will understand that through this field, which seems to me the most urgent and unexploited here, a lot of *our* ideal can be witnessed to. And this is why I really ask you to pray for us.

I have just come back from a ten day course on methods of improving food conditions in the villages and poor areas of the cities. It has been a marvelous experience. I was the only foreigner among twenty-seven home economics teachers, all from government schools in the cities of central and east Java. Only two of this group were Catholics. All the participants were most hospitable and friendly to me, and I was very much impressed by the maturity and the nobility of their thoughts and movements.

This course was held in a beautiful place at the foot of the mountains, with an immense horizon of red earth and green sah-wahs, a place to praise the Lord with your whole being. We had lectures and practical training on diet, common diseases, baby care, agriculture, planting the right vegetables and fruit. I learned to milk goats, as my neighbors have some which they never milk. Most Javanese do not drink milk yet, although it has been proved that it is a basic necessity here too, as a means of fighting the centuries-old malnutrition. Initiatives in this direction are multiplying quickly now in village community development projects in the surrounding area, and prove successful.

Many things in the course were very new to me, and I must confess that my brains were sometimes exhausted! But it will all gradually sink in, and I still have a lot of documents to study. The course has been an opportunity to meet with some sincere and honest Nationalists—in the sound God-given sense of the word—who are working for the people, for the masses, and are deeply rooted in them, with real dedication and faith in God.

Such experiences give one deep faith in the development of this country, whatever may be the influences and the dangers existing at the same time. It also makes us more humble with regard to the role that we can play as foreigners. The Indonesian people are the ones who can feel what is good—and what is not. We may suggest, we may sometimes see things that a person of the country does not notice any more, but we cannot judge what is good or not, by ourselves. In that sense UCCI * is right when it expresses our role as an auxiliary, one that can soon be set aside. *Fiat*. It is a beautiful vocation, and a necessary one, too.

* Catholic Union for Interracial Cooperation.

An important moment in modern history: the opening of the Bandung Conference.

Chapter Twelve

I Meet the A-A Nations

THE FULL stimulating weeks in Indonesia, where I had heard and learned so much, were coming to an end, and just as I was about to leave I got a cable from Father Mark Tennien, M.M., chief NCWC correspondent in Hong Kong, asking me to cover the historic Bandung Conference * for this news service.

I travelled to Bandung from Sukabumi with Maria Malone, who had been in Indonesia since 1951. Back home in Australia Maria loved the bush—she could name every wildflower and bird, and I found that she had transferred this old love to her new land. As the ancient bus heaved its way up the winding mountain tracks, Maria pointed out the rare beauties of the brilliantly flowering trees and shrubs and omitted to prepare me for a particular curve in the road where you could see a sheer drop almost into eternity. We arrived towards dusk at Bandung, a sprawling city bedecked with red flags, many of them bearing the sign of the hammer and sickle. The streets were packed with people, for the most part just walking along and staring at the large auditorium where the A-A Conference was to be held.

Strung across the street was a white calico sign with red lettering: WELCOME TO THE ASIAN-AFRICAN CONFERENCE. I edged my way out of the crowd jostling shoulder to shoulder on the

* Asian-African Conference held in Bandung, Indonesia in April, 1955.

sidewalk, shifted my heavy camera bag and made ready to focus on the entrance to the conference hall across the road. I was hot and sweaty and hemmed in, with an unaccountable feeling of being a gatecrasher at a family party.

Then I saw a group of tall black men emerge from the doorway and walk down the steps, dignified, at ease, smiling into the crowd. The splash of yellow and red from their splendid robes contrasted sharply with the sombre clothing of the Asians walking with them. Straggling behind this group were the big names in the news—Nehru of India, Chou En-lai of China, Nasser of Egypt, Romulo of the Philippines, U Nu of Burma, Sukarno of Indonesia. As a reporter in Asia, I was familiar with these men—the way they looked, their personal histories, their policies. But the Africans were strangers to me—their countries were just emerging into independence and self-government; they were standing in the spotlight for the first time.

The group of delegates converged on the footpath, waiting to cross the road. The Africans stood head and shoulders above the rest. Although I did not know their names, I knew that evening and in the days that followed, hearing them speak in the assembly, that these African leaders were men with a destiny.

This conference of twenty-nine Asian and African nations meeting in Bandung on that hot April day of 1955 was a unique and significant event. Five Asian nations—Indonesia, India, Burma, Ceylon and Pakistan—had taken the initiative in organizing the meeting, and most of Asia, including Communist China, was represented. Twenty-three out of the twenty-nine delegations were from Asia. Most of independent or nearly independent Africa was there, too—Egypt, Ethiopia, the Gold Coast (now the Republic of Ghana, but then just on the eve of independence), Liberia, Libya, and the Sudan. For the first time in history, the people of the "Color Curtain," stretching from Africa through the Middle East, the sub-continent of India, Southeast Asia, continental China, Korea, and Japan, were meeting without any help from the white West, to solve their common problems. "The first intercontinental congress of colored peoples in the history of mankind," President Sukarno, in a voice full of emotion, declared in his opening speech. The range of problems before the congress was impressive: economic and cultural co-operation among the Asian and African countries, questions of nationalism, racialism and colonialism, the promotion of world peace.

Some four hundred correspondents were gathered in Bandung, about eighty of us from the West. I went into the Conference Hall to pick up my press card and programs and for the next week was caught up in a moment in history. The press rooms were chaotic—a tangle of jammed telephone booths and clacking typewriters, avalanches of mimeographed handouts and statements, a dozen different languages shouted across the room, and a young excitement drawing us together for a real exchange and meeting. I remember one evening in the press room listening to Richard Wright, American Negro correspondent and author, who had come to Bandung on his own initiative, drawn by the idea of a meeting of the colored peoples of the world. Pounding his fist on the table, he pointed to a chap from the Manchester Guardian.

"Your world of culture," he said, "clashed with the culture worlds of colored mankind. Traditional beliefs have been destroyed among a billion and a half black, brown and yellow men, and this has set off a tide of social, political and economic revolutions. There's an astounding emotional thrashing about as men seek new objects about which they can center their loyalties."

One center of loyalty has been formed by the growing sense of solidarity among the colored peoples, which had its major expression that April week of 1955 in Bandung. No "white" nation was invited to this gathering. The Asian-African Conference comprised the nations whose people are nonwhites, those billion and a half human beings who for the most part have only recently emerged from colonial status and are often bitter in their reactions to colonialism.

This is not to say that the twenty-nine nations present at the first A-A Conference were of the same political shade. They ran the spectrum from Western allies in NATO and SEATO to determined neutralists to Communist China and North Vietnam. But it is probably correct to say they shared a common hope and desire for economic development and progress, for they belonged to the less developed areas of the world with relatively low standards of living.

Along with this growing sense of solidarity within the A-A nations which was so clear to me at Bandung, there was the widening rift with the white West and an upsurge of nationalism. The burning question for Asians and Africans today is nationalism.

Pandit Nehru of India, addressing a meeting at the Bandung Conference, spelled it out in these words: "There is no Asian nation now where any argument, be it Communist or anti-Communist, is worth mentioning, if it runs counter to the national spirit of the country in question. In any Asian nation you may go to, one fact impresses you: what has imposed itself everywhere is nationalism, and the means of bolstering it up. If you oppose this, you will never be fully understood or fully appreciated."

Nehru's words echo feelings to be found everywhere in postwar Asia, Africa and the Middle East.

A conversation in a plane flying between Djakarta and Singapore comes to mind. A young man from Chicago returning to a USIS * post in Manila complained to me, "I tell you, we're up against it. I was talking to an Indian when we stopped down in Calcutta and he said to me, 'I know it makes no sense, but when you Americans let off a hydrogen bomb, that is a threat to peace; when the Russians do it, that's an example of another undeveloped country making good.'

"It gets me," he continued, "that America is always linked with colonialism."

Carlos Romulo, a friend of America, lecturing at the Univer-

* U.S. Information Service.

Like this Cantonese farm woman, millions in Asia must struggle unceasingly for the bare necessities. Caught up in today's revolution of rising aspirations, they are looking for a way to a better life.

sity of North Carolina, listed six Asian criticisms of the United States, and the first one was this: "Americans continually talk of freedom and human rights. But they have supported the colonial policies of France, England, Belgium, and other colonial powers. They abstained in the United Nations whenever the questions of Cyprus, Tunisia, Algeria came up for decision. In the U.N. Trusteeship Council, they have adopted an amorphous attitude on fundamental questions affecting nonself-governing peoples. How can we believe in the sincerity of the Americans when their preachments and protestations do not jibe with their policy and actions?"

It is not important at this point whether the criticism is justified or not—what is really important is for Americans like the young man from Chicago to know the criticisms leveled by the Asians and Africans and to become more aware of their sensitivity to anything which smells of colonialism or racialism.

An intolerance of the guttering candle of colonialism and tolerance of the raging bushfire of international Communism is a form of suicidal mania in many of the young sovereign nations today.

So many times, sitting in busses, trains, or planes, walking in the paddy fields or markets, talking with students, soldiers, or reporters, I encountered the same pattern of thought. "The white Westerner has to get out: too long he has dominated our country. Everything, even Communism, must be used if it helps us retain our hard-won sovereign nationhood."

It is not easy for the young patriot to see the wood for the trees. How often the Communists have used nationalism as a springboard to put across their ideas. Of course, waves of extreme nationalism following liberation from colonial status are understandable. When a person is insecure he feels the need to assert himself. It is the same with a nation. The new sovereign powers know economic and social instability; they lack a corps of political and administrative leaders backed by solid training and experience.

Indonesia is a case in point. Although the colonial government had opened a number of professional schools on the university level in Java after World War I, still relatively few Indonesians had university training or preparation for administrative posts. So you see a handful of intelligent young men ruling 88,000,000 people. The Indonesians know their own problems. One of them who knows America well summed it up: "If Washington were destroyed by a bomb, there would be many other men to carry on, who are experienced in foreign affairs, taxes, economics, national health. Here, if our capital,

Djakarta, were destroyed, Indonesia would have no government."

Not content with small political units, which are necessarily weak, the Asian and African leaders of the world are planning large-scale federations.

The inevitable fumbling which must follow in the wake of independence as the high hopes turn to disillusionment, the absence of experienced leadership, the lack of capital to develop national resources—all these factors help to maintain an atmosphere of anarchy and discontent. The Marxist dialectic finds in all this a most favorable situation. This is a point many fail to understand. I returned to Hong Kong from Indonesia with a new understanding of the major issues at stake, which affect the lives of men, and I knew that in the coming months I'd have more news items about Africa in the pages of the *Sunday Examiner,* and that the term A-A nations had come to stay in our everyday vocabulary.

A typical street scene in people-packed Hong Kong.

Chapter Thirteen

Christmas in the Sun

ON DECEMBER 23, 1955, I left Asia for Australia, to spend Christmas "down under" in the sun. It was my first visit home in seven years, and I flew out from Manila, where I had been attending the "Asian Meeting of the Laity." Fifteen Asian nations had sent delegates to this first Asian congress of the lay apostolate, united under the slogan "ASIA FOR CHRIST." Valerian Cardinal Gracias of India presided over the gathering, and it was heartening to see the alertness and eagerness of the delegates going up to the microphone before the assemblies of thousands of people, putting their questions, making reports about the development of the Church in their lands. You saw a new world opening for the lay apostolate, Catholic people of India and Japan, of Vietnam, Pakistan, Ceylon, and Korea, Indonesia and, of course, the Philippines, aware of their possibilities and strength. So it was with the brave words of many speeches ringing in my ears that I left Asia.

The plane was filled with Filipina nurses going to Australia on the Colombo Plan * for six months. As we circled over Darwin, one beside me pressed my arm and whispered:

* A program of economic and technical cooperation, initiated by Ceylon, India, Malaya and Pakistan, and now including most of the nations of Southeast Asia, together with Australia, New Zealand, Canada, the United Kingdom and the United States. Its aim is to raise standards of living and promote economic development in Southeast Asia.

"Why, this can't be Australia—it's only a tiny village." But it was Australia. Darwin is the doorway to the sprawling vast empty land. A handful of low wooden buildings with gleaming corrugated tin roofs, clumps of palms, wide stretches of low scrub country—and the same searing heat as Borneo and the Philippines. Had it not been for the Australian officials at the airport, it could have been just another stop-over on one of the islands along the way. We were only four hundred thirty miles from Timor in Indonesia, with another 2000 miles to go to Sydney.

My brother John and his wife and three nephews and niece were at the airport to meet me. I stayed two weeks in the area, as I had stories to write on the Australian aborigine missions as well as to renew my acquaintance with my family.

From Darwin I flew out to Bathurst, Melville and Channel Islands in the Arafura Sea, and as well down to the Adelaide River to take pictures of some of the 70,000 surviving Australian aborigines, a people who are still living in the Stone Age.

The aborigines are generally believed to have come from southeast Asia between 10,000 and 20,000 years ago. They traveled on rafts or in bark canoes via the island stepping stones of Indonesia and New Guinea, where the longest voyages necessary to go from one island to the next were no more than fifteen or thirty miles. About seven hundred tribes, each numbering from two hundred to seven hundred people, have been recorded. Today tribal life is preserved only in remote parts of Cape York and Northern Territory which I visited, and in some parts of Western Australia.

My brother chartered a Tiger Moth plane to fly me to the mission stations, which was a delightful experience. I enjoyed sitting in the narrow cockpit, waist upwards in the open with a heavy leather cap and goggles clamped on my head. We flew as low as sixty feet from the ground to chase wild buffalo in the swamps, and we followed at the same altitude the progress of an alligator up a billabong. It was one of those days when you are suddenly a child again with all kinds of impossible adventures just around the corner! I saw strange sea creatures in the translucent light blue sea which we barely skimmed—then we went over the low mangrove swamps until we landed in a clearing in the bush.

After the roar of the engines the sudden quiet came as a shock. I removed my helmet and felt as though I was on the rim of the world. The pilot was tinkering around inside and called to me to take a walk as he wasn't sure if this was the landing for the mission station which expected us. But we didn't wait long—there was the rattle of a truck and in a cloud of dust there emerged from the bush a battered Ford utility, bearing three Sisters, their veils streaming behind them, and myriads of aborigine children clinging to every available space. Before the truck stopped they hopped off and ran to me, staring unashamedly, then with a call from the Sisters ran off in all directions leaving me standing alone. Now some of their elders came out of the bush to see what all the hullabaloo was about. They were naked except that most of them wore a string or fur pubic-apron attached to a girdle. They had armlets made from shells, necklaces and forehead-bands as other ornaments, and some wore bone nose-pins. After looking me over briefly, they turned their attention to the plane. The Sisters scooped me up on the truck, and within half an hour life was normal once again, as big mugs of strong sweet tea were handed around with generous plates of buttered scones. These Australian Missionaries of the Sacred Heart are *real people* (not in the sense that the beatniks of today use the term); they are strong plain women with clear eyes used to looking into the distance. We talked long into the night, for I was their first outside visitor in eight months, and the event of the year.

The following morning as I woke I heard singing and thought I'd overslept and Mass had already begun. I slid into my clothes and dashed off across the compound towards the tiny chapel on the edge of the bush. But I wasn't late for Mass. What I had heard was a little old nomadic tribeswoman, squatting on the ground outside the church, singing her grandchild to sleep. Her scrawny black arms encircled a fat baby boy, lying blissfully in a coolamon (a curve of bark in which aborigine children are carried), while her old body swayed to the rhythm of a song as old as the Church—*Credo in unum Deum*—in perfect plainsong and understandable Latin. In moments like these, how one loves Mother Church, present here among the most primitive children of men as in the world's great cities, teaching, sanctifying, opening doors. That child, after all, was a potential priest or pope—he has all the essential makings: a baptized Catholic boy!

They were full days on the island missions, and I got back to Darwin just in time to board the plane for the last lap of the journey home. It took eight hours to fly the last 2000 miles over the dead heart of Australia, over the gibber plains with boulders scattered like marbles where some playful giants had been interrupted at play; across dry river beds and the grasslands where the shadow of the plane scares the sheep; over the Great Dividing Range, a mountain chain which extends almost all the way along the east coast—and then Sydney. The untidy metropolis sprawled below, row after row of red-tiled houses, chimney stacks belching smoke, great liners pulled up in the harbor, and traffic packed streets. A final swoop earthwards, and the Reid clan mixed with Grail members waving from behind the barrier. A cycle completed and a new one all lined up to begin.

Sydney is the capital of New South Wales, the oldest and most populous of the six Australian states. When the Declaration of Independence was being signed in Philadelphia in 1776, New South Wales was still a nameless tract of country, part of a land where seas of grass stretched to the horizon and the forests had never bled under the impact of a metal axe. Australia is a country where the world's youngest civilization has been superimposed on one of the world's oldest landscapes. Its people have a vitality one finds only in the young, and the land has a ruggedness that comes only with time. The two opposites have merged to produce a nation that is playing a strong and growing part in the world's politics and economy. The Church has taken root there, sown from the seed of fighting Irish stock—the political prisoners exiled from Ireland to Australia by the British government. Today Australia is nineteen percent Catholic, we have the first Australian cardinal, Norman Cardinal Gilroy of Sydney, and an almost completely Australian hierarchy, with the exception of a few "giants" from Ireland—ninety-six-year-old Archbishop Daniel Mannix in Melbourne, and eighty-six-year-old Archbishop Sir James Duhig in Brisbane.

Australia had changed somewhat during the years I was in Asia. The population had gone up from 8,500,000 to 10,000,000. Some 1,500,000 immigrants have come into Australia as a result of the "Populate or Perish" slogan after World War II. Forty-seven percent of these new Australians came from Great Britain; the rest, including 15,000 Americans and many refugees from the iron curtain countries, came from every white nation in the world.

The same old bugbear, the "White Australia Policy," was still in the air, but there seemed to be a growing understanding of the universal declaration of human rights and a decent respect for our Asian neighbors developing among the student groups, largely as a result of the Colombo Plan. Jim Bowler, leader of the Australian delegation to the Pax Romana Conference in Manila in 1960, showed this new approach in his remark that an Australian with an open conscience cannot help feeling some qualms at his own country's lack of charity, to say the least, in regard to the plight of Asians—refugees from Communism—who seek admission to Australia. We both agreed that there is something paradoxical about an Australian preaching Christianity in Hong Kong or in any Asian city, for that matter.

And Father Kevin Toomey, National Chaplain of the Young Christian Workers Boys' Movement, had even stronger words on his return from a journey to our "near north." "The time has passed," he said in a statement to the press, "when we can sit back content with our immigration laws as they are. Perhaps we can't attempt a solution right now, but I do say this: Let us get rid of the cliches which endeavor to justify our present policy. At present our government is insincere. Proof of a certain amount of European blood is said to allow admission, but when this is done one must survive the scrutiny of officialdom, which still judges the slant of the eye or the pigment of the skin. If our government wants a 'White Australia,' then let us not hide behind meaningless cliches: rather let the world see our narrow-mindedness, our prejudices. If we are not game to do this, then our position as a Christian democracy demands now a complete reshaping of present policies."

Geographically, the great south land of the Holy Spirit is in Southeast Asia, and it was heartening to see that opinion is changing and a greater appreciation of the peoples of Asia is growing in Australia. It was a special happiness for me to see how much the Australian Grail had grown over the years towards her Asian neighbors. The Family Apostolate has sent clothing and food parcels, and members have opened their homes to give hospitality to Asian students in Sydney. In Melbourne, there was a whole organization, sparked by Tay Creggan, for an "Adopt an Orphan Plan," and Sunday night parties and special lectures always included some of the Asian community.

It was good to spend Christmas in the sun at the Grail training center in Springwood outside Sydney: to walk in the bush in the deep gullies covered with bracken, to see again the slender silver-gums reaching up out of the depths to catch sun-glints on their slanted leaves; to hear the sound of twigs crackling under the billy as it boiled, and to drink steaming mugs of tea—all this caught me up and called me to my roots once more in warm contentment. The easy conversations followed by long spaces of silence, the drone of the locusts, the sudden harsh calls of the magpies were among the familiar sights and sounds in which I rested.

The new generations of young Australians coming to the Grail crowded into Springwood. There were three camps during my holidays, each attended by a hundred girls from city or country colleges of New South Wales. Many girls travelled up to seven hundred miles to be with us for a week. Distance means nothing to Australians—even on foot. An eight-mile walk through the bush to cook a picnic supper out was nothing to these students. They walked without blinking an eye—starting at 5:30 in the morning—three and a half miles to Mass at the seminary and back again when the pastor in our parish church went out of town.

Adelaide Crookall, the President of the Grail in Australia, and I worked together before I went to Hong Kong. She also attended the Lay Apostolate Congress in Manila as an observer from Australia, and we travelled in Indonesia and Malaya together in 1955. She briefed me on the latest developments of the Grail at home. There are four Grail centers in major cities of eastern Australia: Melbourne, Sydney, Springwood and Mackay. The southernmost center is 2000 miles from Mackay in the north. The program of apostolic action is brought into effect at one or the other or all of these centers throughout the year, through long or short residential courses, holiday schools, schoolgirl camps and weekly programs of work in the Grail apostolate in Sydney. This latter involves evening training programs for women of the Family Apostolate Movement, working for the Catholic Asian Students, the Sydney Liturgical Guild, and the Catholic Film Center. In Melbourne, our largest house, Tay Creggan, provides a unique apostolic training which begins in autumn and runs through the winter (March–September in the southern hemisphere). The students, who range between eighteen and thirty, work during the day in shops and offices and professions and the course program goes on in their leisure time, evenings and week-ends.

The place for lay people in the missions is being realised

more and more in Australia. Ten Grail members have left the country on mission assignments—to Indonesia, New Guinea, the Fiji and Solomon Islands. There is a growing stream of inquiries from professional women anxious to donate some of their time and skill to building up the Church in the Pacific Islands, Australia's mission area.

On my way to the States from Australia I stopped in Fiji and saw some of our Australian lay missioners on the job. There were Mary Coleman, Pat Kent, Phillipa Green, all old friends from the early days of the Grail in Australia.

For over a decade Mary has been doing secretarial work for Bishop Victor Foley, S.M., and acting as accountant for the Catholic Missions. Pat has a Catholic library and bookshop attached to the Mission office. Other lay people are helping on the office staff, including one Australian who saw an advertisement in the paper for lay workers for Suva and packed her bags for a two-year stint. Two others, both teachers, one from England and one from Australia, are running a school on another island. Phillipa has been there for three years now—first studying at the new Teachers Training College which has a multi-racial student body of Fijians, Indians and other Islanders, and now teaching in her own island school.

All too soon my Australian interlude drew to an end. By February, 1956, both Australia and Fiji were behind me, and I was in the air once again, this time winging into the western hemisphere, to take up a new assignment at the United Nations in New York.

The Grail is a member of UFER,* Paris-based international movement for fraternal union among races, which has consultative status with U.N. agencies ECOSOC, UNICEF, and UNESCO.† With fifty national branches throughout the world,

* UFER—Mouvement International Pour L'Union Fraternelle Entre Les Races et Les Peuples.

† ECOSOC—Economic and Social Council; UNICEF—United Nations Children's Emergency Fund; UNESCO—United Nations Educational, Scientific, and Cultural Organization.

UFER seeks to assist all people by providing needed services at the request of governments or private organizations, without political or economic strings. It maintains representatives in Paris, New York, and Geneva. Majorie Krijnen, who had been UFER representative at ECOSOC and UNICEF in New York, was being called to a new work in Brussels, so with seven years experience in Asia, it seemed that I was the one to fill the gap.

PART II *Africa*

Alice McCarthy of Brooklyn, teaching a class at Christ the King School.

AFRICA

Sleepy giant
You've been resting awhile.
Now I see the thunder
And the lightning
In your smile.
Now I see the stormclouds
In your waking eyes:
The thunder,
The wonder,
And the young surprise.
Your every step reveals
The new stride
In your thighs.

—Langston Hughes

Chapter Fourteen

Africa in Evolution: A World Awakening

WHEN I arrived in New York to take up my UFER assignment at the United Nations, I wasn't too keen about my new task. It seemed like a lot of paper work, and I like to work with people. Walking up 42nd Street, I tossed over some of the positive reasons why it was a good thing for me to be there. After all, the U.N. does bring together all the countries of the world—the large and small, the rich and poor, the strong and the weak, in one global organization. A member of an international movement, I told myself, has a duty to be present.

It was a cold, rainy morning in February, and I tucked my brief case and the New York *Times* under my arm, so I could put my hands deep in the pockets of my coat to keep warm. With my eyes fixed on the icy pavement, I headed towards the East River. Then all at once it was there in front of me, the great glass building of the Secretariat, its thirty-nine floors emerging out of the mist with an unreal quality. To the left, in front of the circular Assembly Building, a curve of flags, red, white, green, blue, and yellow, were blowing stiffly in the wind. A few minutes later I was on the escalator to the third floor, listening to a dozen different languages spoken by the people whose flags I had seen a minute before outside.

I was at home at once in this United Nations family, with its big job of settling disputes peacefully as they arise and, if necessary, checking aggression; of developing economic resources in underdeveloped countries, extending education, combating disease, expanding food supplies, improving the lot of workers, modernizing transport and communications, and elevating the status of woman. No wonder a student from Kenya said to me later, "The U.N. is mother and father to the new African nations," as he carefully outlined the part the U.N. is playing in the affairs of his country. In the months which followed I came to understand the importance of the U.N. in this age of international action, when the nations have pooled their efforts to solve problems too great for single countries to overcome alone.

Many times in question periods after lectures I have been asked, "What does the United Nations do, anyway?" I think at once of the FAO * program which is responsible for the world food situation and wrestles with the problem of how to fill the plates on the world's table more adequately—and at the same time fill more plates for the 100,000 new members of the family of man born each day. Or of UNESCO,† which is extending educational opportunities for the forty-five percent of the world's adults who cannot read and write, and the more than 250,000,000 children who are not in school. Then there is UNICEF,‡ providing milk powder and vitamins for supplementary feeding for half the world's children. The search for new high protein foods, like an international detective story, has put scientists of many countries to work, looking for cheap, plentiful products that can be both appetizing and nutritious. The results include *saridele,* a "milk" made in Indonesia from soybeans and sesame;

* Food and Agriculture Organization.

† United Nations Educational, Scientific, and Cultural Organization.

‡ United Nations Children's Fund.

fish flour; and other foods made from coconuts, peanuts, cotton-seed and sunflower seeds. The U.N. *is* father and mother in a hundred different ways to the family of men in our time, and not so remote from people as I first thought.

Another question often asked by Americans is, "Who pays?" Many have an idea that their country is bearing the brunt of the finances, and they think of the U.N. as an "expensive debating club."

The annual budget from which the U.N. expenses are met is made up of appropriations assessed according to each country's ability to pay. America's contribution costs each American less than a cent a week—forty-eight cents a year. Here is the break-down: Ten cents for membership in the U.N.; seven cents for participation in the specialized agencies; thirty-one cents for voluntary contributions to special programs such as the Children's Fund and the Technical Assistance Program. World War II for the single year of 1945 cost each American $633.57. Forty-eight cents is very little to give to an instrument to work for peace.

It is so often said, too, in Catholic circles that the Communists use the U.N. as a forum to expound their ideas. They certainly do, but nothing prevents us from doing the same. It is true that the ninety-seven member nations run the whole gamut of political views, social systems and cultures, but they do represent a continuing effort to prevent differences from exploding into war and to find a common ground for constructive cooperation.

At the U.N., my specific work as an NGO * observer and UFER representative has been to be present at the meetings of the Economic and Social Council and its commissions and subcommissions, to make available the technical knowledge and experience of all the UFER affiliates to the members of the Council for use in their discussions and resolutions, and to keep UFER members informed about U.N. activities. The members of ECOSOC † sincerely seek the cooperation of the NGO mem-

* Non-Governmental Organizations.

† Economic and Social Council.

bers, and there is ample opportunity to make Catholic voices heard in the deliberations.

And Catholic voices are heard speaking out in this international gathering on such topics as human rights, the family, the freedom of education, forced labor, status of women. Among those who are making a substantial contribution are Miss Catherine Schaefer of the World Union of Catholic Women and Girls, Director of the National Catholic Welfare Conference Office for United Nations Affairs. Catherine Schaefer is a woman of the world with a clear and objective appreciation of the growing world community—no mystique of internationalism in her, just facts, truth and clear thinking based on solid Catholic tradition and living. It has been an education for me to sit in on meetings chaired by Catherine at the NCWC Office for U.N. Affairs. They are brisk, coordinated; assignments which are given are followed up and brought to the utmost degree of accomplishment. Everyone can speak, and everyone can have different ideas, and they are varied because we are of widely differing backgrounds and represent such a variety of movements in the Church. Other Catholic NGO's are Dr. Alba Zizzamia, the chief U.N.-NCWC correspondent, with her warmth and sparkling intelligence; Jean Gartlan, also of the NCWC Office, a journalist who has had two tours of duty in West Africa and follows African affairs closely from her U.N. observation post; Dr. Louis Longarzo of the International Conference of Catholic Charities—a convert to Catholicism, who has an extensive knowledge of community development, especially in urban areas; Ed Kirchner of Pax Romana; Gary McGloin of the World Union of Catholic Press, an Irishman who is an independent thinker and always ready with an argument with an unexpected twist to it; Gerry Thorman of the International Federation of Christian Trade Unions—an articulate young man of intense dedication to his work; Mrs. Carmen Giroux of the International Catholic Social Workers' Union; Dr. Margaret Bedard, of the International Catholic Child Bureau; Rosemary Cass of the World Federation of Catholic

I discuss a point of NGO procedure with Dr. Louis Longarzo of the International Conference of Catholic Charities before a meeting of the Economic and Social Council at the U.N.

Young Women and Girls; and Carolyn Pezzulo of the Young Christian Workers.

There is no doubt that as members of the spiritual community of the Church, as members of the apostolic movements within the Church, we have a duty to take part in the expanding world community which is rising up before our eyes. The strong, wise voice of the Vicar of Christ, the Father of Christendom, invites us, wishes us, points the way when he says: "A Christian, then, cannot remain indifferent in the face of world evolution. If he sees an increasingly close-knit international community developing under the pressure of events, he knows that this unification, willed by the Creator, must result in a union of minds and hearts in the same faith and love. Not only is it possible for him to work for the realization of this community *still in the making,* it is his duty."

From the vantage point of the U.N., I have watched Africa taking her place in the world scene. The glimpse I had of Africa at the crossroads in Bandung, when I watched the tall, colorfully clad delegates to that conference mingle with seasoned Asian leaders, was but the faintest prelude to the *fait accompli* of the present powerful position of the new African nations in international affairs. Listening to debates in the Trusteeship Council at the U.N., discussing with African leaders in Togoland, Ghana and Sierra Leone in West Africa and in Tanganyika, Kenya and Uganda in East Africa their hopes and plans for their countries, talking with African students in the United States, over and over again I have had the sense of Africa as a world awakening and changing with almost unbelievable rapidity.

It is a vast world—Africa is the second largest continent, four times the size of the United States, large enough to fit Europe, China, Japan and New Zealand easily into its borders. Its 230,000,000 people belong to a great variety of tribes and backgrounds and speak more than eight hundred different languages.

This mighty continent is caught up in a gigantic transition as the spirit of self-rule sweeps it like a gale. March 6, 1957, when the flag of Ghana replaced the Union Jack, is a date of tremendous significance for Africans. The breakthrough in Ghana, made possible by the British policy, started the "Independence Parade."

Ten years ago there were four independent countries in Africa—Egypt, the Union of South Africa, Ethiopia and Liberia. Today all this is changed. Month after month, somewhere on the continent, new national flags are sliding up flagpoles and departing colonial officials are saluting their African successors while the whole world looks on, concerned with Africa's destiny.

This is Africa's time of freedom. Sixteen nations were born in the first year of this new decade. By 1962 more than thirty African nations will sit in the United Nations.

Young African leaders, no longer nameless delegates, but men recognized by millions of newspaper readers throughout the western world, walk onto the world stage with uncommon self-assurance.

There are Julius Nyerere of Tanganyika, Tom Mboya of Kenya and Benedicto Kiwanuka of Uganda, all of whom I first met in America and have also talked with in their homelands.

Julius Nyerere at thirty-nine was elected the first Prime Minister of Tanganyika * when his country won internal independence in May, 1961, with full independence to come at the end of 1961. A Catholic, Nyerere was educated in government schools and later attended the University of Edinburgh. He taught in the Catholic schools until his entry into politics, where he has become the leader of the multi-racial elected members of the new government. Seven years ago, Nyerere was unknown at home and abroad; today he is a man of international reputation, known for his policy of moderation, as he takes up the task of guiding his country to a respected place among the nations. His reputation is based on leadership of Europeans as well as Africans.

"All tribes in Tanganyika will participate in our new government," Julius Nyerere explains, "the newer tribes—the Asians and Europeans—will be just as welcome as the Africans."

Education is a major need, and primary schools are springing up everywhere. Integration of schools has begun. Speaking with a disarming smile about integration, Nyerere said, "Integration in education will be brought about by evolution and not by revolution. Our aim is to integrate, not to disintegrate."

Planning for a university college to open in 1962, he pointed out, "A university college is not just a group of buildings; it is first a group of students and teachers." Nyerere knows that there are very few in Tanganyika with the qualifications that will enable them to enter a university, nor are professors at hand.

* A German colony before World War I, Tanganyika has been a U.N. Trust territory under British administration since World War II. A predominantly agricultural country on Africa's east coast, it has an area about equal to that of California and Oregon combined.

"Teachers must come from overseas," he says, and he works to get them and to gather enough qualified students to start the college with schools of agriculture and law by 1962.

Born into one of the smallest of Tanganyika's one hundred twenty tribes, Nyerere has long dreamed of African unity, first in Tanganyika, then in East Africa, and eventually in all Africa. But Nyerere and his people know that the Tanganyika of their dreams cannot be built in a day. "Now," says Nyerere, "our task really begins. We have changed our cry from '*Uhuru,*' freedom, to '*Uhuru na kazi,*' freedom and work."

Tom Mboya, general secretary of the Kenya Federation, was a school boy scrawling his lessons under the shade of a tree at a Catholic mission school not so very long ago. He went on to a Catholic high school. Later he got the chance to study political science at Oxford University. He first made a reputation in 1955 when, at twenty-four, he settled a Mombasa port strike on terms favourable to the African workers. But he was still unknown outside East Africa when he arrived in Accra for the All African People's Congress in 1958. He was elected chairman of the meeting "to unite Africa and to give Africans a chance to speak for themselves and to work for freedom." He shared the spotlight with Kwame Nkrumah, leader of the host country, and overnight his name appeared in the world press.

I met one of the young people from Kenya for whom Tom Mboya arranged scholarships in the United States during his visit in 1959. As I talked with this tall, mild-mannered student of political science, some of the current thinking of the new generation of Africans began to take shape. I had made a remark that the African people are separated by so many different languages and cultures, and come from such an extraordinary number of tribes that it was difficult to see how a United States of Africa could eventuate. Very quickly the young man answered me: "The burning determination to free ourselves brings us together," he said. "The independence of a few states is meaningless without the total liberation of the whole continent,

Grail team in Kampala: Joan Dilworth of Scotland and Kevina Nabwami of Uganda.

including South Africa. Africa is going to be free. By the time my son grows up, Africa will not be looked upon in terms of jungles and wild game hunting, but in terms of people and their human needs. We want to be part of the modern world."

For the 1960-1961 school year, Tom Mboya sent three hundred young African men and women to the United States. They are ready to sacrifice and work to get an education to help bring about the African dream.

This immense political evolution taking place so swiftly in Africa—indeed, never before in history have so many changes taken place in so short a time—is developing among the shifting sands of radical social change. Already in New York I was confronted with some of the ramifications, as I began to meet more and more African students and visitors.

One afternoon, sitting over tea at the Grail International Students Center in Manhattan, the meaning of these winds of change became the subject of our discussion.

I had just returned from the annual meeting of the NCWC-Mission Secretariat in Washington, D. C., and I began repeating a conversation I had had with a White Father who had worked for many years in central Africa and who had closely studied its social patterns. The introduction of western industrial civilization into the tribal societies of Africa, he claimed, was the cause for throwing the continent into such a profound upheaval.

Frances, a young African student taking post-graduate work in the United States, quietly anchored our attention.

"You have to remember," she said, "that in a few years my people have gone through a social evolution that took centuries in the West. Little wonder that there is a crisis in authority and government, in morals and religion, in economic life, in the entire cultural pattern."

A world of difference, we all agreed, lies between the "old" Africa and the modern Africa, and it is this cleavage which brings about the crisis now evident in all phases of African life.

With my head full of what I had heard at the meeting in Washington I continued talking, with one eye on Frances, getting a nod of approval from her from time to time as I outlined the missioner's thesis.

Primitive African society was based on the clan system with the authority in the hands of the older men headed by the Chief. All land belonged by right to the Chief and private ownership was unknown. The authority of the Chief was absolute; he had the power to dispossess the workers or to demand any share he wished of the fruits of their labors.

The coming of the Westerners brought a change in all this; another authority was introduced, higher than that of the Chiefs, in the person of the regional administrator. A further factor has been the rise of the educated class, the *évoluées,* frequently more highly educated than the Chief himself, and representing a real possibility of slighting his authority. All these elements combine to produce an actual crisis in authority with the consequent criticism of all authority. The absolute rule of the Chiefs as it was known under the clan system no longer has an unquestioned hold; but at the same time, in some areas the people have not developed to the point where they are able to accept and respect a more democratic authority.

"Not only that, but in the area of morals there is a problem," Frances interjected.

"Is it true to say," I asked, "that primitive Africa has its own moral laws based on a sound moral sense, and not necessarily contrary to the Christian code?"

Frances' thin, sensitive face warmly responded to my query. "The difficulty now," she said, "is to know what should be kept and what changed to Christian usage. Perhaps too much has already been done away with which could have been Christianized. I think of how the pagan moral law is based on a strong sense of community. 'Sin' is anything done against the community. It's all right to steal something," she laughed, "if you do it outside the community! This is the difference with Africans. Your Western code of morals is individual, ours is a social law.

"For example," she continued, "orphans are almost unknown in an African community. Such children are immediately taken into the home of another member of the clan. The child is seen as a definite gain for the clan, but he is adopted primarily out of a family spirit rather than for the possible benefit he will bring to the group."

We often see this same sense of solidarity among the students here in the States. Frequently the cost of study abroad is borne by the whole clan. This means, of course, that when the years of study are over and the student has obtained a good position, he is usually expected to maintain the whole family, a fact which brings conflicts when a young African has the vocation of dedication in the Church.

The conversation flowed on.

"A few years ago it would not have been possible," I thought, "to have had such an animated discussion on Africa—nor would anyone have thought it the least bit important or interesting. Now Africa crops up all the time, in national magazines, papal encyclicals, radio news commentaries, and over the teacups in Manhattan!"

A social science student gave another fascinating turn to the discussion with a question about the sudden economic development through plantations and industries. "Isn't it the first time that money has begun to play a part in the lives of the ordinary people of Africa?"

"Yes, that is true," said Frances quietly. Once again she held our full attention, this friend whose background and experience were so different from our own. The quiet voice belied the stir of anger I felt in her as she went on to explain how workers are being drawn from the villages to the mines or the great cities, or migrate there on their own accord, attracted by the lure of cash wages. They are far from their own homes; in Nyasaland and Rhodesia there are towns where sixty percent of the men are away at the mines, leaving the women and children alone at home. It is rarely that the men are permitted to bring their own families with them. This is too expensive, for it would mean that the management of the mines would have to build houses for families, instead of barracks.

"Are the men actually forced to leave the security of the clan," I queried, "or is it a situation which sweeps them out of the old system willy-nilly?"

"The pressures are strong," Frances told us. "Of course, there are a variey of reasons why the men leave the villages—for some it is the attraction of having money to spend for a new bicycle, clothes, a phonograph; for others it is a chance to be free from the old customs and the authority of the clan.

"Then, too, there is a sort of snobbery; a man who has not worked in the mines is a poor fellow indeed.

"The old values are collapsing and new must be found to take their place; it is a time of transition, let us say, from shells to money, from the spear to the can opener," Frances summed it up.

"This is a cause of great anxiety for us. It is true we want to attain to European standards of culture, technique, prosperity and comfort. My family have sacrificed for me and for my brother to have higher education in Europe and here in America. But side by side with this is always the longing to remain ourselves, to build a great culture of our own. In spite of everything we want with all our heart to remain African."

In this changing society, women's role is undergoing far-reaching transformations as African women in growing numbers take on paid employment outside the home, attend secondary schools and colleges, become teachers, nurses, social workers, look towards Western ideas of marriage. To live and work together with the women of Africa, to share their aspirations for freedom and dignity, to give what we can of the Christian understanding of woman, to try together to come to a Christian style of life—it was with all this in mind that the Grail began work in Africa in 1951.

Josephine Drabek of Chicago, at work in the lumonde patch with her students. Lumonde is a kind of sweet potato much relished in Uganda.

Chapter Fifteen

Uganda: Rich in Promise

THE SIZE and complexity of Africa make generalizations risky and comparisons difficult. Five thousand miles from north to south, four thousand five hundred miles from east to west, it embraces every kind of terrain: snowcapped mountains and steaming humid jungles; arid deserts, richly fertile plains, vast forests. It has modern cities and primitive villages, areas developed and ready for local leadership and places where it is still a waiting time. Uganda is one of the former, so it was here that the Grail put down its first roots in central Africa. This was five years before Pope Pius XII in his 1957 encyclical letter, *Fidei Donum,* urged "the universal flock of God throughout the world" to "turn your attention to Africa today, in the hour in which she is being opened up to the life of the modern world, and is passing through what may prove to be the most important years of her millenary destiny."

Today Grail teams are at work in ten countries of Africa: Uganda, Ruanda, Urundi, the Congo,* Tanganyika, Ghana, Basutoland, Union of South Africa, Morocco and Egypt; international teams with Grail members from the United States, Holland, Germany, the United Kingdom, Canada, France, Egypt,

* In July, 1960, when political developments made it impossible to carry on effective medical and social work, the Grail teams left the Congo to join forces with the team in neighboring Urundi.

South Africa, Austria and Australia; diversified teams of doctors, nurses, social workers, teachers, agricultural experts, journalists and specialists in community development—all working alongside African lay apostles, trying to carry out in their lives the program which the present Holy Father, Pope John XXIII, has outlined so clearly in his letter *Princeps Pastorum*.

"It is necessary," he said, "that the Church should have Her complete structure—the various grades of the Hierarchy as well as the order of the laity—wherever She leads her pacific forces, and it is hence necessary that She perform Her work of Redemption through the clergy and the laity."

In 1952 Lydwine van Kersbergen, president of the Grail in the United States, and Marguerite van Gilse, then president of the Grail in Africa, visited Uganda on a 12,000-mile safari across the continent to survey possibilities for the lay apostolate.

They had been told, "In Uganda you will find the real Africa, the black man's Africa," and indeed they found Uganda a promising part of the continent from the point of both natural and human resources, and from the point of view of the Church as well.

The blood of martyrs—the twenty-two young laymen who laid down their lives in 1886—has soaked deep into the soul of Uganda, and the Church has sprung up with a marvelous rapidity and vitality. It reminds one of the Church in Vietnam with the same blossoming of the faith, which stems from the Christian paradox of life issuing from death. In Uganda the time is ripe for the development of lay leadership to build up African society and culture. Uganda may well become the proving ground and model for the lay apostolate in other parts of Africa. The Grail has an orientation center there to help young team members from other countries get acquainted with the African people with whom they are going to work.

I flew into Uganda in January, 1961, en route to Mwanza, Tanganyika, where the bishops have set up a Social Training Center to prepare adults for civic leadership in their newly independent nation. In between my duties as head of the Center's communication department and teacher of journalism, I have been able to make frequent trips to Uganda to see at first hand the work of our teams in this fertile land on the equator.

Uganda along with Kenya and Tanganyika make up British East Africa. The latest estimates show a population of about 6,000,000, a figure which includes some 50,000 Asians and 7,000 Europeans, the latter mostly government personnel or missionaries. Unlike Kenya, Uganda has no white settlers and hence is relieved of certain political pressures. Economically the people are relatively well off. The land grows large amounts of cotton and coffee; copper is mined and smelted; and a big hydro-electric project has been opened where the River Nile flows into Lake Victoria. Politically the country is on the eve of independence, and in April, 1961, Mr. Benedicto Kiwanuka, the leader of the Legislative Council, became the first Chief Minister of Uganda.

My immediate impression of Uganda as we stopped down at Entebbe airport from London was one of flashing color—bright blue and red and green from the sky, the earth and the banana plantations. And then I glimpsed the familiar faces of Grail members: Jessica Stuber of St. Paul, Minnesota, who heads an education team training girls for work in the villages, and Esther Johns, a nurse from South Dakota. I first met Esther in Minneapolis, when she had come up shyly after a talk I gave to ask how she, a new convert, could share in overseas work. After training at Brooklyn and Grailville, Esther took charge of a clinic at Bikira in rural Uganda where the nearest doctor is over thirty miles away. She has only bush tracks and a battered car with which to face emergencies needing a doctor's care.

We drove the twenty miles from the airport into Kampala, the beautiful modern city which is the capital of Uganda. The streets were crowded: women in brightly flowing cottons with kerchiefs on their heads, hundreds of bicycles, a jumble of cars, mostly small British makes with a sprinkling of Volkswagens.

The Indians dominate the business section here, as they do throughout East Africa, and some 15,000 Indian nationals live in Kampala. There is undeniable tension between the Africans and the Indians; this remains a problem to be solved in the political development of the country.

Kampala is the seat of the Kabaka, the king of Buganda, Frederick Mutesa II. His palace, high on a hill with a towering wall, dominates the city. It was this present Kabaka's ancestor, Mutesa I, that European explorers first contacted when they found their way into Uganda in 1862. To their surprise, they discovered a closely-knit, well-organized kingdom with a king, a prime minister, a minister of finance, an advisory council, a police force and army, and a people proud of their history and ancestry. Buganda, the kingdom of the Kabaka, has always been on a different footing from the other three provinces of Uganda. Its ancient traditions—the present Kabaka claims to be the thirty-fifth in direct line of succession—have given the Buganda people a strong sense of unity and national consciousness. Today the Buganda number over a million people, more than double the next largest of the thirteen main tribes in Uganda, and Buganda is the wealthiest and politically the strongest province of Uganda. Uganda is now preparing to take her place in the independence parade, but problems still remain to be worked out as to the relation of Buganda to the other provinces.

The almost miraculous growth of the Church in Uganda parallels in its vitality and swift maturing the tropical luxuriance of the country. It was only seven years after the seeds of the faith were first planted that they bore fruit in the twenty-two Uganda martyrs. When Archbishop Henry Streicher, W.F., the first priest in the Masaka territory, began his work in 1891, the Church in Uganda was in its infancy and his own territory had scarcely a single Catholic. It is again characteristic of the quick maturing of Uganda Catholicism that forty years later he assisted at the consecration of one of his own spiritual sons, Joseph Kiwanuka, as the first African bishop of modern times. When this venerable

Constancia, with Paulo peering over her shoulder and Yowana Baptista in her lap.

old missionary, called the "St. Patrick of Uganda," died in 1952, the once infant Church in Uganda was already adult, with over a million faithful, five flourishing seminaries, one hundred nineteen African priests, eight hundred African sisters, and one diocese entirely in the hands of the African diocesan clergy. The churches are crowded with the faithful and there is full joyous participation in the liturgy. The Baganda are a community-minded people; they have a natural tendency towards common worship which makes it easier for them to enter into the liturgy than it is for us Westerners, tainted as we are by individualism.

However, the African laity no longer live in self-contained Christian communities. They must be able to hold their own in the face of strong forces playing upon them. Mohammedanism is filtering in from the north and through the Indian communities, which are everywhere in East and Central Africa. Both the African and the Asian Moslems proselytize strongly, and in many areas there are two converts to Mohammedanism for every one to Catholicism. Although Moslems as yet constitute only five percent of Uganda's population, their over-all figures are staggering—86,000,000 in Africa, or forty percent of the total population, and their influence is increasing rapidly and steadily. Mohammedanism is regarded as an African religion, not a foreign importation like Christianity, which has been cradled in the West; it fits readily into the patterns of polygamy found in many territories of Africa.

Protestantism is another strong force in Uganda today. The Anglicans are well established, equal in number to Catholics (although their overall figure for the whole of Africa is less—12,600,000) with plentiful resources in personnel and funds. Their educational and cultural programs, recreation centers, bookstores, libraries are outstanding.

Behind the scenes is the grave danger of Communism, playing upon racial tensions, exploiting the legitimate aspirations of the people. What happens in Johannesburg or Leopoldville or Little Rock reverberates through the whole of Africa—Communism and nationalism awaken a response in the whole continent. There is a particular danger from the few, who through their Western education are separated from their tribal society and yet are not accepted in the European circles. Belonging nowhere, they become restless, discontented, bitter, and fall an easy prey to political agitators.

Following the same strategy used so successfully in Asia, the Communists are systematically training African leaders. They are at work among the African students in London, Paris and other educational centers. Young Africans trained in Czechoslovakia, Hungary, Moscow are already playing their part in Uganda.

A priest from Uganda told me of the latest Russian scholarship offer to students from his country. It is more than generous, including transportation, books and pocket money, as well as tuition and living expenses at the new Communist Friendship University for African and Asian students. It is not surprising if young Africans, eager for education, accept such an invitation.

In the midst of all these contending forces, African Catholics must do more than hold their own. There must be a well-developed, mature laity who penetrate the social structure around them. Uganda holds great promise as a seedbed of the lay apostolate. If the apostolic seedlings come to maturity with the swiftness which has characterized the growth of the rest of Uganda Catholicism, the Church of the Uganda martyrs may set a pattern for the whole continent of an apostolate at once fully Catholic and fully African.

Marie Therese McDermit of Pennsylvania enjoys a joke with patients at the maternity clinic of the Grail hospital in Kampala.

Chapter Sixteen

Hands Are for Healing

SINCE 1953 Grail medical and educational teams have been at work in Uganda, at Kampala, Kalisizo, and Mubende, with a chain of dispensaries and clinics scattered through the outlying districts. Altogether, outside of the main hospital in Kampala, in 1960 Grail teams were at work in ten dispensaries, one training center for African girls preparing for leadership in the lay apostolate, one secondary school and two social centers. Staffing these works is a little United Nations—Grail members from Germany, the United States, Canada, England, Scotland, Holland, South Africa and the first Grail members from Uganda itself.

In Uganda the Grail teams have won a place in the community, accepted as friends, as fellow workers, as members of the universal Church who have come to share their skills and professions. By 1960 we had passed through the first pioneering stages: learning the language of the people, coming to understand each other. Now, as the women of Uganda begin to enter the professions, the moment is ripe to form lay leaders.

Tremendous changes are taking place in the lives of the women of Uganda. Until very recently with few exceptions the only unmarried women in the country were nuns. Now there are nurses, teachers, and a growing number of women in shops and offices. The first woman to take a degree in medicine has just graduated from Makerere University in Kampala, Dr. Josephine Namboze. She decided to become a doctor when she was just thirteen years old.

"At homework one day we were asked to write an essay on what we wanted to be when we grew up," she recalled, "I looked out the window and saw the nurses in the nearby Catholic hospital giving a treatment under the supervision of a doctor. At that moment I knew what I wanted to be—a doctor, not a nurse. I felt this would be the best way to help my people."

Women like this have a crucial role to play in deepening the Christian spirit and carrying it into everyday life. Through our work with young educated African women, we can help them exercise a Christian influence in their families, in their professions, and not least in their own village communities at a grassroots level.

So the Grail program in Uganda is developing along three major lines: the medical work at the hospital and outpost clinics; the educational program at the secondary school and the lay leaders training center; and finally, working out from the central point of the hospital, clinics and schools, a broad program of community development. Gradually a women's movement is beginning to take shape, a lay contribution to the consolidation of the Church in Uganda.

But to get back to the beginning of the Grail medical work in Uganda. It was two young American nurses who pioneered there, Lorraine Machan and Marie Therese McDermit.

It is a long way from Milwaukee, Wisconsin, to Rubaga Hill in Kampala, Uganda, but anything can happen to you once you're in the Grail! At least, that is how Lorraine Machan, with six years of experience in Central and South Africa, feels about it.

Many girls complete nurses' training, then settle down to a good salary and a new car. But neither of these satisfied Lorraine, though she had both in Montana after taking her master's degree at Marquette University. She was looking for wider horizons, for greater opportunities to reach out to the people of the family of man and to serve the Church. Someone told her about the Grail and how it hoped to fill the urgent need for nurses and teachers in Africa.

"I wanted to go at once," Lorraine told me, "but I wasn't ready. I had enough sense to realize that you can't grab the first boat for an overseas assignment. So I went to Grailville to see what the deal was.

"It was like a new life opening up for me," she said. "I had to relearn the meaning of the Mass and the living out of it in everyday experience. I found out quite a few things about giving service to others. Finally, I was sure that my vocation was to use my professional skill in Africa."

In the spring of 1953 Lorraine sailed for South Africa. At the Queen Victoria Hospital in Johannesburg, she took her certificate as a nurse-midwife with honors. From Johannesburg she went to Kampala, Uganda, where, working under the sponsorship of Archbishop Joseph Cabana of the White Fathers, she began the first Grail apostolic project in Central Africa.

Side by side with her worked Columbia University graduate Marie Therese McDermit, another American Grail leader who had also been trained at Grailville in Ohio. Together they took over administration of the eighty-bed Rubaga Hospital.

When the Grail nurses arrived, the White Sisters who had been in charge of the hospital broke them in to the problems of tropical medicine and gave generously of their experience to get them started. They worked fast to learn Luganda, the language spoken by the patients and staff. "You can learn a new language in a hurry when you have to," drily remarked Lorraine.

The hospital in Rubaga was then a complex of buildings, set on the slope of a hill, covering several acres of land. A cluster of small, tile-roofed mud huts served as private rooms. "Fortunately, each patient brings a member of the family, a 'mujanjabi,' to prepare his meals and to take care of his non-nursing needs," Lorraine explained. "Otherwise we couldn't take care of so many patients with our small staff. The 'mujanjabi' is a real African institution—often people will make great sacrifice, give up a job, leave school, travel hundreds of miles, to care for a sick member of their family."

While Marie Therese was responsible for the administration of the hospital, Lorraine looked after the maternity division and the out-patient department. "Symptoms were usually so dramatic that the diagnosis was easy," Lorraine says modestly. At first her department was open six days a week. Later, it was closed on Saturday afternoons to give the staff some rest. Among other things, like every medical missionary, Lorraine became an expert in pulling teeth.

Second busiest department in the hospital during Lorraine's time was the maternity ward where upwards of sixty babies were born each month. Maternal care is a primary need in Uganda where many women suffer from complications in childbirth. The hospital depends for its maintenance on the small fees which are charged the patients and upon help from friends in Europe and America. Imagine an American mother coming home from the hospital with a new baby for a total charge of $2.25!

In the meantime, a medical team was preparing to come to Rubaga from the International Grail Center in Holland with much-needed doctors, laboratory technicians and more nurses, so the pioneer days for the two Americans came to an end and they went south to fill new posts in Basutoland.

Dr. Magdalene Oberhoffer * led the new team from Holland and is now in charge of the Rubaga Hospital. With her are Dr. Rita Moser of Stuttgart, Germany, and Dr. Johny Storimans from Holland. Another team member is Hanna Arens, in charge of the Maternity Division and the Sanitarium for sick mission-

* Since this chapter was written, Dr. Oberhoffer has been elected international president of the Grail and has left Uganda to take over the general direction of the movement from the international headquarters in Amsterdam. Taking her place in East Africa is Dr. Johny Storimans.

aries. She is one of the first German Grail members. When she was forty-two years old, after twenty years of work building up the movement in both Holland and Germany, she studied nursing and offered herself for the work in Uganda. In charge of the laboratory is a German medical technician, Elizabeth Weigand, who has as her assistant Alice Dougan of Cleveland, Ohio. Ruth Chisholm of Antigonish, Nova Scotia, organizes the outpost clinics with Esther Johns from Aberdeen, South Dakota, and Beatrice Hobbs from Chicago does secretarial work.

Heading the nursing staff is Kevina Nabwami, the first Muganda Grail member. Kevina, like so many African girls, is named after the famous Mother Kevin, the Irish missionary nun who has done monumental work in Uganda. I met Mother Kevin shortly before she died, when she attended the Mission Secretariat Conference in Washington, D.C. She was a tiny dynamo of living faith. Our Kevina has the same smallness and, I believe, the same dynamism. Watching her at work in the large brick building of the outpatients department at Rubaga Hospital, her deft fingers bringing healing to her people, their warm response at having their own countrywoman tend them in their sickness, has been a constant joy to me.

Along with bearing chief responsibility for the hospital, Dr. Oberhoffer is President of the Grail in East Africa and directs the development of the movement there. Her fine humor and talent of making friends with people of other countries and different nationalities come naturally to her. Small and fair haired, she looks at times even fragile. As well there is a still quality about Magdalene which at first glance belies her strength and the force that is in her. She can look at people with a sharp medical eye and judge immediately their physical and even psychological capacities. But along with her physician's diagnostic power she views people with optimism and warmth and love, giving them all the chances they need to develop.

Just as her brother and sister before her had done, Magdalene, the youngest of three children, studied medicine in Bonn,

Innsbruck and Düsseldorf with great success. In 1948 she graduated as a doctor of medicine. The following three years she practiced in Godesberg with her uncle who was also a medical doctor. In 1951 she joined the International Grail Movement. During her studies in Bonn she had been an active member of a Grail student group.

Magdalene received her apostolic training at "The Tiltenberg" in Holland, our international training center, but soon she was asked to help in the preparation of future lay missionaries at the Mission Institute in Würzburg where the Grail for some time assisted in the training program.

Then she finished her own preparation for Uganda by taking a course on tropical medicine in London. After this she gained additional experience in surgery and gynecology in Nijmegen and Amsterdam, so as to be well equipped for the responsibility at Rubaga Hospital.

Rubaga is one of the oldest mission hospitals in the Kampala diocese. It was started by the White Sisters about 1900 when an epidemic of sleeping sickness took the lives of one quarter of the population. Until Magdalene arrived, there had never been a full time doctor resident at the hospital. Now, with three doctors and a well-qualified international staff, the hospital serves a growing circle and builds up an immense amount of goodwill for the Church. People come from miles around for treatment—wives of foreign officials and businessmen, and Indian women who are delighted to find women doctors, as well as the Africans.

Rubaga Hill is a hive of industry from morning till night, what with one hundred twenty bed patients, plus their relatives; the outpatient department, with an average of one hundred fifty patients a day; a new building for private and seriously ill patients; and the maternity ward which is rapidly outgrowing its present facilities. One in three babies in Uganda dies before he is four years old—malnutrition, malaria, worms, all take their toll. Hospitals in mission places are quite different from those at home, and they demand all one's ingenuity to cope with the day to day situation. Until the recent gift of an operating table from Germany, for instance, Magdalene and the others had to perform operations on a wooden table covered by a grass mattress.

Nevertheless, the confidence of patients in the hospital is shown in a dozen ways by the community at large. Rubaga doctors and nurses teach ethics to a group of Catholic nurses from Mulago, the big government hospital. Magdalene serves on the executive board of the Medical Secretariat of Uganda, official liaison between the government and the missions on questions of medical work. But the response that brings the warmest glow to Magdalene's face comes from her African friends. On her name day they arranged a great celebration. Up the front steps of the hospital came the women, one after the other in their graceful, gaily printed flowing Kiganda dress, surrounded by their children and bearing gifts for their friend with the healing hands. All morning they came, then as a grand finale, arrived Constancia, a trained midwife who helped in the pre-natal clinic each morning. Beside her were Petro and Paulo, her two eldest, skillfully balancing on their heads the "ebibbo," flat African baskets with the feast day presents. Yozefu followed, and Yowana Baptista who could hardly be seen as he hid in the folds of his mother's skirt. Elizabeth, the three-year-old, staggered aft, and Anna Maria slept peacefully in her mother's arms. The serene, smiling face of Constancia glowed as she presented Dr. Magdalene with an assortment of oranges, cabbages and pineapples from the baskets—and, as the *pièce de résistance,* a woven satchel from which the inquisitive head of a chicken emerged and which later was found to conceal half a dozen eggs as well as the bird.

That evening there was a community meal and Magdalene was in the midst of the people, playing her guitar and singing in her clear, high voice. Not such a long way from Germany after all, and it is indeed true as the Rhinelanders say, she is "baptized with Rhine water," which means that she has all the sparkling qualities of that famous river, which she now shares with the women of Uganda.

Many doctors are interested only in their profession, but if you talk with Magdalene about the mission of the Church in Uganda, you will get as wide a picture as you can assimilate. She is intensely interested in the whole person and when patients come to her they can be sure of a listening ear, and the intuitive understanding of a sensitive woman's heart. She has made a significant study of the position of woman in Uganda, which is a valuable help for all the Grail teams operating in the area.

Speaking of the role of women, Magdalene explained: It is common custom in the farming communities for the women to carry the main burden of the work. Besides her domestic obligations as housewife and educator of the children, the mother has to grow the food to supply the needs of the family. This means that she must spend many hours a day hoeing in the large banana plantations, so there remains little time for her to care for the smaller children.

"Not only must the woman provide the food, but carrying the water is the special task of the girls. From a medical point of view the carrying of these heavy loads on the head often creates health problems in later life."

"I suppose all this heavy work is one of the reasons why so many women need medical treatment?" I asked.

"Yes, indeed," said Dr. Magdalene, "we see the consequences of that very often in the hospital—women totally exhausted physically and mentally—patients who leave the hospital too soon. How often my patients say, 'I must go home. There is no one to work in the fields, no one to cook. My husband wants me to return immediately'—this is always the deciding argument. Sometimes the assistance of relatives solves the situation, but in general, the problem of the women carrying too great a burden in the fields remains a barrier in the path of a healthy family life.

"The children suffer the most from the overwork of the

mothers," Dr. Magdalene went on. "Often the mother does not have time enough for the supervision and education of her children. And even when she has the time, she is often not sufficiently well informed herself to be able to guide her children in developing a Christian character. She may have married at the age of fifteen or sixteen; from her training at the mission school she remembers the Creed and the commandments, but just the things that would make religion attractive to the children—stories from the Bible, family customs—she does not know well enough to pass on. That is why it is so important to deepen the formation of the African woman as a Christian wife and mother. If we can succeed in this, we win the family; and if we win the family, we will have gone a long way in the consolidation of the faith in Uganda.

"That is why we want to concentrate on more intensive formation for the women at all levels—in the secondary school, after they leave school, in the women's clubs and community development teams. Where the women have had the chance to deepen, they make first-rate educators of their children and build flourishing Catholic families. The woman is in a key position for the whole consolidation and growth of the Church in Uganda."

Mary Mugibwa and Namulia Matilde prepare "matooke," steamed cooking bananas, the favorite food of Baganda people.

Chapter Seventeen

Where the Wind Blows through the Mango Trees

EARLY IN the morning the students began to arrive and to wait under the shade of the mango trees to be registered. There was an underlying excitement, but also a solemnity in the occasion. It was the Feast of Candlemas, 1954, and a new secondary school for girls in the Diocese of Masaka was opening.

The daughter of the chief was brought in a car by her father and many round-eyed little brothers and sisters; some came riding on the back of a brother's bike, others arrived on foot, escorted by serious looking fathers in long white "kanzus." Each had a wooden box and a bundle containing school requisites: a basin for washing, a hoe for cultivating, a blanket, two sheets and a few cotton dresses.

When Lydwine van Kersbergen visited Bishop Joseph Kiwanuka at his residence in Kitovu, he asked the Grail to come and help with the education of the girls in his diocese. Bishop Kiwanuka, now in his sixties, was the first East African to rule a diocese, when he was named to Masaka in 1939. For more than twenty years he governed this diocese with its 150,000 Catholics and eighty priests, two-thirds of whom are Baganda people like the Bishop himself. In 1960 Bishop Kiwanuka was made Archbishop of Rubaga and Metropolitan of Uganda.

As it took a little time to bring to Uganda the Americans scheduled to start the school, Frances Scott, an Australian, travelled up from Johannesburg to prepare for their arrival. The school was named for Christ the King, and Frances, together with a young African teacher, Elizabeth Nabukoza, began the work there.

Shy girls the students were when they came that first day, kneeling every time they wanted to ask something, as is the custom; looking bewildered if words of more than one syllable were used; but after a few months together they were welded into a jolly family. These Baganda youngsters, although shy, are warmly responsive, eager to learn and to advance. They come from villages with a background of rural living and have grown up in simple houses where daily tasks include cultivating the soil, cooking "matooke" (banana mush), and picking cotton or coffee.

"In Buganda as a whole, cotton has been the great means of livelihood for half a century," wrote Bishop Kiwanuka in his plans for the curriculum, "and also coffee, which is a perfect crop for Uganda. The coffee bean requires no preparation but to be left out in the sun. The warm, moist climate makes the fertility almost ooze out of the ground. The coffee trees rise to a great height, with many straggling stems that mean lots of berries. Then, of course, every family cultivates the banana. Bananas and coffee—coffee and bananas—that is the pattern here. Your students should continue to do these things alongside their new learning."

For Josephine Drabek of Chicago, who has been at Christ the King school over the past five years, this combination of agriculture and book-learning was a "natural." Josephine graduated from Rosary College, near Chicago, and shortly after graduation came to Grailville. At the time of her appointment to Uganda,

Josephine was in charge of the 386-acre Grail farm in the rolling hills of Ohio.

Before World War II, when the idea for a secondary school for girls was suggested to the chiefs of Buganda, their reply is reported to have been: "Why yes, of course we are interested and are very glad to have our girls taught. But who will carry the water? And who will hoe the bananas? And after all, is it good for young women to know so much? Won't all this education make them look down on their tasks in the household and the plantations? And won't it make them difficult for their husbands?"

And when they were approached for the building of a new dormitory and for the fee of two hundred shillings a year for each girl, they responded: "What! Two hundred shillings a year for a girl? Why, we can buy another cow for that!"

Times have changed in Uganda as everywhere else on the African continent, and today three times as many girls apply for entrance to Christ the King Secondary School as can possibly be accommodated. And the fathers of these girls, far from raising objections, earnestly plead for the acceptance of their daughters.

"I cannot forget Nalule's father, a tall distinguished African," Josephine told me when I visited Kalisizo, "begging us to allow his daughter to come to the school. He had seen other girls in his district who had learned not only reading and writing, but new methods of agriculture, nutrition and child care, which brought health and happiness to the whole family."

There is a full schedule of classes: all day until four o'clock, English, Arithmetic, Social Studies, History, Home Economics, Geography, Hygiene, and Religion fill the hours. Then, from four until seven, applied agriculture, with everyone working in the plantation that supplies food for the school.

Josephine considers the study of agriculture and nutrition of prime importance for the African students. By and large, the health of the people in Uganda is poor. The local hospitals and dispensaries are besieged by hundreds of patients daily. The people suffer from malaria, malnutrition and a chronic state of low vitality traceable to poor food habits.

At present the Food and Agricultural Organization is conducting a course at Mulago Hospital in Kampala on the subject of agriculture and nutrition. Uganda is suffering from protein and vitamin deficiency, and studies are being made of ways in which the protein intake can be increased through better methods of farming, and a more varied diet. The present diet is predominantly starch—bananas, sweet potatoes, cassava. Beans and ground nuts are eaten as a kind of sauce and there is occasionally some meat, but the amount is negligible.

Josephine and her team are endeavoring through study and practical work to bring home to their young students through a sound agricultural program the need for more varied diet. Classes include the study of nutrition and health, the balanced meal, the vegetable garden, poultry raising, the care of domestic animals, soil conservation. New foods are grown in the school gardens and introduced into the meals. "It is slow work," Josephine smiled. "I think we served millet cereal for over a year before the girls would ask for it voluntarily. But we are making progress."

In Uganda most of the practical farming is done by the women. If a better diet is to be introduced into the country, the young women, the future mothers, must be convinced of its value and educated to produce the crops and cook the food that is needed.

Assisting in our agricultural training program is Marita Nakiwala, a Muganda woman, a government-trained Agricultural Assistant, expert in her field. She receives a regular salary from the government for her services to the Catholic Missions.

"Marita and I are great friends," Josephine told me. "She takes a real interest in the school garden and plantation, and she's very exacting when it comes to soil conservation and fertilizing. When we planted lumonde—that's a kind of sweet potato—she insisted that we run the bunds at right angles to the slope of the hill. The bunds are mounds of earth, and they keep the soil from washing down the steep slope in the heavy rains.

"She helped us set out our banana plantation—all that digging, a thousand holes five feet wide and two feet deep! And then we mulched them with coffee hulls and cow manure." Josephine rubbed her shoulder for a moment, remembering the sweat and the aching muscles, shared with the women of Uganda, who know so well both the cost and the satisfaction of wresting food from the earth for the family. "But it's worth it!" Josephine's eyes sparkled in her sun-tanned face. "Now we have matooke from our own bananas, and of course, beans, and peas and ground nuts. It makes a great difference in the menu and in the monthly budget.

"Of course," she continued, "the most important thing is not the food but the attitude towards work. We want the girls to appreciate the value of work, to see it as a way of praising God and of serving their families in love. It is such a pity when the ones who have been to school look down on manual labor. Marita and I see eye to eye on this. She's always getting the girls together and telling them, 'You will become good women if you learn to work well with your hands.' And she sets them a good example."

Josephine, too, sets the example of one who takes pride in the work of her hands. She loves the land, this young American, rejoicing in the smell of freshly turned earth, the nurturing of growing plants and animals, the reaping of the harvest; and she has the gift of passing on her enthusiasm. Often I have watched Josephine and Marita walking over the plantation side by side, the fair head and the dark one close together, bending over the lumonde plants—a symbol of these transition times, and of the kind of sharing that can produce a rich harvest among the women of Africa.

Headmistress of Christ the King School is Dorothy Smith,

a tall, red-haired young Englishwoman. Born in the English Midlands, of parents without any particular religious convictions, she discovered the Church in her high school days, but after seven or eight years as a Catholic, she was still searching for a really satisfactory way of living her faith. Then one day, leafing through magazines while waiting to meet a friend, she came across a small booklet on the apostolate of woman, published by the Grail. The illustrations first caught her eye: then as she read the text, she found such vitality that it challenged her. "Here is a dynamic approach to Catholicism," she thought. "What is this Grail which publishes such things?" She pursued this first clue in the search, and soon she was in Holland at the international training center, rubbing shoulders with Chinese, Filipinas, Americans, Canadians, Australians, Germans, French and Dutch. It was an entirely new experience for this reserved Britisher but when her first assignment came to help build up the apostolate in Scotland, she already had the desire to go further afield. At first she thought maybe China or Japan, but when the letters began to pour in from the teams in Africa asking for help, she knew that it was in Africa she wanted to work. The opportunity came—and Dorothy was ready to join the staff at Kalisizo.

Dorothy is a born teacher, and the Baganda girls are eager learners, "pushing on well," as they phrase it. So seriously do they take their classes that they often go on studying after "lights out" in the dormitories, and one of Dorothy's problems is how to discourage young scholars from reading by flashlight under the blankets. The standard is high, and the school has a good reputation. All the graduating class last year passed the government examination conducted by the education department.

Also on the staff are Anne Hope, from Johannesburg, who after taking her degree in England and spending four years on the Grailville staff has come to share her understanding of the apostolate with the women and girls of Uganda; Anne Mercier, a teacher from Detroit whose quiet friendliness and warmth soon evoke an answering friendliness; and two Dutch team members, Leny Schaareman and Siny Bootsma.

One of the three African teachers is Ursula Musoke, daughter of the Chief Justice of Buganda. Ursula is the art teacher, educated at Makerere University, and a valued member of the staff. She is most talented herself, and is gradually bringing the girls to appreciate the beauty around them and to use their own creative powers. Some of the art work from Christ the King has found its way to the States—delightful paintings, with an extraordinary sense of color and design and a fresh and distinctly African approach to religious themes. "The greatest problem in teaching art," Ursula told me as she showed me a recent set of drawings, "is to give the girls confidence in their own approach. Once I made the mistake of drawing Our Lady for the girls and then they simply copied my sketch exactly. But when they follow their own ideas, the results are wonderfully alive and often really beautiful, as you can see for yourself."

But there is much more than a school at Kalisizo—there is a family, working, playing, praying, growing together. Sunday is the high point of the week—the parish church packed with people, all the congregation singing the chant and a small choir doing the propers. A new student at the school set down her impressions of the Sunday celebration in her first essay:

> When the bell is ringing we get up quickly and we say some prayers. After we put our uniform on and we clean our hair. Some girls wear white shoes. Then we go to Mass. I see many people in the church and outside. I say: I am coming here to give to God and please Him. I must do everything well like songs and prayers and to hear Gospel. The men nearer to us sing very much too. When we finish we come outside and we see people in the yard. They see their children that they are very happy. After to eat we dance and sing loudly. In the afternoons sometimes we walk to the village and see the shops and the Indians, or we stay here to play our games. There is no good day like Sunday!

On Sundays, too, Dorothy often takes the chance to get better acquainted with the neighbors by visiting in their homes. One afternoon, she and Namirembe, a third-year student, took me with them to visit the village. We stopped outside a small house, made in the original kiganda style—of grass, reeds and clay, looking rather like an inverted bee-hive. In front was a porch, and hanging from its roof were clusters of small flagons of "mwenge"—banana beer. At first glance these shapely vessels looked like very skillful ceramic workmanship, but they turned out to be a kind of gourd from which the seeds had been scooped to form a receptacle.

An old woman came out to greet us, kneeling and taking both our hands in hers, in the traditional gesture of warm welcome to an honored guest. Soon all of us were chattering away nineteen to the dozen. "See this tree," said Namirembe, "this is good for malaria. We pound the leaves to extract the juice." Dorothy sucked a leaf to get the taste—and soon the old one was eagerly pulling leaves from another tree. "Eat this too," she invited, "this is for 'flu' "—and Dorothy almost choked over the strong taste of eucalyptus. There was another beautiful tree which provided the rich brown bark-cloth in which the old woman was swathed. Then, after this preliminary conversation, we went inside the house.

It was windowless, and at first nothing could be seen but a fire flickering at the back. The old woman pulled some folding chairs out of the shadows, and asked her visitors to sit while she herself sat on the dried grass at our feet. The chairs are usually used by men, and she herself had two sons living at home. Tucked away on the sloping sides of the house were some reed beds almost hidden by a bark-cloth curtain. Like all the women in Buganda, she provided food for the family from her own labors in the plantation. She was justly proud of a large stem of bananas which she gave Dorothy as a present. We drank tea together, and finally left her kneeling on the path, repeating over and over how pleased she was with the visit, and how she would sleep much better that night because of it, and finally, as we walked out of sight, calling down all the blessings from the whole litany of saints. What a warmth and sense of community have these people of Uganda!

"Our aim with the school," Dorothy sums it up, "is to develop among African women a sense of responsibility for the contribution they can make to their country as women. This is quite a new idea, especially for the men. Coupled with this understanding, we try to bring about a spirit of service towards the community as a whole."

As evidence of the way the school is succeeding in its goal, let me tell you about Elizabeth Namaganda, one of the first graduates of Christ the King. After graduation, Elizabeth worked for a year as assistant to Joan Dilworth in Kampala, traveling about the villages, helping with the women's clubs, teaching, sharing. I met Elizabeth at Grailville, where she has spent two years for apostolic training, acquiring basic skills and deepening her life in Christ and her vision of the lay apostolate. She has poise and dignity and charm, this radiant young Muganda woman, whether she is teaching a Luganda song to the Grailville family, making a speech about her country in her clipped, British accent, or showing a visitor around Grailville.

"What do you want to do after you leave Grailville, Elizabeth?" I asked her. She answered with glowing eyes: "I have received much and I would like to share what I have received." Elizabeth's desire is now being fulfilled. It was a special joy to me to meet her back in Kampala, where she is part of the Grail staff, helping to train her countrywomen for lay leadership—so it is that the Grail Movement becomes indigenous in Uganda.

Joan and Alice with two of their students.

Chapter Eighteen

Helping People to Help Themselves

IT WAS one of those unexpected flashes of understanding that so many times come "out of the blue"—waiting at a bus stop, looking out a window, in between chatter at a dinner party. This time it came when I was half listening at a debate in the Trusteeship Council at the U.N. The deep rich tones of an African from Togoland broke into my consciousness.

"It is not poverty as such which gives birth to revolutions, but insecurity, confusion and change which do not compensate for what they take away."

At that moment I knew what a concentrated effort we must make in those areas where a vacuum has been created by rapid social changes and family life is disrupted. A woman is the key figure in the family unit—the Grail is a woman's movement—add the two together and something will surely happen.

And it has. Little by little we are establishing community development teams to help people to help themselves. The social invention labelled "community development" is changing the lives of millions of people in thousands of villages in Africa, Asia and the Middle East, and it has captured the imagination of thinking people in America and Europe. In the Grail we have tried to grasp this new social approach at a grass-roots level and apply it to the apostolate.

Because we are only in the beginning stage in Uganda, and some of the work which I shall describe is merely in embryo, I would like to put on record the wide meaning of "community development" as it is seen in United Nations circles.

It is primarily a philosophy, rooted in a belief in self-determination, finding its expression in a process by which people in an area work together, with outside expert assistance, to raise the moral, economic and educational level of their community. In our program in Uganda you can see this structure evolving—the village women working with the Grail team of experts—in adult education, home economics, recreation and catechetics, to build up the village life as a whole. It is a process of teaching people, not primarily that they may possess knowledge for themselves, but that they may pass it on to others—teaching to teach.

There is no question but that the women of Uganda have a deep yearning to learn, and to bring about better home and family conditions; and it is the Catholic women of the area, whose status in society has been changed by Christ's teaching, who have a key role to play within the whole community. And the men who for so long have regarded themselves as "superior beings" now begin to acknowledge the advantages of their womenfolk having this chance to develop and learn. In Uganda as a whole there are now seven thousand women in some three hundred clubs, directed by local women leaders, who in turn draw upon nuns and lay missioners for help, inspiration and teaching personnel. At the first course in Mbale where we are just beginning, sixty women came for three successive days, walking up to twelve miles a day to be at the leaders' meeting, with the full approval of their husbands. Kalisizo area alone has forty clubs and a thousand women involved. Here a significant milestone was reached when a hundred women came for a five-day residential course, staying overnight in Christ the King

School, to receive the necessary training to carry on their village projects. From the men's point of view, this would have been unthinkable even ten years ago.

Spearheading this development in Uganda and working in the Kampala area are Joan Dilworth, a Scottish Grail member, and Jane Namugenyi, a Muganda teacher, who after a year of apostolic training with the Grail has volunteered her services full time for the community development program. Anne Hope of Johannesburg carries on the work around Kalisizo, and a third area is getting under way at Mbale with Irmgard Grasel from Germany. Backing up all these efforts is the Grail Training Center at Mubende, where Alice McCarthy from Brooklyn organizes leaders' training courses for the entire movement.

Joan Dilworth was born in Lancashire in the north of England but grew up and was educated in Scotland. At twenty she joined the Grail, and when Polmont College was founded in Scotland as a training center for youth leaders, Joan was chosen as one of its first students. What she learned there was soon put into practice, when a Grail Caravan toured Scotland, visiting the most remote places, and finding everywhere groups of Catholic girls open and ready in their turn to spread the little seed of Catholicism in a country that for centuries has been stamped with the imprint of John Knox and his successors. Together with Therese Martin of Nova Scotia, a graduate of the famous St. Francis Xavier University in Antigonish, and now head of our International Student Center in New York, Joan went into the jute mills of Dundee in order to make contact with working women and to find out at first hand their needs before beginning a Grail program in the city. From both Therese and Joan I have heard stories of those days—the shock at finding Christmas Day the same as any other day, all the women at work in the mills and no sign of this great Christian feast visible; the appalling conditions in the mills as they huddled together in a cold damp room to eat their lunch; the warmth and genuine kindness of the women for these two "greenhorns," and the friends they made, "Fishy Ella," and "Wee Maggie," who continue to write to them both over the years.

Joan's most striking characteristics are her resourcefulness and readiness. She will tackle any job entrusted to her. To Joan it is all the same, whether she has to cook, direct youth groups, give speeches or run a camp. Equally striking in quite a different field was the uncommon ease with which she mastered the Dutch language when she was at the international training center in Holland. In 1955, when she was chosen to fill the request from Africa for "an all-round person" who could work alongside doctors, nurses and teachers as a community development leader, Joan was delighted. Her gift for languages stood her in good stead in her new task, and she soon mastered Luganda.

On arrival in Uganda, she plunged into the work of community development, beginning with the women and girls in the Kampala area. The club idea—a rather new development for the Catholic women—caught on quickly, and soon Joan found herself with eighty clubs to keep going with her staff. So four afternoons a week, right after lunch, Joan goes off with Jane or one of the others to visit a village meeting.

The women are all chatting gaily when they arrive, but as soon as the first curl of dust is seen from the car the preliminary greetings begin. Joyful shouts, and then the business of untying equipment, offering a drink, taking bags. This is only the beginning, as it is the custom for each to be asked, and to ask in return: "How did you spend the night?" "Well!" And other greetings follow, so that several minutes may be spent in exchanging remarks, a pastime enjoyed by the gracious, well-mannered Baganda. Only after all the preliminaries are duly observed can the meeting begin.

Lively Jane bent over an old grandmother painfully forming the first letter of her name with a yellow pencil clutched tightly in her fist; Joan with a laughing group around a cooking pot showing various ways of preparing peanuts, a much needed nutritive element in the diet of Uganda; the calm face of a woman in her forties, repeating the Gospel story which has just been read from the following Sunday's Mass, and joining an animated discussion on the "lost groat"—all these are only tiny shoots of cooperative effort, yet they are first recognitions of the individual worth of each woman, a growing-together-in Christ, and a deepening of inner resources for the difficult, work-heavy task of the women of Uganda.

One of the elements stressed in the women's clubs is the good use of leisure time. This may seem odd at first, as the women work so hard in the fields and carry so much of the manual labor of the village, that there would hardly seem time for recreation. But around the equator it is pitch dark by seven o'clock. This means that there is a long evening the year round, when people perforce must stay at home. It is usually not possible to go for a walk or visit friends, as the night is unsafe, and people live far away in the bush. Young girls especially cannot leave the house after dark.

Thus every evening finds the family gathering around its little fire or kerosene lamp in half-darkness, and these evenings can either be a blessing or a curse, especially for the young ones. It is in the Catholic families that the problem is most acute. In former times, before their conversion, family members entertained each other with stories and legends, myths and fables about the pagan gods, riddles, songs and dances to the rhythms of the drums, sometimes rites and ceremonies. But these old traditions are so closely interwoven with pagan beliefs and values that Christians cannot take their content seriously any longer and have discarded them. Now we have to show patterns of Christian recreation to fill the long evening hours, and it is not as easy as it might seem at first glance. Many a good Catholic family tries to fill the void with long-drawn-out evening prayers—but endless litanies and rosaries do not appeal very much to the younger people, and they drop them at the first opportunity.

I discussed this question of recreation with Elizabeth Namaganda at Grailville. We were watching a group folk dancing.

"Have you learned this dance, Elizabeth?" I queried.

"Yes, I like to do it now, although at first I couldn't get the rhythm."

"You'd better put the steps and music down in your notebook," I said, "so that you can teach it to the club women for the village festivals."

Elizabeth said quickly: "Oh no, this would not be a good dance for the village, you have to touch each other, and swing the boy by the waist. This is not allowable according to our custom in Uganda."

Touching, I learned from this young African colleague, means much more to her people than to us in the West, whether it is the clasp of a hand among friends, the healing hand of a doctor, the gentle touch of a mother, or the blessing of a priest. The unity of body and soul are realized strongly and the meeting among men experienced in its wholeness.

The question arose then, what patterns of leisure time do we want to introduce to the Africans? One thing is certain, we do not want an indiscriminate transplanting of Western customs or stories or songs or dances. The African has a different way of thinking from the Westerner, a different tradition, and new forms must grow organically out of the mentality of the people.

Joan and the teams in Africa are concentrating on storytelling—stories have a trueness that can be appreciated in a variety of cultures, especially those about animals and the seasons. There are also special festivities for the high points of the liturgical year, home decorations, processions, dramatic presentation and tableaux.

"Most of our dances," Elizabeth went on to explain to me, as we continued to watch the square dances being called in the heartland of Ohio, "are quite different.

"You see, we don't learn certain steps which we all do together, but we make different movements to the same rhythm, except for dances that we all know for certain occasions, like a marriage, or at a birth, or before the King or an important guest."

Elizabeth knows the needs of her people and she can discern which skills she can use in Uganda. It is a constant source of wonder to me, looking at Elizabeth, mature, radiant, loving and being loved in the midst of our international family, what immense cultural chasms have been bridged in such a short time.

Alice McCarthy from Brooklyn, New York, heads the Grail Training Center at Mubende. Alice began her work in Uganda on the staff of Christ the King School. From there she branched out into community development, going out to the villages after school hours, organizing women's clubs, helping people to help themselves. Her most recent assignment, taking charge of leaders' training programs and courses at Mubende, gives her an opportunity to carry the community development work a step further as well as to prepare leaders among the unmarried girls.

After graduating from St. Joseph's College, Brooklyn, Alice went to Grailville for a year's course. One of her first assignments with the Grail was work among the international students attending Columbia University in Manhattan. One day she received a circular letter in the mail—just one of those stenciled things which we often barely glance at, then throw away. This one came from Grailville. Enclosed was an extract of a letter from Bishop Kiwanuka to Dr. van Kersbergen, with an earnest request for teachers to staff the school in Kalisizo.

"I knew this was it for me," said Alice, and less than five months later she was on her way to Africa. At first the language challenged her. The greetings were so long and complicated, the names unfamiliar, and the language structure complex.

There were other strange experiences for a native Brooklynite: to be called to Mass by drums instead of bells, to have a thatched roof overhead, and reed mats underfoot, to listen to

Luganda sermons, join in Luganda hymns. But soon Alice was part and parcel of the countryside and the people.

Her father died a few months after she had left the States. She is an only child and her mother was left alone. But this Irish mother with her laughing eyes soon discovered that she had twenty-five other daughters in Brooklyn as she became a regular caller at the Grail Institute for Overseas Service.

Sitting at the end of the kitchen table with "Lady Mac," as she is affectionately called, we chatted over the latest news from Uganda. A couple of Institute students with one foot already in Africa pushed her on to read one of Alice's letters out loud. As Lady Mac's glasses couldn't be found, I began to read:

"The new Center at Mubende is developing beautifully. It is marvelous to have a place entirely free for leaders' training, and such a pleasant place, too. The house is whitewashed brick, light and airy, with a wide veranda and a lovely view. We have our own small chapel, but most of the time we go to the parish church. Our pastor is anxious to have us help in developing more congregational participation in the Mass.

"Already we have been able to have leaders' courses for many different groups—the presidents of the village clubs, the young nurses and teachers, the school girls and the girls out of school. We just had a week's course for twenty-six girls from all the different provinces and five different tribes. Some of them travelled as far as three hundred and fifty miles, which is no light journey on the bush roads with African transport. We're always astonished to see how eager they are to come.

"Most of the girls had just finished school or Teachers' College. Several were already working as teachers or staff nurses in Mulago, the big government hospital in Kampala. It was truly inspiring to see how open they all were, and how completely they joined in everything, whether it was the feast day celebration of the Epiphany, or a discussion on the place of the Church in the world, or the setting up of an exhibition, or a practical session in singing, dancing, drama, and this was all the more remarkable because almost every idea was new for them.

"Quite the most entertaining part of the week were the plays put on in small groups, with a minimum of help from the staff, to illustrate the lives of different women saints. Africans certainly have a gift for acting and the Baganda especially are masters at impromptu dialogue—not so easy in a language not one's own! Saints Monica and Perpetua and Felicity went down extremely well, of course, since they were all African women. The most novel was the drama of "Miss Ruth" and "Mr. Boaz," with marriage negotiations conducted in local style and most impressive cornfields of elephant grass stuck in wastepaper baskets.

"The program of the week was based on the encyclical *Fidei Donum*—the hopes that the Church has for the future of Africa, and the present problems of materialism, Communism, and Islam which have to be faced.

"We were greatly helped by lectures from Father Tourigny, a White Father who is in charge of Catholic Action in Rubaga Archdiocese, and who has made a special study of Communism and Mohammedanism in Uganda. He told us how the Communists are actually working under cover of various nationalist organizations, even penetrating certain women's groups, and how they are spreading anti-Christian propaganda in the cities and villages.

"The spread of Islam is even more remarkable. In Buddu, one district of Buganda, for instance, the Moslem population has increased from 8,000 in 1941 to 42,000 in 1958, and this in one of our most Catholic districts. The Moslems in East Africa have an organized 'Moslem Action' comparable to our Catholic Action, with a 'Three Point Plan' for making converts: through business, through getting possession of land, and by marrying Christians.

"This last method touches our African girls closely. Moslems like to marry Christian women because they are less spoiled and more likely to have children; and since the Moslems are for the most part rich, they tempt Christian parents by offering a far higher bride-price than a Catholic boy could ever pay. The girls themselves are offered all sorts of presents of dresses and trinkets —very hard to resist for a poor girl in the bush, who has never had such nice things. In the maternity ward of our own hospital in Rubaga we have noticed what a high proportion of patients are Christian women married to Mohammedans.

"All these things we discussed during the course, but of course we weren't so solemn during the whole week! There was plenty of singing and dancing, miming, cooking, treasure hunts —all things African girls love to do. They especially like religious dancing and many have a great aptitude for it.

"When the girls leave, they say 'Katonda Abakume'—'God keep you,' just as you always said to me, mother, when I went to school; and we reply 'Nawe'—'and you.' Not such a distance from Brooklyn to Mubende, and truly, mother, I cannot help thanking God for putting me among these charming people, and praying that I shall live up to their needs and expectations."

"Lady Mac" looked happy, too, as I folded the letter and gave it back to her. The years alone have not been easy, but this Brooklyn mother knows that the great God is not outdone in generosity.

The three community projects in Mbale, Kampala, and Kalisizo, although only in the beginning stage, show promise of rich development. Already the planning teams are discussing the possibility of a youth movement growing up beside the women's clubs to give young girls an opportunity for Christian formation in the few years after they leave grade school and before they marry.

"There are so many girls who don't get a chance to come to secondary school. There are a hundred applications each year, and only room for thirty first year students." Alice explained to me, and her face lit up as she outlined the advantages a youth movement would offer the hundreds of girls who have to be turned away from Christ the King School.

"You see, they often lose the skills they had from grade school in these years. They even forget how to read and write as there are no books in their homes and no occasion to write. At the same time, they are receptive like newly plowed ground. We can be the ones to sow the seeds of Christian thought and action, teach customs for the home, fill in this gap in their lives, or leave it to the Communists.

"It is not possible, of course, to force this growth," Alice emphasized, "but what we can do is this: we can help the African Church, just as we can help a young plant by digging and fertilizing it, and keeping away harmful insects."

So the teams go on, using all modern techniques and apostolic approaches, striving to bring a Christian dimension to the status of women in newly-evolving Uganda.

Sunday afternoon story hour at Christ the King School.

Chapter Nineteen

Soybeans Save the Day!

HILDA CANTERS was born and grew up in Holland. I doubt if she ever saw a soybean in her life before she went to the Congo, but with her never-failing resourcefulness, Hilda used the little brown bean to turn a serious situation into a real success story.

But don't let us jump our fences—Hilda just didn't mushroom up in Kasongo; a whole lot went into her life before that. At nineteen, straight from boarding school, she joined the Grail. She had a great longing to give herself to the work of world conversion and the express desire of going to Africa. But she had given herself unreservedly, and as other work presented itself over the years, she took it all in stride. In Amsterdam at one stage there was a great deal of Communist propaganda and influence among servant girls. Hilda volunteered to become a servant, to share the life and problems at a grass-roots level, and put all her young enthusiasm behind a Christian counter-action.

Hilda in the dead of night, with a glue pot and brush covering Communist posters with others having Christ instead of Marx as the central figure. Hilda in the Rural Movement, traveling in a motorcycle all over the country organizing farmers' daughters, Hilda as a National Catholic Girl Guide leader, Hilda as a nurse preparing at long last to go to Africa.

It takes four years to become a double-certificated nurse, and Hilda spent her last year of training in Scotland at the famous Western General in Edinburgh, where in her final examination she topped the marks of the city's student nurses. Now she was ready to go . . . but then the assignment was announced: Hilda was to go to the Congo, and because of the nature of this area, another year was needed to study tropical medicine in Antwerp.

Once again Hilda settled down to study, to differentiate among hundreds of tropical insects, and to plunge into the mysteries of tropical diseases. But to get back to the soybean.

First of all, let us look at the problem. When Hilda arrived in Kasongo, she began work in its maternity hospital. For two years she battled with the problem of finding adequate food for babies to tide them over the period between breast feeding and the taking of a solid diet. She found that mothers, in order to conserve breast milk for their babies, refused to have any marital intercourse for at least a year after each birth. This brought a multitude of problems, but most significantly the end result that there were hardly any Christian families in the area. The average husband did not even attempt a life in which eighteen months of abstinence were followed by a few months of normal married life and then separation once more as soon as it became apparent that the woman was again with child. For her part, the woman kept consciously aloof from the man, and so was debarred from taking the influential position in the family that should have been hers by right.

"For two years," Hilda wrote back home, "we have been seeing the sad results of this lack of proper food for the babies, and we could very well go on for another fifty years preaching that people must live according to the moral law. But words will not help unless there is a real practical possibility for keeping the law.

"The government authorities have been busy now for five years, seeking a solution for the problem but without much result. I believe the Mission has to take the problem in its own hands if anything practical is to be done."

So Hilda went to the bishop to discuss ways and means of dealing with the dilemma.

"My Lord," she began, "my holidays begin on May 11th, and I would like to offer my services plus the Volkswagen and the petrol to explore this question. If you give me the addresses of the Fathers and Sisters who will understand what we want and will help us, I will try to get the information you need about food and the growing of vegetables. For me it would be a real pleasure, My Lord, to be able to begin at least to find a solution."

The bishop was full of enthusiasm. "Bunia," he said, "Bunia is the place—there the Sisters are already busy with the problem, but it is so far away and we have little communication."

"Distance doesn't matter if we get where we want to be in the end," laughed Hilda, "but I don't want to go to just one place. Wouldn't it be better, My Lord, if I tried to meet as many missionaries as possible, and got their advice and made them enthusiastic about the project? If, perhaps, Your Lordship could give me a note of recommendation. . . . "

The bishop beamed. Not easy to be the shepherd of a flock scattered over a vast area, trying to implant the Church with inadequate resources, insufficient personnel, and never enough money to meet the growing demands of a time known to sociologists as an acceleration of history.

Just because it is this time, the Hildas and the Gails and the Jeans and the Josephines are needed to throw their whole weight behind the thrust of the Church in the second half of the twentieth century. It was a deep happiness for this missionary bishop to have Hilda come to him with her plan that morning.

"Not a note, child, but a whole letter. If you can solve this problem of my diocese, you will have already earned your place in Heaven. If we can show the way, it will not be merely a plan of action for this diocese, but I believe it will contribute to the well-being of the majority of the missions in this part of Africa. I have not had the chance to assign anyone to look into it thoroughly."

So it was. The following day the bishop brought Hilda a complete plan for the journey, with maps of the possible routes to be taken.

Hilda scribbled a hasty note before setting out. "I feel so enthusiastic about it all, for this is really the problem that lies at the heart of the matter here. In pre-Christian times people could live with polygamy and recognized prostitution, but any true Christian life is impossible if we do not first solve this. How I wish you could see it for yourselves, practically every difficulty in the apostolate here stems back to this faulty Christian family life. . . . "

Hilda loaded her little Volkswagen for the journey. Water and oil and petrol took up a lot of space—no gas stations or drive-in restaurants on this route. Food, and a change of clothes, maps and compass, and an optimistic heart. "Who are the feet of the Lord?" asks St. Augustine. "The apostles sent through the whole world. Who are the feet of the Lord? All through whom the Lord journeys through all the nations." A modern quest, this, not by foot but by Volkswagen, in search of a practical, scientific answer to the problem of infant nutrition in the Congo—and so much more besides.

Hilda kept a diary during the weeks which followed, carefully recording each evening at one or other of the mission stations the findings of the day. By the way, don't forget this was Hilda's holiday after a year of gruelling work in the hospital—not lazy days on the beach in Florida, or doing seventy on the turnpikes and "taking in the tourist attractions." No hours of reading under a tree with a box of chocolate peppermints—all perfectly legitimate things to do if you are minded to take a holiday that way. Each day Hilda bumped mile after mile along dirt tracks in the bush. A stark blue tropical sky above, sometimes the sudden pouring rain, more often choking clouds of dust, the endless green of the jungle, then the clearing and the wooden buildings of the mission stations. Questions and interviews, facts and figures, all carefully stored in the notebook, but day after day disappointment. Everywhere the same problem, but no solution which had worked.

Some notes from Hilda's diary:

Wamaza: Mission of the White Fathers. I met the Procurator on the way to the mission. He told me that he faces the same problem we do in Kasongo. He assured me he would be delighted to help in any experiment to find a solution. One priest has begun planting soybeans, but has found no way of using them for feeding the babies.

Kalole: Mission of the White Fathers. Here again the same problem, and again the Fathers assured me they would be glad to cooperate in an experiment if a solution is found. The Rector has begun to grow arrowroot, says it develops easily, and hopes maybe this will be a possible food. He believes that it might be possible to use goat's milk. He once tried this in a district where animals were never milked, and although it had taken time for the local people and the goats to get used to the idea, he thought it had begun to work.

Kamituga: Mission of the White Fathers. Again the same problem and the same desire for a solution. I must say I am urged on to find some way out—bad enough when I saw it in Kasongo but now in all these places the same big barrier to a real Christian life. One of the priests here has tried milking goats but with very little result. According to his findings one goat gives barely half a pint of milk per day. In the hospital soybeans are used for the older children and adult patients, but the recipe calls for boiling the beans three full hours. We will never be able to get the women to cook anything for three hours at a stretch! I wonder if this *is* a wild goose chase after all.

Mulungu Irsac: I met Dr. de Maeyer here and he could see no possibility for the use of soybeans as there is an anti-enzyme in the beans which neutralizes the juices of the stomach, and which is only rendered harmless after ten hours of cooking. Me, O me, ten hours! What a length of time! Dr. de Maeyer had also tried goat's milk. It seems that with regular milking he was able to produce sufficient milk and from this the necessary proteins can be obtained. As a supplementary source of carbohydrates he suggested the addition to the children's diet of a gruel made of powdered bananas and a certain type of bean, with a juice extracted from sunflower seeds after they have been soaked in water, mashed, boiled, and wrung out in a cloth.

Burhale Ngweshe: Here I stayed with the White Sisters who have a high school. They give lessons in nutrition, and if a solution is found they will be glad to propagate it in their school, in both the theory of nutrition and in the practical work in the gardens. So much goodwill, surely, Lord, we will find a solution!

Katana: A delightful spot, the Motherhouse of the African Sisters. The superior will be happy to help by allowing the Sisters to have the necessary experience in learning how to plant and prepare the feed *once we have found* the correct solution. Here we heard of a gruel of eusine flour, which has been used extensively by the local people to keep orphans alive in the villages.

Djemba: White Sisters. Here there are cows so the problem is not encountered.

Musicene: This mission hospital is not troubled with this difficulty, but in *Buniuka* the same Sisters were busy trying to find possible means of solution. Here they found a soup which can be used for all, from babies of six months to adults. A large pot suitable for sixty adults and sixty children is made from: six kilos of beans, one litre of rice (this is used against diarrhea), three litres of maize flour, one bucket of potato flour, palm oil, as much green stuff as grows each day in the garden, meat (twice in the week). This recipe may look vague to you back home, but the orphans looked very healthy, and the death rate amongst them is low.

Bunia: Here I am at last where His Lordship hopes for the answer. This is the mission of Monsignor Mattijsen, who is a great supporter of soybeans as the best means to combat the malnutrition prevalent throughout the diocese. Monsignor explained that the first harvest of soybeans is always poor. The soybean breeds its own organisms in the ground. If a new field is begun, it is always best to bring along some of the soil from the old plantation. In warm climates the soybean organism dies quickly, but there are over a hundred different varieties, and information about the most suitable variety can be obtained from Station d'Ineac, Rubena, Ruanda. The inquirer writes details of the soil, average temperature and rainfall. The beans when planted must be fresh, and those from the preceding year cannot be used. From Monsignor Mattijsen I received two addresses where experiments are being made now with soya milk. It looks as though we are getting somewhere.

Kilomines: The soybean experiment is finished here. I felt so disappointed when I discovered this after a long journey. Mother Superior told me that the mine authorities distribute an abundance of milk powder, and so there was no need to find another source of nutrition. She told me, however, before the milk powder was available she had experimented with goats, but found that the young goats frequently died because of lack of suitable food. I think I have given up the idea of goats as a suitable answer.

Mongbwalo: What a joy to write tonight. Here in the last place on my list I think I have found the object of our search. For the past two years orphans on this mission station from the age of three months have been fed with soybean milk; there is no animal milk to be had, and no possibility of powdered or tinned milk. But a quite different recipe is used here. Everywhere else the beans were *cooked.* Here this is not the case, and it seems to me that it is just *this* which makes the difference, and that this is the reason why it agrees with the digestion of the children. The recipe used is this: Soak two hundred grams of beans in water the evening before. The following morning drain and peel the beans (the peel falls off easily when the beans are rubbed between the hands). Mash, add one litre of water and stir well. Wring the whole out in a cloth. Boil the juice extracted in this way steadily for a short time, and milk sufficient for one day is ready. The difficulty of soybean milk is that it needs a large quantity of sugar, and so would be expensive if it were not possible to replace the sugar with home-grown sugar cane. The sugar cane has to be peeled, cut into short lengths and crushed. The juice is then mixed with the soybean milk. The remains of the soybeans left in the cloth are still a good protein-rich food for grown-ups. The Sisters make a cake from it, or use it as a pili-pili sauce for the cooked bananas.

So Hilda finished her holiday. Back at Kasongo she reported to the bishop the following conclusion: the planting of soybeans and sugar cane can provide a simple substitute for breast milk

Joan Dilworth discusses future programs with the leaders of the Catholic Woman's Club in Kampala.

for a growing baby, from its fourth month onwards, if necessary. This soybean milk recipe worked out by the Sisters at Mongbwalo proved to be suitable and effective for the nourishment of babies. A long, hard journey—but a most satisfying holiday.

A hasty note from Hilda reads: "Back home. Dead tired

physically, but truly refreshed in spirit. Now we can plan ahead. It is a matter of educating the women to lay out the gardens and prepare the food. Maybe it will take a few years, but in this Diocese we have three posts ready and willing to start the experiment right away—Moya, Kibangula, and Kasongo. And start we will. How thrilled I am about everything I learned and understood during this journey. It is difficult to put it on paper, but to be able to discuss day after day, person to person, with experienced people has been a tremendous help. What a privileged person I am! Of course I know that I am only a small piece in the whole beautiful mosaic, but to see even a little glimpse of the whole, and of the direction in which to go, makes one happy beyond the telling. Indeed, nowhere could I be happier than I am here and now tonight."

Well done, Hilda!

Father Romeo Guilbeault confers at Grailville with Sunku Mofeking, Emilia Charbonneau and Mariette Wickes, before Emilia's departure for Pius XII University in Basutoland.

Chapter Twenty

Ruanda and the Refugees

RUANDA AND its neighbor, Urundi, lie in the heart of Central Africa, between the Congo and Tanganyika, and together they make up the U.N. Trust Territory of Ruanda-Urundi, administered by Belgium. This mountainous land is densely populated, almost 5,000,000 people in 20,000 square miles, and its farmers and herdsmen must utilize every square foot of the steep hillsides if the people are to be fed.

Mariette Wickes from Rochester, New York, and Viola Lafosse of Gueydan, Louisiana, arrived in Ruanda in October 1959, just in time for the outbreak of a civil war between the country's two racial groups: Batutsi and Bahutu. The Batutsi, who make up fifteen percent of the population, are famed for their outstanding height. They are supposed to be of Ethiopian origin and to have migrated to central Africa about 1500 with their herds of cattle and pastoral way of life. For movie-goers, they are the people of *King Solomon's Mines* and the Batutsi dancers of the *Seven Wonders of the World*. Because of their undeniable political shrewdness, the Batutsi peacefully took over the leadership of the country and the political and economic direction of the remaining eighty-five percent of the population who belong to the Bahutu group. The Bahutus are an agricultural people, related to the other Bantu tribes of central Africa, and were regarded as peasants by the cattle-raising aristocrats. The earliest efforts of the Church were directed to the Batutsi, and most of the African priests in Ruanda are Batutsi.

In Ruanda, as everywhere else in Africa, the revolution of rising expectations is astir, giving the Bahutu a new personal consciousness and desire for economic and political rights. The tension between the Batutsi, the traditional rulers, and the Bahutu farmers, claiming their rights, has been mounting and finally exploded in 1959. The violence was subdued by government forces after a few weeks, but of course major tensions and resentments remain. About four thousand Batutsi men were killed by the Bahutus, but not one woman or child was touched, in keeping with the traditional restraint of the people. In the struggle, thousands of Batutsi lost their homes and possessions and fled to the missions for safety.

So one of the results of the civil war is a refugee problem. The Belgian government has built a "centre d'accueil" for them near Kigali, and this is where Mariette and Viola have been at work since December 1959. They had just arrived in Ruanda as the camp was being established, and so were free to accept Archbishop André Parraudin's request and to become acquainted with their new country by sharing the lot of these homeless people.

Mariette is one of the first American Grail members, the elder sister of Francine Wickes, whose work with the Grail in Indonesia has already been described. Born in Rochester, New York, she, also like Francine, is bilingual, and her knowledge of French stands her in good stead in French-speaking Ruanda. During the fifteen years she worked in the lay apostolate in the States, she held responsible tasks at Grailville, helped begin the work in Philadelphia, and at the time of her appointment to Africa was director of the Grail Center in Detroit; but her major contribution to the Grail in America has always been her sense of community and her ability to forge bonds of friendship. To work with Mariette is to work with a team—not just in theory, but in actual day to day practical doing. Wherever she is, a rich life begins to develop, with every member of the team bringing her talents to the whole under Mariette's gentle encouragement. I remember during my first months in America, when everything seemed so big and organized, that Mariette was one of the people who made me feel at home. I had come to Detroit to lecture after my first experience of being "on the road" the previous month in New York City, Brooklyn and Philadelphia. I was feeling homesick for Hong Kong and the House of Our Lady of Joy, and I needed all my courage to face the auditoriums of high school students, the parish groups, the Communion breakfasts and dinner speeches which had been scheduled. Then Mariette came into the picture. The lectures in Detroit were not just isolated gatherings—they were needed to help build the movement there, to explain what we as members of an international team hope to accomplish. Hong Kong was not apart from Detroit and I was needed to bring an international dimension to the national work in America.

No wonder then that in Mariette's work with Viola and Melanie in the camp the element of the team is most important. The five thousand refugees of the camp, about one thousand family groups, are housed in aluminum barracks, divided into rooms of about ten feet square per family. They receive daily rations of peas, beans, rice, with milk and sugar for the sick and the children, and occasionally potatoes and fish. Mariette's team helps organize the food distribution, especially for the children, the sick and the old; they also distribute whatever clothes are donated—what a job to divide thirty dresses among three thousand children, most of whom have nothing to their names but the shirts on their backs! Viola became the camp midwife, constantly in demand at all hours of the day and night. She is also the director of the "Foyer Social," which gives classes in sewing and knitting to the women and girls. Eight girls in and around the camp with some teacher's training help in this work, and also in a kindergarten, and in reading and writing classes for older girls. The regular primary school is in the hands of men teachers among the refugees and is directed by one of the priests.

Besides these services there is the daily visiting of the women, the old and the sick, listening to their desires, needs, worries, encouraging them as much as possible to find their own solutions to the problems they face, interpreting their wishes to the responsible African men of the camp and to the administrators. Says Mariette: "We tried to encourage them to go themselves as a group to the leaders, with their desires for such improvements as outdoor kitchens, garbage pits and so on, but this is outstripping the rhythm of their emancipation, as the women themselves make clear to us. Their daughters will be ready for this."

Out of these personal contacts has come what Mariette considers the most important work of the team: the formation among the women of groups of "Bakuru"—the responsible ones. As the refugees arrived, the team gradually met all the women of the camp, one barrack at a time. Each barrack houses ten families. Mariette suggested that each barrack choose two responsible women with whom they could keep in closer contact, an idea that met with enthusiastic response.

"To begin with," Mariette told me, "the women managed quietly and wisely to agree on whom they wanted as their bakuru. It was a case of common consent, rather than secret ballot, apparently fully satisfactory to everyone."

The workers, Mariette, Viola and Melanie began having meetings once a week with these bakuru in small groups, with the purpose of developing their concept of personal responsibility and group action. At first many of them were afraid of their position of authority. They thought it meant passing on to the women orders they would receive from the team.

"I have wondered," reflected Mariette, "if this is a mentality created by the colonial system or by their own traditional authoritarian set-up. In any case the women have understood that we mean something else and they have risen with real dignity to the demands made on them. We have spoken together a great

Dr. Margret supervises as the local men prepare to build a new building for the hospital.

deal about having an influence through love and confidence, through creating unity and peace.

" 'Umutima'—heart—is the word that comes over and over in our discussions," continued Mariette. "This the women understand well and respond to with a wealth of experience as mothers of families, and as people who know the strength of community. Before I came to Africa, I wondered with a bit of apprehension if communication, dialogue, such as we had in the U.S. would be possible. No question is left in my mind. The 'Inama' is a great tradition in the life of Ruanda—the Council in which each one speaks his mind so that a common wise consent can be reached. These women know how to express themselves freely and wisely and they know how to be peacemakers in their own immediate circle."

Mariette's big hope is to be able to expand this circle of concern and influence by opening up the implications of Christian love toward all men, because she feels very sure that the women of Ruanda have great capacities for influence in their own country and beyond it.

Where and how do the team members live in this refugee camp of Nyamata? Situated in a wild and beautiful region, before the flood of refugees the mission at Nyamata had only about a thousand Christians scattered over a wide area. As soon as the team arrived at the mission, the Belgian administrators promised them a pre-fab house in about a week's time. But three months later, true to their promise, the house was to be ready "in about a week's time!" In the meantime they lodged in one room of the mission, and shared meals with the three priests.

"It is a real bush mission, life is simple, sometimes a bit rough, always hospitable and open to everyone who comes our way," says Mariette.

For the first two months the pastor was a Swiss White Father with fourteen years of experience in Africa and a generous supply of common sense, a great hunter, who kept the table well supplied with meat. Mariette and Viola got a taste for big game hunting, especially antelope, as they accompanied the missioner on some of his expeditions.

Early in 1960 the mission was turned over to the local clergy—a rare chance for the Grail to be in a set-up where the leadership is fully in the hands of Africans. Abbé Aimable is the pastor, a man of goodness through and through, completely absorbed in his priestly dedication—of the Bahutu race, but loved by his Batutsi parishioners for his honesty and charity that rise above the racial conflict. With him are Abbé Eustache Byusa, a member of one of the leading Batutsi families, an aristocrat, a musician of artistic sensitivity, who is responsive to modern currents of thought and the trend towards universality and at the same time bound by his loyalty to his own people; and Abbé Telesphore, a young worker who gets things done, full of boyish good spirits. It is rather an unusual family that the six make—

the four Banyaruanda and the two Americans—with its own family spirit, appreciation of each other and plenty of good humor. Mariette and Viola are learning volumes about Ruanda, and the others a good deal about the USA.

The African priests and the Grail team were gathered together one hot June evening at the mission. It was the dry season, very hot at noon, exceedingly cold at night, with never a drop of rain, and the seven months of camp life with its limited diet was now taking its toll with a vengeance. As they sat and chatted over the possibility of getting more CRS-NCWC food supplies, the first typhoid death was announced by a young man of the camp, tense sorrow written on his face. It was Emertiana, a seventeen-year-old girl whom they all knew well, and this news brought the sense of tragedy that many more were to follow.

For the next month the typhoid epidemic cost two to three lives a day, especially among the children. Viola, an efficient nurse, did a first-rate job of finding the children in the most serious condition, housing them together, and feeding as many as possible back to health, while Mariette launched a campaign throughout the missions of Ruanda, through the Catholic Charities Organization, to keep Nymata's children supplied with fresh foods. The immediate and generous response of the missions is what kept them going in these days.

And what of the future? The people have decided to settle permanently in the area around the camp. The government promises to give them land—two hectares per family—and help them to get it into a productive state. The European market is investing large sums in the project and technical teams are constantly at work to study questions of water supply, cattle raising, and elimination of the tsetse fly. The work at hand is to divide the land and to build at least temporary homes as soon as possible. It is a vast undertaking which requires the joint action of everyone in the camp, and it holds much promise for the future. The women, a good many of whom were ladies of leisure in the past, have said to Mariette, "We want to learn to work." This then is the value they have learned from their sufferings. Mariette hopes that a Grail team—perhaps with some French-speaking Canadians—will be able to stay with the people as they settle permanently, to help the women with the practical skills as well as the spirit needed for rural family and community life.

The work at Nyamata has been a gateway leading to the possibility of contact with girls throughout the country. Working with Viola and Mariette in recent months has been Philomene Karekezi, a teacher, a girl with a strong desire that all the women of her country should become free personalities, able to shoulder responsibility for Ruanda's development. Philomene does more than desire, she is ready to give herself with determined energy for what she believes in. In May 1960, after taking part in a Grail study week in Urundi, she got together with four other teachers from nearby Kigali, friends of hers; together they went to Mariette with the idea of forming a movement among the teachers of Ruanda, so that these young women, the most educated, might help each other to understand and to live out their responsibility to all the women of their country. They wanted to start with a study week during their holidays, and asked Mariette to be their "advisor" in this project.

"You can imagine how encouraged I was," says Mariette, her dark eyes shining. "Such an initiative coming from a group of Ruanda girls." They had a number of meetings at Kigali and Nyamata, threshing out ideas and plans for the study week. Mariette, stimulated by the old team spark, and inspired by the sound judgment of the group, was in her element. The program included African priests on "The Value of the Person in the Community," and "Woman's Present Position in Ruanda"; a largehearted Belgian laywoman on "Practical Aspects of Family Life"; a layman on "The Value of Work"; a teacher on "The Christian Responsibility of the Lay Person in the Teaching Profession"—subjects and speakers all chosen by the team.

Now the Grail in Ruanda is coming to the end of the first

stage of its work there. Viola Lafosse has just left Nyamata to work with a doctor of the I.C.A. (International Catholic Auxiliaries) in a center for crippled children—the first in Ruanda—and the mission for which Viola actually came. Mariette is waiting for another teammate to arrive, and in the meantime is deeply grateful for the experience of living and working so closely with the people of Ruanda. She writes:

"We appreciate the value of each exchange of love and confidence as an enduring force in itself; we pray and we ask you to pray with us that the hearts of all the people of Ruanda and of Africa may be opened wide to build a unity beyond clan and tribe, race and continent—and that we may help to support the people of Ruanda in this painful crisis of growth towards mature nationhood."

Palm Sunday at Kpandu.

Chapter Twenty-One

Training Ground for Greatness

LIFE IN South Africa today is a training ground for greatness, for it is not a place for lesser things.

It is a place where the wound on the family of man is swollen, sensitive and inflamed, and only a living Christianity can heal it. In such an area it is not surprising to find the Grail standing squarely with the bishops and the people, sharing the problems, the longings, the hopes and the plans for the Church in South Africa.

It is a region of far horizons, sharp blue skies, jagged mountain ranges, dry in winter, rain-fresh in summer; of gold and precious metals buried deep in the soil for man's seeking; of modern cities like Johannesburg, six thousand feet above sea level, and slums like Alexandra Township with eroded streets and shabby shacks; of vitality and of brooding trouble.

When we think about the continent of Africa we see three major divisions—North Africa, stronghold of the Moslem world; central equatorial Africa with its lush tropical terrain studded in the last twenty years with a mushroom growth of cities and towns; and finally southern Africa, most widely settled by the white Westerners, with its temperate climate, its advanced industrial development, and racial tension like a power-keg ready to explode.

South Africa presents a complicated picture—almost 15,000,000 people, diverse in race, language, religion, culture, thrown together on the tip of the continent. Unlike central Africa, where the whites are a small minority and generally transient, South Africa is home to a large, stable white population. Of the 3,000,000 "Europeans," two-thirds are Afrikaners, decendants of the Dutch who settled along the Cape about four hundred years ago. They are one in language (Afrikaans), religion (Dutch Reformed), and generally belong to the Nationalist Party. The other 1,000,000 whites are a motley group, mostly English-speaking, but drawn from many parts of the Western world primarily by the prospect of making a better living. The 12,000,000 "non-Europeans" divide into three groups: 10,000,000 Africans—forty percent living in a tribal pattern, sixty percent fully involved in the urban industrial system; 500,000 Asians; 1,500,000 Cape Colored, the result of intermarriage between Europeans and Africans or Asians.

Plant trees and in a few years stands a forest. Let the rains come, not the gentle, seeping rains of the northern hemisphere, but the bold hard beating rains of the South pierced with lightning and thunder—and in three days the world that was parched and dead is green and living. Let it be summer and there is a passion of growth, at night the stars brilliant in an indigo sky. All through the year the sun shines unhindered, defining the shapes and colors of things, giving space and distance.

Australia and South Africa have much in common, and it is from the island continent, one hop across the Indian Ocean, that the Grail leader in South Africa comes. Beatrice Sheehy from Brisbane, Queensland, a real bringer of joy as her name indicates. Beatrice, a spoiled child of God, warm, deep, a person made wise by loving and by being loved, helped build up the Grail movement in Australia by driving hundreds of miles at a stretch, speaking in cities and townships, directing courses, making programs for the youth movement, bringing a lightness of touch and a sparkle to the work, a gift lavishly communicated from her Irish forebears. After graduating from the University in Melbourne with a degree in anthropology and English literature, she sailed for Holland. During the following three years, she assisted in the training of the young leaders from all six continents who gather at this focal point of the movement, bringing new life and ideas to each succeeding Grail generation.

South Africa with its need for love and understanding attracted this young Australian. There is quite a team at work with her in Johannesburg and Rivonia, as well as the group at Pius XII University in Basutoland.

Vera Kelly is Beatrice's right-hand woman. Big and strong, with the same Irish warmth, she was born and grew up in Southern Rhodesia. She met the Grail in England during her student days and, after taking part in a major-scale Passion Play which the Grail directed, felt drawn to find out more about the movement. When she returned to South Africa, she found the Grail already at work in Johannesburg. The program was in the beginning stages, so it was arranged that Vera should go to the United States to receive her apostolic training. Three years of prayer, study and work in the international community at Grailville and Vera was ready to take up her present task in South Africa: organizing the program for the Junior Catholic Federation.

Also with the team in Johannesburg are two South Africans, Ann Monnick and Lesley Webber. Joanna Waite from Sydney, Australia, runs the downtown center, and brings to the team in South Africa some of the pioneer spirit of the early days of the Grail in Australia, when we were a band of young adventurers for Christ, proclaiming the then new idea of the lay apostolate to our prosperous countrymen. Working beside Joanna is a young Canadian teacher, Mary Ann Weber from Toronto.

"Jo'burg" is a city to challenge any apostolic team. It is a closely populated, cosmopolitan city of Jew and Gentile, Afrikaner and English-speaking, pagan and believer, black and white, where Christianity constantly struggles to keep a foothold.

Phily Fuchs of Austria, nursing a bad case of malnutrition.

Look at Johannesburg and you will find none of the qualities which characterize a nation—uniformity neither of language, nor culture, nor race. It is a conglomeration of peoples thrown together by fortune but as yet in no way welded. And such is South Africa as a whole.

"A nationwide apostolic movement of women from different situations in life," reads the folder put out by the Grail in the Union of South Africa. In no country is it easy to weave such a network as this implies, but in complex South Africa it hardly stops short of folly. Yet the teams have begun building bridges of understanding, drawing disparate groups together, sowing seeds of unity.

The program is organized through five Grail councils, small trained groups carrying responsibility for developments in a particular field. There is a council for meeting non-Catholics and new converts; one for the family apostolate; one for the apostolate to the Afrikaner people—conversions have been growing steadily among them in recent years. Another council is responsible for the apostolate among young professional women—nurses, teachers, social workers. Marie Therese McDermit from Pennsylvania plays an important part in this field. As instructor at the General Hospital, she trains student nurses and is a strong support to the Catholics, faced with many a difficult situation in this neutral establishment.

Most important is the council concerned with programs of formation for leaders in the movement. "A movement of women from different situations in life"—and the situations are indeed different. There are the white Catholic girls in the high schools and parishes; there are the African girls in the locations, the segregated areas outside the cities which the government has set aside as living quarters for the urban Africans; there is the small Grail group in Pretoria, a city so predominantly Afrikaner that the few Catholics are almost submerged; there are the young African teachers struggling to keep the Catholic mission schools going in the Archdiocese of Durban. In each case, bonds are formed between Europeans and Africans. The Catholic high school students in Johannesburg, along with their own training through meetings and study weekends, pay a weekly visit to one of the location missions, where they help to enliven interest in the Church. The group in Pretoria reach out to the African nurses in the hospital in one of the locations outside that city.

From time to time, the Johannesburg team makes the four hundred mile trip to Durban to give a week's course for the

African teachers in the mission schools. Beatrice writes of a recent session:

> The course was held at the Mission on the edge of the Cato Manor location near Durban. Cato Manor is one of the better locations; it is built up a hillside; each tiny house makes place for two families and has some green around it. But very recently, the whole area has been declared "European," and within a short time the inhabitants must gather their few belongings and be on their way in search of another location spot.
>
> Many of these young teachers are terribly isolated, alone in their mission schools, Mass only once a month or once in two months. The government refuses to recognize the Catholic teacher's certificate, so the girls who go to the Catholic teacher's training college must sacrifice the possibility of a government-paid job. This is a real sacrifice, for the Catholic education authorities cannot manage to pay much more than a pittance.
>
> All the problems of the Church here seem to go together —the extreme shortage of priests (the government is discouraging priests from entering the country), the growing difficulties in the question of education, the great poverty of the Church, the problem of the great number of African families where the man has simply left the woman with all the children to sink or swim. . . .
>
> The week was completely a shared experience, practical as well as spiritual. With these girls, we saw again the vision of the real Christian community on its way through life—the worshipping family of the Church, the call to the apostle here and now, the woman answering that call, and all that in the world of the young woman who occupies herself at this phase of her life with the deep and responsible task of educating little Christians. Not one of these profound ideas was lost on any of these young teachers. The reaction, the openness, the receptivity were a source of new wonder to us. As one of them said at the end, "This thing is a thing of the heart." But they need oceans of practical and spiritual help. Please pray for them. . . .

Outside Johannesburg, at Rivonia, is the Grail Training Center, with facilities for residential courses, with its three houses —"Ora," "Labora," and "Canta"—the names sum up pretty well the spirit of the training. On the staff is Mary Imelda Buckley from Brooklyn, New York. Of Irish-born parents, this quick-thinking redhead brings a tang of Irish wit and scholarship with her. A graduate of Hunter College in New York, she was one of the first Brooklyn girls to join the Grail. After a time at Grailville, and the experience of a long lecture tour, she returned to Brooklyn to open the first Grail city center, "Monica House," in a store-front that had formerly housed a Chinese laundry. In 1952, Mary Imelda said goodbye to her friends in the Gaelic Society and Monica House and sailed off to South Africa. For seven years she has worked there, first as Dean of Women at Pius XII University in Basutoland; then as secretary of the Catholic Federation in Johannesburg, a task which brought her into contact with a cross-section of the community. Back in the States on leave, she is taking a graduate degree in political science at St. Louis University.

We met on the wide, shady porch at Grailville during her holidays. Mary Imelda is a keen analyst of a situation and always has the words to convey her ideas to others. In a few minutes we were deep in conversation on the theme close to both our hearts—Africa and the future of the Church in Africa.

"You see, Elizabeth," she explained, a toss of her red head giving emphasis to her words, "we Catholics are a very small minority—only about 5 percent of the whites and a bit more of the Africans and colored. For a long time, the Dutch Calvinists wouldn't allow any Catholic establishments on the Cape—the first Dutch priests didn't arrive until 1805. Besides, the Church has developed from two sides in South Africa: the priests who came to take care of the European Catholic emigrants, and the missionaries who came to convert the Africans. It's only recently, in the face of all the problems, that these two branches have become deeply conscious of their unity and have drawn close together.

"But in spite of all the difficulties, the response is often marvelous. Think of the school question. When the Bantu Education Act was first passed, and the bishops decided that the Catholic schools could not cooperate with the apartheid policy and would have to forfeit a large part of their government subsidies, the Catholics raised almost $2,000,000 for the schools. When you realize that most of this came from the 140,000 white Catholics, you can see it was a real witness to love and unity."

The hierarchy has taken a daring, courageous and strong position against the Union of South Africa's official policy of racial discrimination, known as "apartheid." "There is only one race, the human race," the Catholic bishops declared in a joint pastoral in February, 1960. "God planned that we should all be united in Him and to one another in this world as well as in the next." Calling for a "change of mentality" to solve the country's race problems, the bishops urged all to "see our fellow human beings as human persons, not thinking of the color of their skins, or of where they come from."

The Catholic stand on education has given rise to bitter words from the government, but many thoughtful non-Catholic South Africans agreed with a statement issued by Archbishop Hurley who is Chairman of the Administrative Board of the South African Bishops' Conference, publicly replying to the government criticism.

The Archbishop announced that the Church could not give up its educational work among the Bantus "while the future of South Africa is hewn out with massive apartheid measures that fall like hammer blows on the soul of the black man, and the conscience of the white man." He went on to ask: "What is the future to be? It is the agony of that question that makes us so eager to retain contact with the education of the African. He can put up with a lot, cheerfully and patiently—poverty, undernourishment, disease, low wages, separation from wife and family—but one thing he cannot abide forever is the insult he sees in every law and regulation of apartheid. What will happen when the point of utter exasperation is reached?"

From Johannesburg a team has gone to Pius XII University

at Roma in Basutoland. African leaders are setting in motion forces capable of transforming Africa, forces which need a Christian direction. The reagent necessary to capture this moment in time is the provision of a higher education invested with spiritual values and this is what Pius XII University strives to do.

From the shores of Lake Victoria, from the highveld of Kenya, from sunny Tanganyika, from the Angoni highlands of Nyasaland, the savannahs of Northern Rhodesia, from the Kalagadi Desert fringe of Bechuanaland, the well-watered valleys of Swaziland, the passes through the Blue Malutis of Basutoland, from the shanty towns of the Transvaal, the sugar plantations of Natal, from these and other areas young African men and women set out on an educational pilgrimage which brings them to Roma; having come, they quickly settle down to university studies which have no cultural barrier on the grounds of race. Into the midst of these African students, with their varied backgrounds, have gone two young Americans, showing by their physical presence the universality of the Church.

Students of Pius XII University in Basutoland discuss plans for graduation day.

Chapter Twenty-Two

Part of a Bold Experiment

WHEN Mary Emma Kuhn of Pittsburgh received her Bachelor of Arts degree at Pius XII University in Basutoland in 1957, she was the first American Catholic girl to earn such a distinction on the African continent.

Diminutive Mary Emma—she is a breath over five feet—stepped off a DC-7 Skymaster at Jan Smuts international airport in July, 1953 to embark on her unique career as the first white student of Pius XII University. Four years later, she was the first white graduate in the school's history.

Mary Emma was in the first team from Grailville to work in the British Protectorate of Basutoland in the heart of South Africa. With her on the flight from Cape Town to Roma was Mary Imelda Buckley, first dean of women at the University. Later Lorraine Machan took her place as dean and lecturer in science.

During her high school days in Pittsburgh, Mary Emma was a straight "A" student at St. Mary of the Mount, and captured honors in Latin, mathematics and religion when she graduated. Her older sister, Doris, was a student at Grailville, so each summer from her thirteenth Mary Emma had been visiting. It was natural for Mary Emma to enroll at Grailville as soon as she could qualify.

"I was puzzled for a while about what to do," Mary Emma recalls. "I was thrilled with the international community at Grailville and the world vision which was presented, and I knew the importance of training for lay leadership, but frankly Africa never entered my head at the time.

"I think my special interest in Africa grew out of a series of lectures and discussions in 1952, when we studied the needs and growth of the missionary church on this continent." Not long after, Father Romeo Guilbeault, O.M.I., the dynamic rector of Pius XII, visited Grailville.

"He talked about the university," Mary Emma explains, "as a bold experiment in Catholic education which held out promise to African young men and women university students who are eager to take their rightful place in the world of the twentieth century. He told us that Pius XII would be a source of redemption for all of Africa and that its goal was nothing less than to save a continent—to save all Africa. I must have caught a spark of his enthusiasm, because when he offered me a scholarship at the university, I was delighted when the Grail leaders agreed that I accept it."

Mary Emma has lived in the women's hostel, a short ten minute walk from the University, with African girls from the four provinces of the Union of South Africa as well as from Basutoland, Uganda, and Northern and Southern Rhodesia.

"There has always been a very real oneness among us," Mary Emma says. "We have helped each other as much as we could with our subjects. We have worked together and have had our recreation periods as a family. Altogether, it has been a terrific experience."

Mary Emma's work now? She regards the training of an elite among the Catholic African students as an immediate and urgent need for the future, because Mary Emma is totally committed to the task of bringing Christ into the very heart of African life.

When Mary Emma was about to graduate, Father Guilbeault

made another visit to Grailville. He told us that the experiment had been a success and that he would like another Grail member for the student body of Pius XII.

This time it was Detroit-born Emilia Charbonneau who volunteered to carry on in Mary Emma's place. Emilia is the fourth child of French-Canadian parents who immigrated to the automobile city in the '20's. It was while Emilia was studying at Girls' Catholic Central High School there that she first heard of the Grail.

Father Donald Hessler, M.M., went to the school to speak to the students, and in the course of his talk he stressed the missionary needs of the Church and the very real need for the lay apostolate.

"He suggested that some of us should go to a summer course at Grailville," she told me, "and in order to encourage us he himself would pay the fees for anyone who would find the transportation money. I worked after school and managed to get the necessary cash together, and five of us divided Father Hessler's scholarship."

The five young Detroiters returned to finish their last year in school, and their main concern as seniors was to graduate. However, the following summer Emilia returned to Grailville and in the ensuing two years was a staff member at the Gateway, Detroit's Grail Center. Emilia joined in this experiment in cooperative living, concentrating especially on the family service and children's recreation programs.

"The group was international and interracial," Emilia recalls, "and my two years at the Gateway were very important to me. There I began to grasp the vision of the apostolate and to get experience in many fields.

"The Gateway program was broad and flexible. We worked in the parish with the liturgy, converts, children, families, recreation, parish councils, credit unions, interracial contacts; in the city through family service, art and culture discussions, foreign students, professional women."

After two years in Detroit Emilia came to Grailville for the year-long school of formation.

"What led me to Africa? I can truthfully say," Emilia smiled back at me, "that my desire to serve the Church overseas goes way back, but I'm afraid I would never have accomplished this desire without the opportunity offered me in the Grail. You see, I had no professional training, and so I thought it was impossible for me to contribute anything overseas. When Jeanne Plante, the Director of Grailville, asked me whether I would like to go to Basutoland, you can imagine my surprise and my answer!"

Emilia arrived in February 1957, and she is there now with Lorraine Machan and Josepha Gall. Lorraine teaches a full schedule of classes in chemistry and zoology, and heads the science department at the University.

On the average, students are older than those at a corresponding level in the States, Lorraine reports. They are mature, eager to learn, and work hard. For the rest, they have the same talents and are bothered by the same difficulties as students anywhere. After a year of work, Lorraine was convinced that they were capable of carrying on at the University of Natal Medical School in Durban, so she made a quick trip to that city, where she convinced the Dean of the School, Dr. Gordon, that the science courses at Pius XII University would qualify her students as pre-medical trainees. Her work increased so much with this step forward that she is looking forward to an assistant.

Josepha is from the Grail in Holland and Scotland and more recently from the Union of South Africa. She is the librarian at Pius XII as well as the Commissioner for Catholic Girl Guides in Basutoland. Gabrielle Miner from Chicago, another librarian, is a recent arrival from Grailville who assists Josepha in her work and is in charge of women students.

Nothing can be written about Pius XII University without introducing Father Guilbeault. For years he and his fellow Oblates struggled and sacrificed to make the University possible. When it became clear that a Catholic college at Fort Hare Uni-

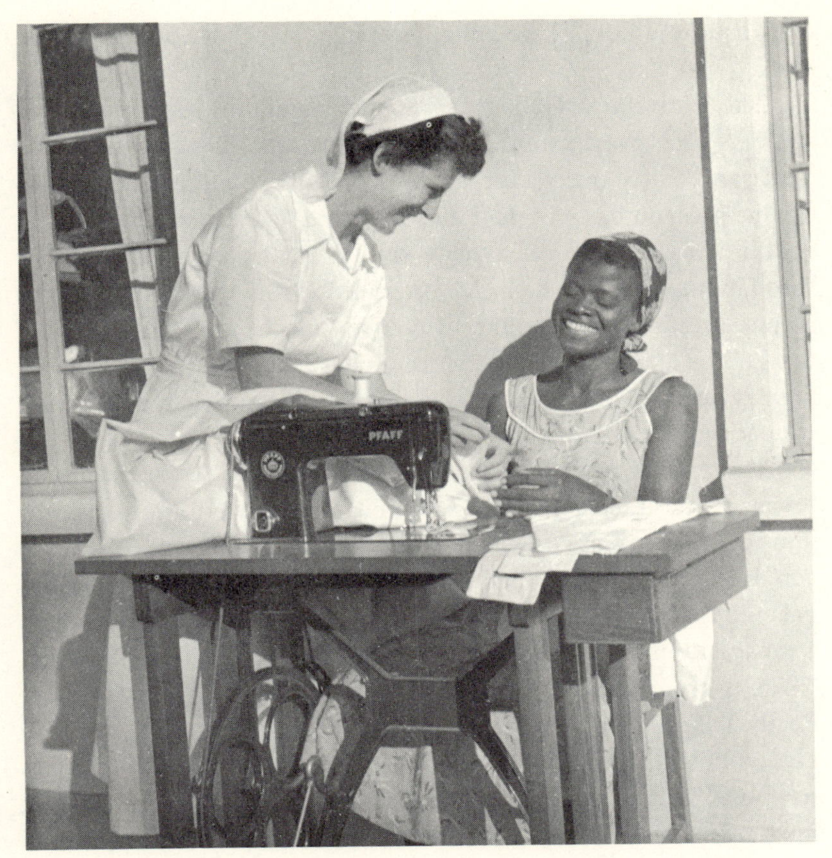

A nurses' aide gets a lesson in sewing on the porch at Kpandu.

versity could not be erected, the Oblates responded in a magnificent fashion to the plea of the hierarchy of South Africa and assumed the huge burden of building and staffing Pius XII Catholic University in Roma, Basutoland.

The Oblates pin their hopes on finding funds in America. I have met Father Guilbeault in the States, his face lined and weary after days of tramping in and out of Manhattan offices seeking help from foundations to build up the University. I have heard him speak to plead his cause as many as five times in one day, always, in spite of his weariness, in spite of the difficulty and distastefulness of begging, keeping the whole vision before him.

The University College at Roma began in 1945 with five students and five lecturers. Today it has one hundred fifty students and thirty-one lecturers. It is growing continually, but up to the present has not had the financial backing which would enable it to develop on a scale similar to the other universities throughout Africa which are financed by the various governments. Funds are important, of course, but they are not the main thing. "It's a small show but a great cause," says Dr. Jowitt, leading lay lecturer at the University and outstanding authority on education in Africa.

The aim of most of the other universities in Africa seems to be academic integrity, Father Guilbeault reported after a recent journey to various universities for African men and women across the continent. When asked if there was a Christian background to the particular university, the answer always came—a university is an intellectual work and not necessarily Christian, "This is true," insists Father Guilbeault, "but only partly true. Partly true because if you train the intellect properly, you will give your students a right outlook on life, life on earth and life to come. The African is afraid that there may be no real truth; he longs for truth that is certain, that is sure and applies to everyone. The Christian doctrine that there is one truth for all people everywhere is the foundation on which the work at Roma is built.

"There is a high academic standard in all the universities. In the main, the African students seem to know one world—the world of their lecturers. In a British University, they know the British world. This gives a rather limited outlook, which has both advantages and disadvantages. Nearly all the students—roughly seventy-five percent of them—are pro-Russian in sympathy, not Communist but pro-Russian. I had not known this pro-Russian sympathy was so strong," Father Guilbeault continued, "until I made this journey, and it came as a surprise to me. The Russians present a world to the African which welcomes him fully, not debarring him because of race or color, and this has a very strong appeal.

"University education is intimately connected with race relations," Father Guilbeault insists. "Often when the students first come to Roma, there is a real work to be done in breaking down racial prejudice that has grown over the years. There is only one basic way to do this. It is essential to teach the truth that we are all part of mankind, that we all have God for our Father and therefore are brothers. The student wants to know that he is part of mankind, not a segregated minority, nor, for that matter, that he comes from a segregated continent. The African has a longing for unity, and we build on that."

In practice, at Pius XII University College there are certain concrete expressions of unity and oneness that Christianity brings, which are a great help. The staff is international in character, drawn from ten nations. Also, as much as possible, the students are drawn from different tribes and different countries. There are two European students and one American taking full and equal part in all the student life. Non-Catholics make up about thirty percent of the student body.

Jimmy and Joan Stewart, Cambridge graduates, head the English department. They have two small sons and a daughter and their home is a constant rendezvous for the students. Joan is a sister of Anne Hope, who is on the staff of the Grail secondary school in Kalisizo, Uganda. Anne and Joan were born and grew up in Johannesburg, daughters of English parents.

Alexa and Joe Kane, a young American couple with two small children, the second born in South Africa, are also on the faculty. Alexa is Emilia Charbonneau's sister and she met Joe while she was on the staff of the Philadelphia Grail Center. Shortly after the birth of their first daughter, Joe and Alexa decided to offer their services to AID* and give the first years of their married life to the missions. Great was the joy when the two

* Association for International Development, a lay mission group.

Detroit sisters were reunited, one a student in this African university and the other a faculty wife.

Lorraine Machan, when she was home on leave, told me that there is one dream in the heart of almost all her students, and that is to continue their studies overseas. To see the determination with which some of these young people have pursued that aim is, in itself, a study in potential leadership, she maintains.

"I think of my friend Charlie from Rhodesia, whom I met shortly after my arrival in Africa. Since his childhood he was bent on becoming a medical doctor, but for economic reasons he had to interrupt his education and take a job, a thing which happens frequently in Africa, so often that many never complete high school. But Charlie had made up his mind that he would be a doctor, so the job he took was one which fed his ambition as well as his pocket; Charlie became a medical orderly. Last year at the age of thirty-three he graduated from a North American medical school with an academic record among the highest in his class.

"I think of Johnny, a would-be dentist in South Africa. There is no school in the whole of Africa where he (or any other African for that matter) can achieve this goal. For months I watched him exhibit all the prowess of a professional sleuth as he tracked down dental schools whose degrees would be recognized in his country. At the time I left for home, he had no scholarship in view; still I cannot but have faith in his determination.

"And I think of how much the opportunity for study overseas given to one member of a community means to the rest. I recall how in order to obtain a passport for a girl coming to the U.S.A. from South Africa, it was necessary that her legal guardian, her uncle, report to the township superintendent. This meant that Uncle Walter had to forfeit a half day's work and a whole day's pay. Anyone familiar with the wage scale for an African factory worker in South Africa knows how much those few shillings in a day's pay mean to a man with a family. But with a big smile on his face, Uncle Walter vowed that he would gladly lose a month's pay if it would help his niece get to America for study."

The community waits hopefully for the day when the young student will return, ready to use the knowledge and skill he has acquired for the benefit of all.

I have met six students from Pius XII doing postgraduate studies in the United States today, all of them outstanding for leadership and for a mature approach to the common problems which beset Africa in the 1960's. Among them were Percy and Monko Rangongo, a young couple whose first child was born in Milwaukee. I met them on their arrival by plane from Africa. They had only a few days in New York before going on to Wisconsin, and they stayed with us at the Grail center in Brooklyn. At once, they fitted into our activities—Percy reading in a warm, vibrant voice the lesson of the day at Vespers; Monko, tall, serene, enchanting the family with her stories of African family life. Monko is an anthropologist and was assistant lecturer in the African languages department of Pius XII before she came to continue her studies at Marquette University. Percy, voluble, charming, was a lecturer in education. Here in the U.S.A. he will receive his doctorate and then return to help build up the University of which he and his wife were foundation students. They are well known on the campus at Marquette where they contribute to faculty and student discussions, and are welcome visitors in the homes of young Catholic families like themselves.

Sunku Mofeking was the first Pius XII student to come to Grailville. Sunku contributed to the life and program at Grailville, and was the "bridge-person" for the other Africans who followed her. In Detroit, where she completed her bachelor's degree at the University of Detroit, she exerted a real influence and apostolate, especially among other African students, and in interracial groups. To sing with Sunku is to experience community in its fullest. In a twinkling she can have a hundred people in the palm of her hand, and with the driest of humor change an awkward moment into something of rare happiness.

Another of the Pius XII students at Grailville told me a story about life at the university which gives quite an insight into the problems which beset African people in these changing times.

A man student wrote an article in the university paper, *See,* making certain allegations against the supposed behavior of African university women. This caused such a rumpus that the women students boycotted all student functions from August until October! No woman appeared at any entertainment, at any discussion, at any sports meeting, until a full rebuttal was published.

In the meantime, witty letters composed by the girls appeared in each issue of the paper, pointing out to the men the true role and status of Christian women.

A year later, as she told me this story, we could laugh about it, but then for a minute her thin, sensitive face was serious.

"You know, Elizabeth," she said, "we had to show those men that they cannot treat us in the same way as they used to. The old ways are passing, and we as university women cannot overlook such false ideas. We have to speak for the women who have not had the chances we have had with our higher education. Our education has not been given us for nothing, and it is our responsibility to show the true role of woman to our people, even in such a small way as this boycott."

"Didn't it make student life difficult in those months?" I queried. "Of course it did, but we did have a point to make. At home we were taught that women must be docile and submissive, and I do believe that is proper for us too, in the family especially, but if we take this type of criticism without fighting, it will only get worse. If we want to change, we must begin, and we must face difficulties."

Mary Joyce, another of the trio at Grailville, hails from Natal. A girl with an irresistibly sunny smile and endless good humor, she has a canny sense of what to do to smooth over a jagged situation and was warmly received by the Americans in less time than it takes to write.

And yet, it was this sunny outgoing one who remarked to me, the morning after we got the result of the South African elections: "I know it is no use crying about it. For myself I have no bitterness. I am a Catholic, but for my friends who are not, I know how they will feel. It isn't just a fair share of the land they want any more, what they want more than anything else is a chance for education so that they can govern themselves."

Throughout Africa there is this intense hunger for learning, and no matter what the sacrifice involved, an impassioned determination to achieve it. The new sense of economic and political expectancy has swept away indifference and apathy, and has given place to a compelling conviction concerning the crucial importance of higher education. Here is something new and vibrant in the making—it may be emotionally colored, but it is vital with purpose, energy, and sincerity. Pius XII University is a significant response to this tempo of the time.

Gail with a group of children in a village in upper Egypt.

Chapter Twenty-Three

From the Hudson to the Nile

GAIL MALLEY has lived most of her life a stone's throw from the Hudson River in New York. Today you can see her walking along the Nile in the history-heavy city of Cairo, capital of the new United Arab Republic.

This slim New Yorker has many friends there—the sweet potato seller in Heliopolis, drably dressed but with a song that rings through the early morning silence, mixing with the fragrance of jasmine; and the mending man, sitting long hours in his little cubby, wielding his needle with fairy fingers to mend—with unbelievable skill—holes his friends the moths have made, accepting humbly a price so low that it is painful to think of it. Then there is the blind man who walks through Zamalek, his hand on the shoulder of a little child, calling out his haunting refrain to say that he has needles to sell, ten for half a piastre; and the young woman sitting on the floor of a tram, with a big sack full of chicks—and her face grave and full of concern for them; and the bird seller in Suk el Tewfikie, whom Gail makes a detour to see each morning, who has half a dozen naked skinny little birds dangling limply from his grasp and punctuates his walk with a loud short cry, "Asafeer," that breaks through the chaotic noises of the swarming street.

Gail has many more friends, but these seem to be her favorites, as she has told me about them. "I think," she said, her warm grey eyes alight, "they must be the ones Christ thought of when He told us that the poor are blessed, because the kingdom of heaven is theirs."

How Gail got to Cairo is quite a long story—and it all began with the visit of Father Habib Ayrout, S.J., to New York, where he met the Grail.

"It was a providential meeting," smiles Samira Megally, Egyptian Grail member, "because through his conversations and discussions with Dr. Lydwine van Kersbergen, he decided to arrange for a representative of our group, the 'Responsables de Haute Egypte' to come to Grailville, and soon I was on my way."

Samira loved the Grail and all that it stands for right from the start. As the months went by at Grailville, Samira became convinced that the Lord wanted the Grail to be present in Egypt "so that many of my countrywomen would find in it the source of radiating happiness and total giving." When Samira left Grailville, she went to the international Grail training center in Holland, and after much discussion and prayer, it was decided that one of our Grail people would accompany her back to Egypt to begin orientation and preparation for the work. For this task, Gail Malley from New York was chosen.

Gail had already been two years in Holland. She had worked in The Hague in one of our movement projects for people of the Eastern Rite so she knew something of the mentality, and as an added gift, she is brilliant at languages. She has an ear for those "sounds of the heart," as the Chinese call words.

Gail registered at the University of Cairo as a student in Arab language and culture. She and Samira live in an apartment in Zamalek, and, as friend and fellow-worker, Gail is daily with the "Responsables," the group of Catholic girls and women who have taken it upon themselves to aid the desperately poor Christian peasants in the villages along the Nile.

Egypt is the No. 1 limb of the newly-formed United Arab Republic, right at the crossroads between East and West on the northern shore of the pulsating continent of Africa. It has a population of some 23,000,000 people, most of whom are Moslem. But it is a nation steeped deep in Christian tradition. What Catholic child does not know of the flight of the Holy Family into Egypt? This was the first foreign country to give refuge to Christ—the forerunner of those nations in our time who receive Christ in the person of the refugees. It was on the soil of Egypt that the Christ Child first walked, that Mary our Mother knelt in praise of God and lived by faith, until she and Joseph could return with the Child to Nazareth.

But we have to make a big jump to modern times in order to understand a little the complex problems to be faced by present-day apostles in Egypt. During the last hundred years the country has passed through many stages. First it was a British protectorate, then an independent kingdom for thirty years, and finally, after the military revolution of 1952 which dismissed King Farouk, it was proclaimed a republic. In 1958, Egypt joined with Syria and Yemen to become the United Arab Republic with Gamal Abdel Nasser at its head.

The Islamic faith has been dominant in Egypt ever since the Arab invasion in the seventh century. Eighty-seven percent of the population are Moslems; the remaining 13 percent, almost 3,000,000 people, are Christians. The great majority of these—2,500,000—belong to the Coptic Orthodox Church, which is headed by a Patriarch with the title "Pope of Alexandria." The remaining half-million are divided among the other Orthodox rites (100,000), various Protestant denominations (200,000) and Catholics (200,000). Among the Catholics, seven different rites are represented—the Coptic, Armenian, Chaldean, Maronite, Greek, Syriac, and Latin. In one Jesuit community, three rites are represented. Even for an Egyptian Catholic, this complex picture is quite confusing. He must face the problem of relationships with the other rites within the Catholic Church, with other Christian communities, with the Catholics of other lands, as well as with the Moslems.

A further complication arises because the Christians, and very especially the Catholics, owing to their education in schools run by foreign missionaries, are mostly French-speaking, and hence are considered less Egyptian than the Moslems. There is a whole generation, at least of women, who are barely able to read and write Arabic and feel much more at home in French. Strenuous efforts are now being made to change this situation.

One of Gail's primary objectives is to understand the position of women in Egypt, which is also quite a complex question. There are many types of status for women, as a result of varying social conditions, cultural formation, racial origins, and above all differences in religion. Old and new still go side by side in Egypt as regards woman's role. This is an Islamic country, where for centuries women have had to remain hidden and covered by a veil, where it has been taken for granted that the woman is inferior to the man and must live under the patriarchal power of her father or husband. But the old patterns are changing rapidly now.

It is only thirty years ago that a movement sprang up, called "Bent el Nil" (Daughter of the Nile), which started to struggle against arbitrary divorce, polygamy, and the wearing of the veil. Now an educated girl can be a teacher, nurse, doctor or lawyer, and she can assert herself in many fields and prove her efficiency.

From Morocco to Indonesia, the drive of Islam's women towards emancipation has kept pace with the drive of their countries towards independence. In Pakistan, where ten years ago cars were heavily curtained to protect women from the vulgar gaze of passers-by, hundreds of still devout women now drive themselves, unveiled, to work or their social rounds. In Tunisia, where in 1947 polygamy was accepted practice, in 1960, according to a report in *Time* magazine, a husband landed in jail for having defied the law and taken a second wife. In Egypt and Lebanon, Turkey and Syria, where for centuries the life of a woman was described proverbially as "from the womb of her mother to the house of her father, from there to the house of her husband, from there to the tomb," women shop unveiled in the markets, train as nurses, drive cars unescorted, and many have the right to vote. In the last ten years Islam's women have achieved a greater change in status than in the preceding ten hundred.

It is understandable then that this new awakening of woman and her appearance in public life are tremendous events, not only for the Moslem women, but as well for the Christian women in Moslem lands.

In Egypt there is still a transition period, which, painful though it may be, is rich in possibilities and promise for the time when women will be fully free. It is in this situation, then, that our Grail team is at work.

For several years before coming to America, Samira had worked with Father Ayrout in the Catholic Association of Egyptian Schools which had been founded by him in 1940 in an effort to improve the condition of the "fellaheen," the Egyptian peasantry, so called from the Arabic word for labor. The fellaheen, who make up roughly seventy percent of the population, go on living, working, suffering in the same pattern as a thousand years ago—cultivating their little fields along the Nile with the same primitive wooden plows without wheels, dwelling in comfortless mud huts, filling their earthen jars at the banks of the Nile each morning for water supply.

Among the thousands of villages are a number of Christian peasant communities in the Nile valley, and these are the special concern of the Association. In spite of centuries of isolation and even persecution, with very few scantily instructed priests, these communities have stubbornly, miraculously remained Christian. Many of the people no longer really know what it means that they are Christians, except that it is something to be faithful to. Between these poverty-stricken, disease-ridden fellaheen and the wealthy, well-educated Christians of the big cities there is a tremendous gap which the Association tries to bridge. As the heart of the work Father Ayrout chose a group of women and girls of the highest class and called them "Responsables," for they were to carry in themselves the responsibility for these neglected brothers in Christ. The Association provides schools—at present one hundred thirty schools in villages scattered from Cairo to Luxor, where 12,000 children receive an elementary education together with training in manual crafts. At the same time, the truths of the Catholic faith are presented to their growing minds.

The Responsables do voluntary administrative work for the schools, help to find teachers and funds, operate dispensaries, teach child care to the women, visit the families, organize recreation for the children. This is no abstract charity, to be accomplished by signing a check at a safe distance. Every Responsable goes each year for at least two weeks into a village and lives in the midst of the people. This caused a revolution in the beginning—public opinion was so much against it. The villages with their primitive way of life were no place for gently-nurtured women and sheltered girls—they would be exposed to all kinds of diseases and indescribable dirt! After a few years, however, the venture has become commonplace, but the conditions are no less painful. These Egyptian young women mean business in the apostolate—no half-measures for them.

"It is a tremendous experience for the Responsables to be in contact with a way of life so different from their own," Samira explains, "and with a faith so simply lived. And for the fellaheen, it is an event, this arrival of city people who come to serve and to help. The school building with its white cross—often the best building in the village—gives the people a sense of pride and dignity. They begin to feel that they belong to the great, strong Catholic family."

Gail Malley, laden with a big case of medicines, soap, sweets and demonstration equipment, and going off to a village with her Egyptian friends would not trade her experience on the banks of the Nile for a jaunt down Broadway or for the Easter parade on Fifth Avenue. Enough for Gail to see the hundreds of small, eager faces and the waving hands as she goes towards the school where they greet her, "Glory be to Jesus' name," to which she answers, "Forever."

A letter has just arrived from Gail and I would like to share it:

Cairo, Egypt

Dear Elizabeth,

I am so glad to tell you something about Egypt and the Grail here, and at the same time apprehensive that the picture I will give you won't be very exact. In learning about a country, I guess it's the same as learning anything. I've noticed it with learning a language, for instance. After the first very blank time when you just don't understand anything, there comes a consoling moment when you have sudden flashes—when without understanding more than one word in twenty-five, you feel you have the gist of the thing. You intuit what people are talking about from a few subtle clues. This is a wonderful time. After this follows a time of increasing darkness, where the more words you learn, the less you understand, and this lasts a long time. Sometimes you think you have recognized up to ninety percent of the words—but missed the point. You don't see the woods any more for the trees.

This is the point I am at, both with Arabic and with Egypt. But I will do my best now at least to tell you about a few trees.

In Egypt you are really overwhelmed by the diversity of everything. Cairo especially is a kaleidoscope—of peoples, languages, religions. . . .

If you just sit in the metro on the way to Heliopolis, you hear Arabic, Armenian, Greek, French. In the tram that goes to Zamalek there is often quite a bit of Italian. You will see the women in different degrees of veiledness—some draped in black from head to foot, once in a while with even the vestiges of the veil before the face, in a symbolic net affair balanced against the nose with the help of a little golden cylinder. Others wear the black veil over bright clothes that vary from the fellaha's long unsophisticated "galabeya" to the most modern dresses. A great proportion of the younger generation in the cities have abandoned the veil altogether and are completely western in dress.

When I wait for the bus in the morning on my way to work, I am tempted by many other means of transportation: patiently plodding donkeys, haughty camels. . . . This morning two gamossas passed. I think they were on their placid way to be slaughtered.

Cairo is not a quiet place. Of noise, too, there is a great variety. Through the clanging of the trams and the wheezing of the buses in a busy street, you can hear merchants praising their wares, and the call to prayer floating from some minaret: "God is most great. There is no God but Allah, and Mohammed is His prophet" (or the pointed reminder towards four o'clock in the morning: "Prayer is better than sleep"). If you are lucky, you can be caught up into a lusty argument where—when voices have reached their loudest and most threatening, and you begin to wonder if this is not a good moment to edge away quietly—suddenly, inexplicably, there is peace, and everyone is smiling and laughing together.

There are terrible contrasts, too. The huge, luxurious apartment buildings and majestic villas of the residential section, in spacious tree-shaded streets, house only a small proportion of Cairo's 3,000,000. There is a whole scale of degrees of other kinds of housing, ranging down to districts of which it is almost impossible to believe that they belong to so modern a city. There is a corresponding range of social differences, hard for me to appreciate accurately, though I have the privilege of being in contact with almost every level of it, what with my contacts at the University and living at the Kahils'.

It is, however, at the Association that I come into daily contact with the two extremes of the range. It is also to the Association, ultimately, that I owe every contact I have in Egypt, for it was through it that I came to Egypt, and it was under Father Ayrout's dynamic guidance, in particular, that I became acquainted, in a few months' time, with more people than I have ever known in my life, received by them with a warmth that made me feel at home from the very first.

It is through the Responsables that the Association has become not just a work to be accomplished, but a spirit to be communicated. This Christian spirit of love and concern for our neighbor, if it is strong enough, concrete enough, will be the solution to the overwhelming social problems that exist here. It is tempting to say "If it were strong enough, it would be," but this would be an admission that it is already too late, and we should have faith that God can operate even the interior revolution that is necessary in the hearts of the rich. The change will come in any case; whether it happens in love or in hate is what is up to us. Already the change has begun: the revolution of 1952 was its effective beginning.

I hope I have conveyed a little of what I feel so strongly—the tremendous, complicated richness of Egypt, which expresses itself in every field. There are so many other things to tell you—so many problems that I have not even been able to hint at. You have been able to guess some of them: the unequal distribution of wealth (such a detached way of saying such a real and gripping thing); the divorce between city and country; the complexity of the religious picture. Perhaps you have suspected the less bright side of the rich diversity of rites: it tends to give Christianity a divided look, just where it is important that we be one. I have not even touched the problems of overpopulation, of undernourishment, of disease. . . .

Please God that Egypt may grow and may gradually solve its gigantic problems in a positive, balanced way, without bitterness or distortion.

With love to you all,

Gail

Gail is at work in Egypt today with Simone Tagher, Egyptian leader of the team, and Rosaline de Villaines of France. I saw her last in Holland on my way back from West Africa in June, 1960, and as we stood looking out over the dunes facing the turbulent North Sea, Gail said to me, "It was wonderful to visit America and the family after seven years, but I know now that I really belong in Egypt, and I can't wait to get back there and go on with the work." The tall, still young American, with her dark curly hair blown by the wind, was a sign and a symbol for me of the quiet strength of womanly dedication.

Simone Tagher of Cairo and Gail Malley of New York carry on an informal discussion with fellow Christians in Cairo.

Chapter Twenty-Four

Toumliline: A Flame of Hope in North Africa

INCREASINGLY in our time, Catholics begin to have an eschatological outlook—an orientation towards the Second Coming of the Lord at the end of time. Perhaps only from this vantage point can we understand fully the value of the international meetings which have been taking place the last few years at the Benedictine monastery in Toumliline, Morocco. They feed a tiny flame of hope glowing at the northern point of the African continent, as followers of Islam, Judaism and Christianity meet each year to discuss some of the major issues facing us as a world community today.

On two occasions our Grail representative at this significant gathering has been Lucia Leichner. Currently a member of a team at work at the Grail International Secretariat in Amsterdam, Lucia was born and bred in Berlin.

Beginning her studies of Slavic language, Greek, and archaeology at the University of East Berlin in 1945, it soon became evident to her that this seat of learning would become completely dominated by Communist thought. In her third year of studies, Lucia, along with a small group of other students—she was the only girl—decided to do something about the situa-

Catherine Bagley of Australia and Evelyn Pugh of Brooklyn pick up household supplies in the market at Tamale.

tion. They could see only one way out and that was to help build up a free university in West Berlin—out of nothing!

After three months they were able to prove to the authorities that they had gathered together students, while six professors were prepared to start teaching in the first faculties to be established.

Lucia became the assistant of the rector of the university and at the same time the right hand of her professor as he built up a Chair of Islamic Studies. Up to this time, Lucia was not yet a Catholic. Her four years of study had brought her in close contact with religions of antiquity, while archaeology became for her the means to discover that the New Testament was the fulfillment of the ancient promises and beliefs.

The quest for knowledge made her search for the truth in her own life, and she presented herself, with thirty-six written questions, in the office of the Catholic chaplain at the university.

When it became clear to her that Catholicism constituted the only direct line to Christ, Lucia had but one wish: to be admitted to the Church at once. And on the Vigil of the Ascension, 1949, she entered into this fullness.

A few years passed, and towards the completion of her studies, Lucia heard about the Grail, travelled to Holland to spend a few weeks at The Tiltenberg, and knew at once that a life of dedication was meant to be the outcome of the "golden string" she had been following ever since she began to seek after religion at the age of sixteen. With this background, Lucia was captivated when she heard about the work beginning at Toumliline, and soon found her way there and threw herself into the program.

Morocco is on the western rim of the Mohammedan world. A few years ago Benedictines from Encalcat, south of Toulouse in France, began to build a monastery at Toumliline, in the neighborhood of Azrou. Soon it became a meeting place for an exchange of thought among those who were interested in the development of the country, and it grew naturally to be a place where Islam and Christendom could come to know each other better. Since the monastery is so strategically located on the European-African frontier, making possible mutual knowledge and understanding, its aim lies in the direction of being a scientific-religious center for Islam, Christianity and Judaism.

An international study course on the theme of Community, held in the summer of 1956, was the first of a series at Toumliline. Thanks to the indefatigable activity of the monks, the cooperation of the King of Morocco, Mohammed V, and outside financial assistance, it was possible in succeeding years to hold similar study meetings on a larger scale.

The theme of a recent meeting was Education, and Lucia has written a glowing account of all that took place:

> How I would have loved you all to be here. Lectures and workshops were presented and led by eminent professors and outstanding personalities. Among these were: Professor Louis

Massignon, of the *College de France,* Paris; Osman Yahya, Alimiyya of the University Al-Azhar; Emmanuel Levinas, Director of the *École Normale Israélite Orientale,* Paris; Reverend Louis H. Regis, O.P., Dean of the University of Montreal, Canada; O. Lacombe, Dean of the University of Lille; F. Northrop, Professor of Yale Law School, U.S.A.; Mr. Eustache, Cabinet Minister of Education in Morocco.

The two hundred participants in the study course came from twenty-two nations, and it is significant that we were united not so much by *what* we believed, as by the fact *that* we believed. Because of this link a personal exchange was possible among Moslems, Catholics, Jews and Protestants—an exchange which was occasionally rendered rather difficult only by the diversity of languages.

The hospitality with which the international guests were everywhere welcomed and received made it easy for us to feel at home in this land of contrasts, and the experience of living together enabled us to have a good look at the Arabic-Islamic life. I cannot stress enough the need for tact and sensitivity, if all are to profit from such a meeting of different worlds. We can so easily hurt people without realizing it, and so close doors forever. From practical experience I have learned how important mutual trust and respect are, especially in the meeting of different religions.

The events of daily life very naturally stimulated informal discussions on religion—for instance, mealtimes, during which the Christians ate and drank everything; the Moslems took no wine or pork; and the Jews had quite another bill of fare. Five times each day the Moslems were conspicuous by their observance of a time of prayer, and almost as frequently this practice provoked a discussion. We discovered that for Christians it is far easier to come to a mutual understanding with a deeply religious Moslem than with a "modern" Moslem—that is, one who practices his religion only halfheartedly or not at all. We had many conversations with Moslems in which sympathy, respect and concern for each other were expressed. Here I think particularly of the real effort of the different currents in Islam today to keep the spirit and practice of the faith without the existence of a protecting hierarchy or leading institution. We, on the other hand, experience the need for a more dynamic

Alice receives a lesson in basket making, a skill highly developed among the Baganda people.

Christian spirituality. Here Islam and Christendom meet in the quest for the life-giving spirit.

This experience of the Moslem world was for most of us a never-ending series of new impressions. The striking customs of daily life and the beauty of the culture often left us silent in admiration. Yet from our Western point of view, some of the expressions seemed strange. Just a small example out of many: often, particularly on festive occasions, the people had a communal dinner, a so-called "diffa," during which they ate out of a common bowl with their hands and divided the large pieces of meat without any utensils. No one there seemed to have any difficulty in joining in this communal way of eating, or in drinking out of a common glass—nor did it seem to anyone to be "unhygienic." It was the custom of the people, and certainly provided us with a vivid expression of community. By the way, it is not at all easy to eat gracefully with your hands, and to sit in an "elegant" manner on carpets and cushions.

During our long excursions together, we had an opportunity to get to know the towns and general landscape of Morocco. Everywhere we were struck by contrasts. In a small area one finds two patterns of life next to each other, but so different it seems almost unreal at first glance.

For instance, each big town—Rabat, Casablanca, Fez, Meknes—has both a Medina and a European quarter, which exist side by side under very different social and cultural conditions. The Medina is the Arabic city, surrounded by high walls with strong gates at its entrance. On the inner side are concentrated the houses, whose smooth mud walls close in the narrow streets on both sides. One discovers small gardens in the inner courts of the houses, often decorated with colorful mosaics, and centered around a fountain at which the ritual washing is performed before the periodic prayers. There are also palaces of the king and the rich Moslems, with large, well-cared-for parks and an extraordinary wealth of flowers, trees and cactus, again closed off from the outside by high walls. The sewage system, water supply, electric power system, sanitary and medical facilities in these Arabic towns are difficult problems which have not yet been solved.

Particularly conspicuous, side by side with the Medina, is the existence of the "European city," which, with its modern public gardens, streets, businesses and houses, could hardly be distinguished from our ordinary western city. It is here that the Europeans and the well-to-do, "progressive" Moroccans usually live.

The problems typified by these sharp contrasts are many and complex, but their solution is gradually being worked out.

I had a chance to visit the town of Goulmina where the people gave us a gala reception, although it was already very late—a "diffa," at which we sat on colorful carpets under palm trees, with rows of tiny lamps between them. After midnight the women of the village came in their festive costumes to show us some of their dances, while the men sang and played on big tambourines. It was really a great spectacle!

After a night under the stars of the Sahara, the next morning we visited the Casbah. Here the influence of the West stops; no European lives within the Berber community. With wide open eyes one is aware of "the other" and enjoys the differences. Most women have a tattoo in a geometric pattern on their forehead or nose or along the chin, and they wear heavy, simple lead rings as bracelets, and coin-necklaces, which look very attractive on their colored dresses. With enthusiasm we admired each other's jewelry and understood each other very well, though we didn't speak the same language!

Of course, a Westerner cannot help but be struck by the position of the women in this part of the Islamic world. Here one is in daily contact with the veil and with the problem of polygamy. We Europeans attracted attention not only by our dress, so different from the "galabeya" and veil of the Moslem women, but also by our general bearing, our attitude of independence, our obvious lack of a sense of inferiority. Secondary schools for girls are slowly being introduced in Morocco, and there is a great need both for formal education and for work outside the home to give the Islamic woman the opportunity to find and form her own personality.

Thus the communication with "the other" goes on at Toumliline. And behind the fruitful dialogue stands the silent witnessing to Christ by lives of prayer and love. In response to an obvious need, the monastery has begun a dispensary, where nurses recruited by the Grail assist in the care of the sick. The team also goes out to the women in the surrounding villages, making contact, helping to solve social problems, building bridges of understanding and sympathy.

A meeting of different worlds has begun at Toumliline—a small but significant step towards that wonderful gathering of "the multitude which no man can number, of all nations and tribes and peoples and tongues" before the throne of God.

Dr. Margret Marquart with the Hospital Committee in front of the hospital in Kpandu, Ghana.

Chapter Twenty-Five

On the Road to Anywhere

THERE'S AN Australian bush-ballad which runs through twenty-six verses with a recurring theme—the joy of being "on the road to anywhere." When it was suggested in February 1960 that I should make a study journey to West Africa to help set up Grail teams in Ghana and have a look at neighboring countries for possible placement of American Grail members, I found myself humming this ditty a dozen times a day. In the subways of New York, as I went about the endless unravelling of red tape involved in going from one country to another, it continued with me; I sang my song (not loudly) across the Atlantic to London; I walked happily to it down the Appian Way in Rome; and I was acutely aware of the ramifications of such sentiments when I landed in Accra on a blistering hot morning to find the airport deserted. I felt like a child at the dead end of a paper chase unable to find any more clues. It was March 6 and the third anniversary of independence in Ghana. Everyone, it seemed, was enjoying the celebrations somewhere else. After I waited a long time, a Syrian trader gave me a lift to the city.

Accra crowds down to the ocean front and swarms along a ridge, then slips away to abandoned flats which reach toward the sea. It is a city of remarkable personality and a history that dates back to the seventeenth century. Harboring more than 150,000 Africans and a handful of Westerners, Accra is a city of contrasts, sprinkled with palms and flaming flamboyant trees, trading stores and mansions, tar paper shacks with rusty tin roofs and modern office buildings. There are imposing new ministry buildings, designed by British architect Maxwell Fry, who has done a new community center, large and airy, with a bas-relief over the entrance of umbrella-covered Ashanti chiefs and a handsome reproduction of Salvador Dali's *Crucifixion*. On the highest point in the city is the Cathedral of the Holy Spirit, presided over by American Negro Bishop Bowers, S.V.D.

Ghana, a nation of 7,000,000 people, occupies an area about the size of Oregon (92,000 square miles) on the west coast of Africa between the Ivory Coast and the Republic of Togoland. It was the first country in black Africa to achieve independence, and Kwame Nkrumah, the first president of the republic, is a symbol throughout Africa.

Ghana's frontiers, hastily drawn during the scramble for Africa in the late nineteenth century, cut across both natural and tribal boundaries. There are four distinct parts of the country, and one of the problems facing the present government is how to weld these sections into one nationally conscious whole. The majority of the western-educated, and therefore more nationally-minded, leaders come from what was up until 1957 the British Gold Coast Colony. North of the coastal district lies Ashanti, a heavily forested area inhabited by the Ashantis, a warrior people. This also was a British protectorate and later a crown colony. Farther north still, from the Ashanti forests to the Sahara desert, stretches a wide expanse of grasslands called Northern Territories, formerly also a British protectorate. Tamale, its capital, is the base for the Grail education team. Across the Volta River, to the east from Ashanti and the Gold Coast area, is a strip called Togoland which has also become part of Ghana. At one time under the German government, it

Old and new in West Africa: Kwame Nkrumah, President of Ghana, greets a tribal chief.

became a British protectorate after World War I and joined the new Republic of Ghana in 1957.

Ghanaians have established a constitutional democracy aimed at uniting a divided people. There was little violence in the break with Britain. They had a well organized political party, the C.P.P. (Convention People's Party), and a popular leader in Kwame Nkrumah ("Show Boy" to his people). Born in 1909, educated in Catholic mission schools and in Achimota College, Nkrumah in 1937 sailed to the United States for university education. He graduated from Lincoln University in Pennsylvania, majoring in economics and sociology, then went on to the University of Pennsylvania, where he studied theology and education, taking the degrees of M.A. and M.Sc. He worked his way through college in American fashion by going to sea as an ordinary seaman and working in the shipyards. He became President of the African Students' Association of North America, and naturally turned towards politics on his return home. When independence came, he was a standout to lead the new country as Prime Minister and then as its President when it became a Republic within the British Commonwealth on July 1, 1960.

Out of Accra, an inland road escapes to the upland forests north and east, and I headed this way to Kpandu in Trans-Volta Togoland, the most easterly region of the country. Here in the Diocese of Keta, invited by His Lordship Bishop A. Konings, S.M.A., a medical team headed by Dr. Margret Marquart had arrived five weeks before to carve a hospital out of the jungle

The morning I left Accra, the road was jammed with brightly painted trucks hung with charms and boldly lettered slogans fore and aft. *Clean Boy* and *Fear Women* wobbled along beside us until we came to a mountain pass, when they were left behind, radiators boiling, and passengers lolling on the road-side, lost in the dust from our tires. The *Hour is Near* loomed ahead, and *Lord Have Mercy* swirled up beside us, as we frantically rolled up the windows to save choking from dust.

But it was a beautiful ride, villages at intervals with closely packed houses of red earth, markets every dozen miles, their narrow lanes packed with booths, flowering with a feverish press of women in brilliant printed cloths. I grew to love the markets in West Africa, those vast foregatherings of private enterprise stacked with the riches of the land—local fruits, large and luscious, and earthen pots made from the red clay and splashed with black glaze. Goods from afar are to be had, too. Once, shopping in Kpandu, I counted tinned foods from thirty-seven different nations on sale in this unpretentious town at the edge of the mountains. The cloths which draped the quicksilver bodies of the children at Mass on Sunday had come as imports from faraway Indonesia.

Kpandu is a strongly Catholic center 146 miles from Accra. The hospital, three wooden school buildings with cement floors, is on the edge of a wide stretch of tropical bushlands which throw out a haze of heat. Everything is deeply green, and the plants bursting out of the red earth show a thrusting bigness of desire. Great lilies, white with crimson splashes, peep above the grass; bushes are all ablaze with wild gardenias; tall ground orchids cluster together, their spikes a mass of gold, light green, mauve and white. There are groups of ragged bushes—half trees—laden with purple and yellow and scarlet flowers; shrubs with giant tendrils several feet long are a glaring vermilion. There is nothing trivial about Kpandu—the tall straight coconut palms beneath the molten sun, the fifteen foot cobra caught in the hospital compound, the swift sudden fevers which bring death.

I first saw Margret walking through the long grass and stooping to pick a bush lily on her way back to the staff house from the ward. We waved and soon were talking together as if we had known each other for years. She asked keen questions about the journey, and I liked her at once when she said she had not been able to meet me because of the pressure of work, but that she had figured if I could find my way half across the world, the last 146 miles wouldn't make any difference to travel with or without escort. That's a sound way of thinking, and one true to type as I came to know her better.

Margret is in her thirties and she has packed quite a bit of history into her life. She was born and brought up on a small farm high in the mountains in southern Germany. As a child she cut wood in the forests, carried water on her head, studied in the village school, resisted the Nazis, saw her farmer father go off to war leaving her mother with a young family of eight; towards war's end Margret was strafed with shrapnel from a passing U.S. plane, and her consequent stay in the hospital confirmed her childhood longing to be a doctor in Africa. Not just anywhere, she was quite sure of that; her reason for waiting to study medicine was clear from the start—she wanted to use her skill in Africa. Margret starved and studied in Stuttgart to get her degree, went on to Würzburg Mission Institute to prepare specifically for overseas, and there met a Grail member on the staff, Jacoba Schaper. Jacoba told her about the Grail and our vision of the lay apostolate, to go not only with her medical skill, but to go as part of a team with a variety of skills, to bring Christian values into the various levels and structures of society. Margret listened, and the conviction grew that this was indeed what she wanted, and the following year she went to our international training center in Holland. Then, after a year of internship at a hospital in Germany, Margret was assigned to Rubaga Hospital in Kampala where she worked alongside Dr. Magdalene Oberhoffer. Now after three years of work there, and three months of leave in Holland and Germany, Margret, together with two Austrian nurses, Anita Linninger and Phily Fuchs, had come to Ghana to begin the Grail in West Africa.

The hospital is a real "felt need" of the people and has all the earmarks of a genuine community development project. The people have urgently wanted a doctor in their midst for some time, and many chiefs and queen mothers had petitioned the district commissioner, asking for government help. Everywhere the Ghanaians are working hard to build up their country —no easy task, when you consider that in Ghana the percentage of persons in the category of administrators, executives and professional personnel is about 3/10 of one percent compared with 2 percent to 5 percent in advanced societies like the United States or the United Kingdom. In all Ghana there is an average of one doctor to 25,000 people, and the government was unable to supply a resident physician for Kpandu. Finally, the district commissioner asked the bishop whether he could find a doctor and nurses who could come until the Ghanaians were themselves ready to take over medical facilities. Great was the delight of the people when final arrangements were made and the word came through that the medical team were already on the ocean on their way to Ghana.

Suddenly faced with the actual fact of having a doctor and nurses in their midst, the people began to think about a suitable building. It was decided to evacuate a girls' school and turn over the buildings to the hospital. The people formed a Medical Board, and began to make preparations for the doctor's arrival.

"The welcome we received was overwhelming," Margret told me. "I don't think Anita and Phily and I can ever forget it. Father Beckers met us at Takoradi harbor and drove us to Kpandu. About a mile from the town a large sign stretched across the road—'Stop, Doctor!' it read. We had to get out of the car and were received with much ceremony at the home of the head catechist. Later on," Margret twinkled, "we discovered that the preparations for the official reception were not quite finished, so someone had the bright idea of intercepting us!

"Then the community welcome began. Hundreds of people lined the road from the catechist's house into the town. There was dancing and singing as the people showered gifts of yams, bananas, eggs, pineapples, beer and even a sheep upon us. We went on foot then to the hospital buildings, where the chiefs and representatives of the community welcomed us with long speeches. Every speech had to be translated, to be sure that everyone present understood—some of the small boys stretched out on the ground and went to sleep during the process! A copy of the climax speech was presented to us to keep as a souvenir of this memorable occasion."

At the reception, as during several conferences since, each chief brought his queen mother to the gathering. The queen mother is an influential figure and plays a part in all important decisions made by the chief. It is an interesting fact that a king's son in Ghana can never become king, but the poorest woman of royal blood is the potential mother of a king. When a chief is to be chosen, it is the queen mother who has most to say. Whenever the chief travels, except to war, she must accompany him, and when he sits in court she is beside him. She alone has the privilege of rebuking him, his spokesman or his councillors in open court, and of addressing the court and questioning the contending parties.

When I arrived, the hospital was about to open, and in the work of preparation it was immediately apparent how much the people themselves wanted the hospital and how ready they were to shoulder responsibility for it. The Medical Board came forward with common-sense, practical suggestions, and help that would cost the people time and effort was offered spontaneously.

The days were full right from the start—we had to acquire and set up in their places beds, equipment and instruments; to sew sheets and pillow slips and layettes for the babies; to get in stocks of medicine, find bottles and containers; and, most important, we had to make the choice of local staff to help us. Applications for work in the hospital came from one hundred and fifty girls with Middle School Certificates, and it was difficult to choose the twelve we wanted to train as nurses' aides. One trained nurse, Victoria Dzimomooh, was found right in the town. She has become Margret's right hand, translating with ease from one local language to another during the long clinic hours each day. One week after we actually opened our doors, the forty-five-bed hospital was filled with patients, and the out-patients during the first ten days numbered nearly one thousand.

The blackboards are still on the walls of some of the wards, and the children who moved out of the school to make room for the greater need can be seen carrying their desks to the shade of a tree near the church until the new school is ready. But the people of Kpandu have demonstrated the strength of community effort, and of what can be accomplished when they know how to transform a felt need into a fact. It is exhilarating to be in the midst of a people learning to read and write and manage their own affairs, who are becoming interested in the world beyond their village, in their own African government, in what is hap-

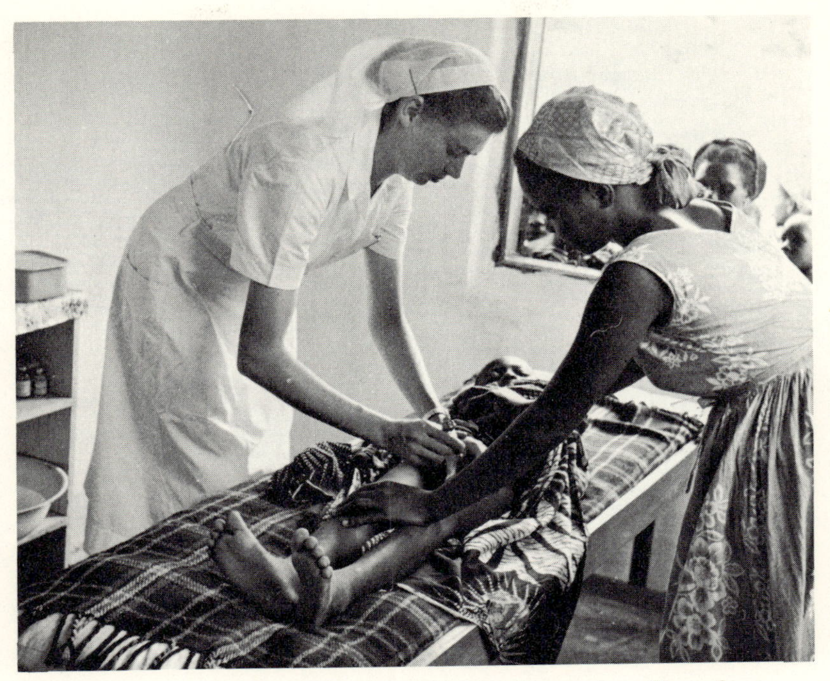

Anita Linninger of Austria, in the children's ward at Kpandu.

pening in the rest of Africa, and even in what is going on overseas.

And in the midst of all this, there is Margret, with the strands of her reddish hair limp on her forehead as she works hour after hour in the clinics, bending over the old Moslem with an open sore on half his leg, he chasing the flies with a languid hand as Margret snips and cleans; greeting the young mother fearfully edging her way into the surgery with three small children feverish and bumpy with measles. She has walked eleven miles in the blazing sun, spattered by the dust of a hundred lorries, to come to us, and her tired eyes take on a new light as Margret tells her she can stay in the hospital to receive treatment for her family. I remember a man with acute abdominal pains and the anxious concentration on Margret's face, as she has to decide whether or not to operate on what she diagnoses as a

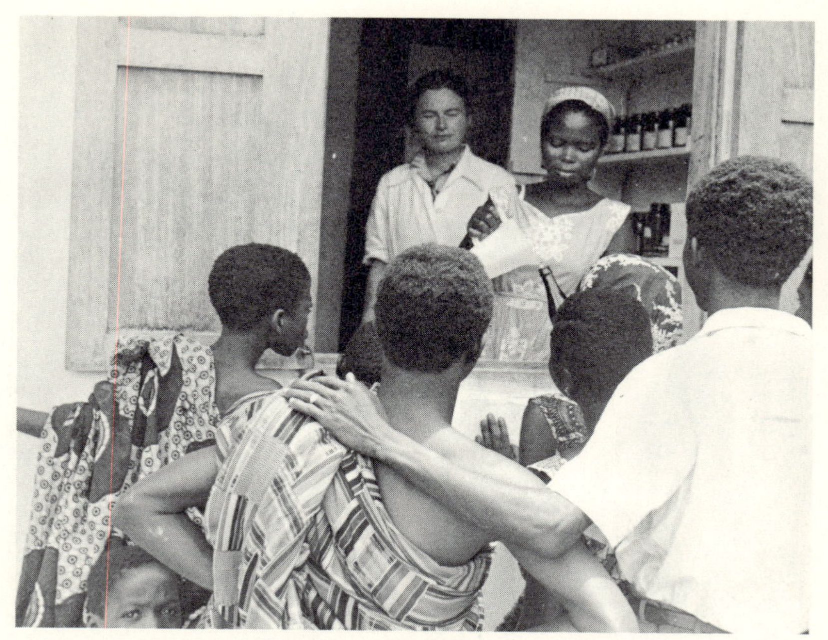

Morning line-up at the dispensary: the patient has brought a soda bottle in which to receive his medicine.

ruptured appendix. The decision is not easy; we had no proper operating room in those first weeks, no autoclave, no sterilizer—it means an emergency and all the surgeon's skill this young doctor can muster. But the man has seven children, and if we don't risk it he will surely die. He is a Catholic, so I dash off in the Volkswagen to get the priest from the neighboring mission and to ask his advice about the risk of death on the operating table. We are still strangers in this country and confidence has to be built up. But the priest says, "Go ahead." By the time we are ready, it is pitch dark with the heavy blackness of a tropical night. I pump the Tilly-lamp, the beetles quickly gather round the flame, as I hold it high and Margret, scrubbed and gloved, waits for a minute over the figure on the table. We pray the *Veni Sancte Spiritus* swiftly together, the comforting words moving quietly along from the heart "what is soiled, make thou pure;

what is wounded, work its cure. . . ." It is a gentle dialogue between us, one so fearful and rigid with pain, and God the Comforter, and the heart knows that every word is heard and answered. Then with sure swift strokes Margret begins her work, Anita and Phily passing her the instruments in quick succession. Unusually difficult circumstances, but for us the immense satisfaction of knowing that we are in the right spot at the right time and that we have helped to save a life.

The weeks I shared with the team in Kpandu were filled with that rare joy of making bonds of friendship effortlessly. Each morning I woke with a sense of expectation at the demands the day would surely bring. It is a splendid thing to be healthy and alive and working with a team in a place where you are needed. The Ghanaians are a laughing friendly people, confident in themselves and ready to accept you for what you are and do. I remember one meeting with the Church Committee, at the home of a committtee member. One of us said something to the effect that we appreciated their kindness and helpfulness to us "foreigners." Mr. Theodore, the Head Christian, replied earnestly: "You are not 'foreigners'—we do not like that word here; we are brothers and sisters in Christ."

On Holy Thursday night we had just come back to the hospital from the paschal celebrations. We had prepared a small supper for the occasion, rolls baked in a clay oven in the village, and red wine from the Rhineland, a white Christ candle alight on the table. Margret was just about to say grace when we heard a shuffling of bare feet and a wave of excited voices which were lowered as they came up to the window. They were as surprised as we, and I think were quick to recognize the symbols of the sacred banquet on our table. The leader clapped his hands together softly. In Ghana a visitor doesn't knock or shout, but gently claps hands to attract attention. As we went to the door, a small boy, eyes sharp with fear, was pushed out in front. Everyone began telling how when he had come out of church, he chased another boy into the long grass in the compound and had been bitten on the foot by a very poisonous snake. I held him in my arms as Margret reached for her bag: a quick incision, a plunge of the hypodermic needle, accompanied by a long sucking intake of breath on the part of the watching villagers, then the small body relaxing in my arms as the lad understood that all would be well and he wouldn't die after all! Then the thanks of the people, the same gentle phrases spoken over and over with clapping of hands. Finally they turned to go, and the head man looking once more at our table, said, "See, they have a little church here; these are good people who have come to help us. We will return and help you with what we know."

That was our introduction to Victor, and he was as good as his word, coming often to work at the hospital. He is a man of parts, this African gentleman, who speaks German and English well, along with his own Ewe language. As a child growing up in this region, he had his first formal schooling in German. But before he had completed school, World War I had ended, and German Togoland was divided into two territories—half under the protection of the British, the other half under the French. But the African people who lived in these territories were for the most part from one tribe, the Ewes. Victor explained all this to me as we split bamboo sticks to make a fence around the vegetable patch. He also told me how he and many of the elders hope that one day the Ewe tribe will be united territorially. Many of Africa's present problems arise from the boundaries drawn by the European powers in the 1880's and rearranged after World War I. Often these lines are arbitrary, cutting across natural economic regions and dividing tribal and linguistic units. The problem is further complicated by the new linguistic frontiers—English, French, Portuguese—which grew up under the various colonial administrations. As Victor said, leaning against our new bamboo fence when we paused to rest, "Do you know, my own first cousin's children cannot speak with mine—and they live just eleven miles from here across the border."

One evening as I had just finished taking a roll of pictures

Dr. Margret with a young patient.

of Margret and Anita and Phily around the hospital, I heard a great commotion—chattering, shouting, wailing, and the thud of bare feet running. Looking out across the compound, I saw a procession which immediately brought to mind the Gospel story of the widow of Naim. On a litter in the rear, a young man was being carried, his limp, lean body in sharp contrast to the white cloth on which he lay. A woman kept stopping the bearers and wiping the boy's forehead—and with each stop came a fresh wail of anguish. The boy was already dead when we got to him, and I think the mother must have guessed it, but she wanted to make quite sure whether the new doctor from far-away could still do something. He had died from tetanus. Margret told me that he had stepped on a rusty nail as he drove the cows home to the village—but he could have lived if he had come in time. Now we are beginning a series of classes after Mass each Sunday morning to educate the people in preventive measures and to let them know what is available for them at the hospital.

One night I had just fallen asleep after a work-packed day when I heard the familiar soft clapping outside my window. I sat up sleepily and pulled the curtain aside, and have for the rest of my life a picture in mind to ponder at suitable intervals. Standing a few yards away was a young man in the blue striped robe of the northern tribesman, wooden staff in one hand, and a lantern held high in the other. Beside him was his wife, a young woman heavy with child, beads of perspiration on her forehead, and a cloth bundle balanced on her head. I called Margret and soon the thin cry of a newborn child sounded out across the compound. I heard next morning that this Catholic couple had walked eight miles in the night to come to the hospital, praying as they came that this would be a good delivery. A former child had died at birth, and this time they wanted to be sure. I was asked to choose a name for the child and, fresh from an audience with the Holy Father, suggested that he be called John after the pope. Everyone was delighted. The following Sunday the family came back to have his papers signed by Margret, and we discovered that the moppet was indeed named after the Holy Father. There it was on the official paper for all to see, "Pope John Moshi."

It was from Kpandu, too, that one of the chief catechists wrote to the Holy Father about local matters which he wanted cleared up, and addressed his letter to "Catholic Mission, Rome." I thought of this a few weeks later when the announcement came through that Pope John was inviting the new African bishops to come to Rome for their consecration. One is close to the heart of the Church here, and it is good to have a strong bond with "the Mission in Rome."

The Church in Ghana is already established in seven dioceses which have been built up during eighty years of apostolic labor by three mission societies in particular, the Society of the African Missions, the White Fathers, and the Society of the

This young broadcaster is a representative of the new generation of African women eager to play their part in the development of their country.

Divine Word. There are already two Ghanaian members of the hierarchy, His Grace Archbishop Amissah of Cape Coast and His Lordship Bishop Peter Dery of Wa, consecrated by Pope John XXIII in Rome in May, 1960. Ghanaian priests are working in each diocese and there are Ghanaian religious brothers and sisters. Schools and teachers' training colleges are operating effectively, and the work done by lay catechists is greatly in evidence. Lay mission groups have sent people with professional and practical skills and they are at work as valued personnel in five of the dioceses. The Church is not lagging in its efforts to use new opportunities presented by this emerging nation.

With Abbé Pierre at Lomé

Chapter Twenty-Six

Freedom Feast in Lomé

AROUND THE middle of my stay in Kpandu, everyone began talking about the forthcoming independence celebrations to be held in Lomé, the capital of Togoland, at the end of April, 1960. For months I had followed the proceedings in the Trusteeship Council at the U.N., and I wanted very much to be actually present as this new nation was born. It presented quite a problem to get there, however. Although Kpandu is only eleven miles from the former French territory, reports were coming thick and fast that there was trouble brewing along the border as independence came closer. Police reinforcements were moving in from Accra, and it was hard to get a driver to make the journey. Only someone who knew the roads well over the steep mountains could risk our precious Volkswagen, but just when I had concluded that this experience was one which I wasn't going to have, an opportunity came.

An Ewe priest of the diocese decided to drive the long way round, down the coast to Keta, where we could cross the border into Lomé on the edge of the sea. Father Joseph is young, with a hundred ideas, each a surprise package, and one deep-rooted desire—to visit the Holy Father in Rome. Over the rough three hundred miles, across bush tracks and swamps and five police barriers we went, talking of the Church and the possibilities of having some American nurses come to help him in his parish. Late at night we arrived in Lomé, and early next morning I got accredited with the International Press Bureau.

I stood in the midst of these men and women of Togoland as they saw their green and yellow flag with its white star for freedom unfurl in the harsh blue skies for the first time. I saw men and women weep, great bushmen shoot arrows into the air from wooden bows and dance to the rhythm of a hundred drums. I saw educated men with degrees from Paris and London marching past dressed in their former prison clothes, proud of their part in the struggle for freedom; and the blank passionless faces of the boys and girls who seemed never to tire of singing their national song. The roar of 50,000 voices, the intensity of the singing, the awareness of the solidarity of the crowd, all caught me up as I listened, and I was carried on wave after wave of the people chanting "Emblade, Emblade"—"Freedom, Freedom." All their longing for a better life for themselves and their children was centered in that single word.

A French frigate in the harbor lowered the colonial colors and gave a 101-gun salute to the new nation, while photographers and reporters pushed and shoved to record this moment in history. The Apostolic Delegate, the local Archbishop and two visiting African bishops sat close to the new Prime Minister, Sylvanus Olympio, who is a practical Catholic and a man of stature apart from politics. A Pontifical High Mass marked the opening of the celebrations, and this tiny splinter nation—about one million people—started off with a high hope on the road to freedom.

Among the hundreds of correspondents in Lomé was Abbé Pierre of Paris, modern apostle of love, who had come across from Dahomey to take part in the celebrations. I stood talking with him one night at the unveiling of the new Freedom Statue in a public park. Dressed in a khaki cotton cassock with a brown leather belt, this tall scrawny priest, with three cameras strung around his neck, was perfectly at home in the glittering gathering of diplomats and politicians. Sylvanus Olympio was making a long speech—it was hot and soggy as we stood there in the open park, a small boy began to whimper and cry that he couldn't see. Abbé Pierre leaned over and gave me his cameras as he picked the little fellow up and put him on his shoulder. The mother, obviously one of the high ranking Togolese officials, was pleased, and whispered to me, "My son has a right to see and hear; our new Prime Minister is his grandfather." So it was that this young son of Togoland saw part of the independence celebrations from the shoulder of a Frenchman.

The following day I was with Abbé Pierre again as we attended a Solemn Pontifical Mass in a mountain village. The sermon was in the Ewe language, and true to style it went on and on for over an hour—and we skipped the last half and sat on the back of a jeep talking about what had brought us both to Africa. Abbé Pierre was visiting the missions in the former French regions so that he could go back to France and speak about the needs of the Church, open up channels for scholarships in France and technical assistance to the missions. We made a pact to pray for each other as we go about our tasks in the United States and France, and I know that I have the best of that bargain!

At the celebrations, women were much in evidence. I heard that they had played an important part in the preparations for independence. It was in Lomé too that a twelve-day seminar was held in 1959, organized by the World Union of Catholic Women's Organizations and sponsored by UNESCO, to discuss the difficulties women face in trying to lead Christian lives in a predominantly non-Christian society. Three hundred African women attended. It would seem that in the newly created republics of Ghana and Togoland and in other West African countries, a major scale social revolution is quietly taking place. According to Jean Gartlan of the NCWC office for U.N. affairs in New York, who attended this seminar in Lomé, the movement is spearheaded by Catholic women, most of whom have been educated by Catholic missionaries.

The delegates in Lomé concentrated on problems that affected them immediately—ranging from the abuses surrounding the customs of marriage palaver and polygamy to how to cope with in-laws and how to take up women's new role in civic and social affairs.

Marriage palaver, which encompasses all the protracted discussions and negotiations involved in arranging marriages, is generally conceded to be a considerable obstacle to the growth and practice of Christianity in Africa. The talks are carried on by male relatives of two families and include such questions as the bride price to be paid by the groom to the girl's family before the wedding, the possibility of the husband's taking a second wife, and the amount of interference to be expected from his relatives after the wedding. The prospective bride has no official voice in the arrangements (though she is often able to make her wishes felt). Sometimes the girl over whom the families haggle has not even reached the age of puberty. Too often marriage palaver is reduced to the level of a mere business transaction in which women are treated as chattels.

The bride price varies from territory to territory, in some places cash, in others cows or the groom's free labor for a year. The negotiations preceding the marriage, however, follow a rigid pattern of visits by the boy and his family to members of the girl's family, and then presentation of the prescribed gifts—tobacco and liquor for the father, a cloth for the mother to replace the one she carried the girl in as a baby, a complete trousseau for the bride, and, since African society has become more westernized, expensive items such as a sewing machine or a refrigerator.

These customs must be strictly observed if the marriage is to be considered valid according to tribal law. Generally the Church insists that at least the essential preliminaries be observed before a marriage is blessed, since these arrangements help to safeguard the stability of the union. The Church strongly discourages exorbitant bride price, since it tends to delay marriages unduly and increases the temptation for the young couple to start living together before the conclusion of negotiations. This often happens anyway, and it is not considered a disgrace if the girl becomes pregnant before the wedding. Indeed, having had a child may make it easier for the girl to find a husband.

A young African couple frequently starts married life heavily in debt. The wife never knows how much money is owed because her husband would feel himself disgraced if she knew he had to borrow to pay for the wedding. Nor does the husband tell his wife how much he earns—there is no such thing as joint planning of the family budget in West Africa—but he does give her "chop-money" for food and living expenses for herself and the children. There are several reasons for this financial secrecy: women are considered essentially inferior and a husband never treats his wife as an equal; and in the African extended family system both husband and wife remain separate entities whose first loyalty is reserved for their individual families. While the extended family—husband, wife, children and numerous relatives—provides innumerable occasions for the practice of charity, it does cause friction and is the main source of in-law trouble in Africa. Relatives often make unreasonable demands, largely financial, on the man, to the extent that he is sometimes obliged to contribute to the education and support of his sister's children to the detriment of his own. At the same time the wife finds herself in the dilemma of trying to make her husband and children happy without alienating his relatives.

Polygamy is one of the severest challenges presented to African Catholic women. If a husband takes a second wife, or concubines, his first wife is expected to put up with the situation and say nothing. In some cases she must even help her husband to make arrangements with the second woman's family. Among the non-Christians, the wives usually get along well together, helping each other with the work and in caring for the children, with each wife living in her own one-room house opening out on a central yard. Polygamy is a strong obstacle to the conversion of non-Catholics and recent political events have only served to entrench the practice. Now that some of the territories have become independent it has become fashionable to be ultra-African in clothing, names, and customs. Since the view is common that polygamy is an African phenomenon that cannot be changed, many men, some of them Catholics, who before would have been ashamed to confess that they had second wives, now flaunt their polygamy openly, claiming that it makes them more African. The Church's position, of course, is that polygamy is strictly non-Christian, and that there is nothing irrevocably African about it.

One of the most pernicious family problems in West Africa today is the widespread malnutrition which stems from poor distribution and preparation of foods rather than a shortage in the area. Malnutrition is not restricted to the poor but is found also among the educated who eat imported foods whose value is more in prestige than nutrition—white bread, for instance, in preference to some of the cheap but nutritious local beans and grains.

In spite of their repressed social conditions, West African women are usually financially independent. They earn money by farming, trading, cooking and selling food at small stands, or by teaching, nursing or working in offices. While this financial independence is responsible for the growing political strength of women—there are currently ten women M.P.'s in Ghana—it has also created difficulties.

Single girls who leave rural areas to work in towns and cities have the problem of finding decent places to live and also friends and recreation; there is a great need for hostels and social clubs under Catholic auspices. Working mothers in Africa, as everywhere else, have the predicament of what to do with their children during the day. Among the poor, children may accompany their mothers to the fields or trading centers, but among the educated the habit has arisen of leaving the children at home with maidservants who are mostly illiterate and even of questionable moral character. Still, work is an economic necessity for most women and with the emergence of independent African nations

Women in Ghana are beginning to take jobs in industry.

it has become a social necessity as well, since the young states need the services of educated women particularly in order to accelerate their development.

It has been said that if you educate a man you educate an individual, whereas if you educate a woman you educate a family. The women of West Africa want education, they want a better life for themselves and their families, and are certain to play an important part in changing family patterns. The visit to Lomé showed me an independence celebration typical of the enthusiasm for national freedom which is sweeping over Africa today. It showed me, too, that the women of West Africa mean business.

A village scene on the road to Tamale.

Chapter Twenty-Seven

Nation on the Move

THE ROAD from Kpandu to Tamale is three hundred miles of sheer delight for a traveler, if not for the owner of a car. The road begins as a dusty red dirt highway to Keta Krachi, a town developed by German settlers at the turn of the century and still bearing the orderly marks of their colonization—long avenues of mango trees, strong bridges which have worn well for half a century, civic buildings in the center of the town. Driving on from there the country is open bush variety, and one can get views over wide areas until reaching the eastern frontier of Ghana, where there is a range of mountains, thickly forested at the base, but ending in grass and bare rock. The mountains rise to about three thousand feet and are very steep. They boast waterfalls, torrents and great pools of crystal-clear water, as well as shaded forests within which the dark shelter of gigantic trees tempts one from the boiling sun of the road.

But on from Keta Krachi the road changes into a track with deep furrows made by countless wheels grinding into its sandy surface. The small Volkswagen in which I was driving to visit the Grail team in Tamale constantly had its "belly" scraped as we see-sawed between the ruts. But I was glad that we could do only about twenty miles an hour because the people on the road fascinated me.

It was like a giant pageant, passing along this road to the north, which leads to Tamale, Nandom, and then on to Timbuktu and the mysterious reaches of the Sahara. I have found none to put beside it among all the roads I've traveled across five continents. Here come a group of women on the way to market, teasing and laughing, with baskets of bananas and yams on their heads, bare of breast and with vivid cotton cloths wrapped around their waists and hips, and tagging along behind them an incredibly small girl with a bundle of firewood twice her length. Now a man wobbling along on a bicycle with a bow and arrows slung over his shoulder and a dozen pelts of small furry animals tied to the handlebars. A bicycle and a bow and arrows keeping company together—thus old meets new on so many roads of the world today. Now come a band of singing, shouting young men and boys with an assortment of dogs—they too have been hunting and carry bows and arrows, and call to us, "Yani-Yani-Yani," as we pass. Now a flock of sheep, trotting briskly along, then pausing to nibble at the vegetation beside the road; they don't look tired and yet our driver told me they may have been driven several hundred miles already on the way to market to be slaughtered. Not far away is a herd of cattle crossing the road, and two skinny imps dressed only in grass hats cracking their whips and jumping up on the back of the last animal to take a neat dive away from the wheels of the car. Here come a pair of wandering troubadours with crude instruments in their hands, calabashes covered with iguana skin and stringed with horsehair—such is the road with its thousand pictures, scuttling guinea hens, intense heat, and, for me, endless fascination.

The last fifty miles is surfaced with bitumen and we sped along in comparative ease through a monotonous stretch of undulating grass country covered with small trees. We swept past ramshackle trucks crammed with persons and produce, so tightly pressed together that bodies, clothes, sacks and baskets looked as one. *Iron Boy, Love Thy Neighbor, Don't Say Die,* were some of the names adorning the sides of these pell-mell rickety transports on this final stretch of road.

At journey's end were Catherine Bagley from Queensland, Australia, and Evelyn Pugh from Brooklyn, New York, who have just begun work in the Tamale Diocese with Bishop Gabriel Champagne, W.F. This bush bishop, with his finger on every new current in the Church, was among the first of the bishops of West Africa to ask for Grail personnel. After a visit in 1958 from Rachel Donders, our international president, it was decided our best contribution to the northern territories of Ghana would be an education team, so Catherine accepted a government post at Women's Training College and is the only Catholic on the teaching staff there, while Evelyn is working out a diocesan program of adult and mass education in collaboration with the government community development department.

Tamale, where they live in a pink stucco government bungalow, is the capital of the northern region, and is a large market town, administrative and educational center, surrounded by many villages. Until quite recently the Diocese of Tamale included the newly-created Diocese of Wa, where through the work of the White Fathers, thousands of the Dagarti tribe came into the Church in a miracle of mass conversion just over twenty-five years ago. The new Bishop of Wa, Bishop Peter Dery, was the first of the tribe to be baptized, and has the astounding record of making the step from baptism to the episcopacy in a quarter of a century—almost unheard-of in the Church up till now—but then everything is moving more swiftly in Africa than in any other part of the world. With the division of the diocese, Bishop Champagne begins all over again to build the Church, as the Tamale section of the former diocese retains only a handful of Christians in a largely Moslem and pagan area.

Catherine, the only daughter in a large family of boys, was born in the coastal town of Mackay and grew up there in tropical North Queensland. Her family likes to tell how she was born during a hurricane, and was baptized at once under the tap at the kitchen sink, as the whole town was in danger of destruction. But in spite of this tempestuous entrance into the world, Catherine has an immovable quality, a sureness and right judgment, which was a staff for many of us during the hectic pioneering days of the Grail in Australia.

After graduating from Queensland University, Catherine was one of the first five Australians to join the international Grail team then at work in Sydney. Soon she was taking responsibility at the *Arrows Club,* which the Grail established as a service for women of the Armed Forces during the war years. At war's end, the movement had to be developed nationally, and Catherine became state president of the Grail in New South Wales. During this time she managed the Catholic Central Library in Sydney, which was a headquarters for new ideas in lay apostolic circles there. The now eminent Australian poet, James McAuley, read his poetry for hours on end to students and young family people as they crowded in between the stacks in the basement library. But being a member of an international movement, you can't help knowing the universal needs of the Church in the mission areas to which the Grail is committed. Catherine began taking postgraduate studies in education at Sydney University, and in 1959 she was ready to take her present strategic post at the Women's Training College in Tamale. At the college she is in close daily contact with those precious people in a new nation, the educated women, who, because they are still so few, exert an influence far outweighing their numbers.

Working alongside Catherine is Brooklyn born and bred Evelyn Pugh, a large, warmhearted, laughing person who is "natural" for community development. Evelyn, with her seven years' experience in charge of the Women's Section of the Extension Department of St. Francis Xavier University, Antigonish, Nova Scotia, and her flair for making friends, brings a special gift to the work in the arid, dustblown north. I was with her one of the first days after her arrival. Catherine wanted to show us the big market at the height of its bargaining in mid-morning. It lies in sprawling disorder over about two town blocks in the heart of Tamale. It was packed with men, women and children, dressed in every conceivable color and type of clothes—the long white flowing robes of the Moslems, the blue and white striped short tunics of the northern tribesmen, the large colorful turbans of the Nigerians. Then there were the traders from Navarongo, surrounded by glaring multicolored baskets, who looked like a walking cloud of color as they pitched their stalls on the edge of the throng. Over the meat market hovered huge vultures whose wings would touch you as they swept down to gather a sliver of flesh from the new-cut skins lying in the mud and filth. In these teeming warrens, everything is on sale: chickens, sheep, cows, goats. Cheap European goods—razor blades, beds, iron pots, enamel bowls—nestle side by side with kola nuts, ginger roots, yams and silk kente cloth for chiefs and kings.

Evelyn was in her element. Without the language, she still managed to hold conversations. I watched her spend half an hour with a market woman whose soapbox counters sold rice, cigarettes, peeled oranges and roasted bananas to passing townsfolk. One by one Evelyn fingered the items and repeated the names after the woman, who was happy to have this foreigner as an added attraction to her store. Other women gathered round, and then Evelyn got the idea to try and balance a basket on her head like the rest. There was a great flurry of excitement and everyone began to gather as time after time the big basket toppled off and Evelyn, laughing with them all, would begin all over again to set it on her head. It was the sideshow of the day, but Catherine and I, with our stiffer Anglo-Saxon inhibitions, left the field to this jolly Brooklyn Celt, and retreated to a dignified distance to enjoy it all from afar. Evelyn's work is with the people, and week after week now finds her in the villages and markets, in the meeting places and on the streets, getting to know the women, their needs and hopes in this time of swift transition.

I was told by mass education officers in Ghana that the success of the community development programs depends on the extent to which the people themselves become emotionally identified with the program. Such identification gives community development the character of a movement, providing strength and a sense of purpose over a whole country.

At the village of Tolon about sixteen miles from Tamale, Evelyn and I attended a local meeting with Johanna Gordon, a senior government mass education officer, a Scottish Catholic with eleven years service in Ghana. We were greeted on arrival with a crowd of singing people; the chant rose and fell, growing more and more dynamic as the people danced to the rhythm. I asked what they were singing which created such a wave of enthusiasm. This is the literal translation they gave me.

> Education is good, knowledge brings health and happiness.
> We listen, we do, we grow strong in knowledge.
> Welcome, welcome, welcome.

These people were literally caught up in an idea, and as we walked through the village, we observed the prestige of the voluntary mass education officer. He wore his community development badge, a large celluloid affair, and stood beside the Chief when the inevitable picture was taken. A year before, I was told, he had just been one of the crowd, and Tolon had no visiting clinic, no drains, no covered well, no literacy program—but "knowledge is good," and now the whole village was behind him.

This volunteer had been trained in Tamale at the Social Welfare Rural Training Center, along with twenty-two other leaders from twenty-two villages in the area. Johanna Gordon with her staff of three African women is responsible for the programs there, and it can be easily seen what a wide influence a very few informed skilled people can have on a large number of local people. It is with Johanna Gordon and her team that Evelyn has begun to work, and their approach is completely in tune with this period of history in Africa.

In Ghana there are four phases in the community development program, which is considered by U.N. officials as the most advanced in Africa today: adult literacy campaigns; women's work; village improvement; extension services in cooperation with other government departments.

Adult literacy campaigns are run once a year for a period of three months. During this period the people are taught the elements of reading and writing, chiefly in their own local language. This work is done by voluntary instructors, who are gleaned from officials, teachers, or any other literate persons in the vicinity. In a period of six years, according to a government report, 150,000 persons have been made literate.

Women's work is carried on through organized clubs and groups, led by voluntary leaders from among the women themselves. These groups are a pillar of strength to the village communities when the people discuss their needs and try to meet them. The women also strongly support the literacy campaigns as they have suffered far more than the men from lack of education. But by far the most important part of the women's work is the instruction which is given regularly for women in nutrition, health and hygiene. According to an official report, more than 14,000 women are enrolled in various groups throughout Ghana.

Women in Ghana have a special place in society. In large areas of the country, mostly in the south, matrilineal succession is still the custom, and by tradition the queen mother plays an important role in the selection of chiefs. Women are an important element, too, in Nkrumah's party, the C.P.P. They dominate most of the petty trading and make a substantial contribution to the economy of Ghana. Their importance in bringing about a Christian social order should not be underestimated.

The women are quick to give expression to that element of "movement." You see groups of them dressed in special "community development" cloth—printed cottons, emblazoned with various slogans: "education is good," "knowledge gives freedom," or simply the letters of the alphabet and the President's face.

The third and fourth phases of the community development plan in Ghana embrace village improvement and extension services. The former comes about when the villagers have seen both the need to improve their conditions and way of life and the practical possibility of doing so. It is best to direct enthusiasm to a project that can be rather quickly achieved. An extensive scheme should be avoided as a starter. Across the country I saw roads, bridges, school buildings, community centers, dispensaries, water facilities, road levelling, street tarring and concrete drains as common village improvement projects. As well, there are dozens of village brass bands which certainly enrich life and entertainment for this warm, joyful African people. In Jirapa in the Diocese of Wa I saw a village improvement team go into action to obtain the use of a bulldozer to scoop out a new dam for the hospital of the Franciscan Missionaries of Mary. And perhaps the biggest village improvement project tackled as yet is the Apapam-Akropong Road in the Eastern region. The people of Apapam, a small village of under a thousand inhabitants, had to travel one hundred twenty miles around the mountain to Akropong. Finally, after thirty years of pleading with officials for a road, an engineer was called in and he estimated that the road would cost 80,000 pounds, if all the labor came from the people. With the capital expense taken over by the Cocoa Marketing Board, the people themselves began work. They divided into gangs, each working one day a week on the road, starting from both ends. The top of the mountain has now been surmounted and success is in sight.

The extension services are carried on in collaboration with other government departments—agriculture, health or education. When I was in Ghana, a campaign was going on in behalf of the Ministry of Local Government which had undertaken to educate the masses on the role of "the policemen as a friend, not an enemy of the people."

The importance of the work of an education team such as the one in Tamale with Catherine and Evelyn can hardly be overestimated. Self-help without any domination from above hardly needs stressing. Community development is part of the challenge of progress; political independence in Ghana has accelerated the pace. Given the continuing cooperation of all concerned and the enthusiasm of the people themselves, it cannot but succeed.

After a month in Tamale I was on the road again, still going north—this time accompanying Bishop Champagne "on trek" as he visited all the White Fathers' mission in the far end of the diocese.

Moses, the silent driver, sped along in the cool morning air, the kindly French Canadian bishop beside him quietly giving out the decades of the rosary, with Evelyn and myself answering from the rear. We were heading for Nandom, the farthest northwesterly section of Ghana, through Damongo, Wa, Kaleo, Diffiema, Ko, Jirapa. The early morning coolness was left behind and the heat of the midday sun scorched down on us. The bush by the road was wild now, and suddenly out in front of the car scuttled a family of monkeys; a little farther on were a group of women and girls carrying water. They were thin, and quite tall, with straight backs, and wore just a girdle with a bunch of leaves between the loins. It was the first time I had seen women without clothes, and the bishop explained to me that they may have come from a tribe across the border to the north looking for water. It was an experience for me, as once again I understood the immense transition for so many millions of African people, from age-long customs to the second half of the twentieth century. Here we were with communications and roads and transport and here were these bush women, walking miles to look for that basic necessity, life-giving water. A few miles farther on we stopped near an almost dry waterhole. I saw a man take a handful of dry grass, place it over the small muddy hole into which water had seeped and bend low to suck the water through his primitive filter.

During the week, Bishop Champagne confirmed seven hundred people—it was a deep experience to travel with him, to watch the people running to kiss his ring, to be part of a vast congregation at Mass—two thousand deeply praying people at Nandom in a huge barn of a church made from mud bricks with cement floors; to walk to the Communion table in the great jostling throng of women dressed for the most part in one cloth draped around their waists, and men in short woven tunics, with tribal scars on face and bodies; to listen to the surge of virile singing of the people as one by one they stood to receive the Bread of Life, to watch the babies on their mothers' backs with waving hands reaching out to touch the ciborium—so very much like Asia in a hundred different ways. It is truly we of the West who are so stiff, so conscious of ourselves, when it comes to corporate worship. But here participation was spontaneous, the people of God at worship, singing and praying and eating at the table of the Lord.

Outside I saw two boys chasing one another. The one behind stretched out his hand and pulled on the other's cloth which was draped around his naked body and in a flash the verse from St. Mark was in my mind, "And a certain young man was following him, having a linen cloth wrapped around his naked body, and they seized him, but leaving the linen cloth behind he fled away naked." So many times in Africa the Scriptures come alive: the mud houses and the women at the well drawing water and carrying it away on their heads in round stone jars; the man with an animal skin slung over his shoulder, the skin filled with "pito," the common drink in these regions; the woman mixing meal in a stone jar; the backs bent over yam-mounds as people patiently hand-hoe field after field; the children squatting under a tree, listening to a catechist telling stories; the sick being carried by their friends to the dispensary outside the church on Sundays, one being brought in on a litter and left at the doorstep of the church, to "be present" while he waited for medical treatment.

The great gaping wounds, the leprosy, the blindness, the crippled limbs were all there. And we had so pitifully little to offer, in spite of the time in which we live—no real hospital, no real drugs, no X-ray, no laboratory—but wave after wave of suffering people. I remember the pain on the face of the White Sister as she told me: "This one must die; I have nothing I can help her with. This one, I am not sure what disease she has; there is no doctor here and I cannot diagnose this."

There is a lack of water and the land is dry and parched as the people wait for the rainy season to come. Some women when I was there in April were walking six and seven miles each way to a waterhole, and carrying the water back on their heads. They had been doing this daily for the preceding five weeks. These same women fetched their water in the night so as to be ready for Sunday Mass. They walked to the church another eleven miles in the opposite direction.

The faith of the people is deep and strong, their participation in the liturgy is vigorous and genuine, their lives seem remote from the changing times. One prays earnestly for a peaceful transition here. Yet there are shadows in all this light, as an educated son or daughter here or there goes off to Kumasi or Accra and comes back with new ideas and hot talk of freedom and rights and bitterness against the white man from the West. Of course it is good and inevitable that the changes come—the Church desires this, but how clearly we must understand the situation, and how swift we must be to witness to Christian justice and social teachings. And yet it is not always possible to meet the need. The mission bishops have very little money or personnel to do a giant's task. I understood this as we drove those hundreds of miles with Bishop Champagne, and he discussed some of the problems facing him, and the urgency he feels to have the Church's social teaching made swiftly available to the educated Catholics, in order to give them practical knowledge for the handling of everyday situations. Trade unionism is just beginning, and in Ghana there needs to be a Christian "presence" in its structures. The north is the strength of the Church, and the north is underdeveloped compared to the south, but we have the advantage that for the most part the educated men are Catholics with strong ties with the missions and the White Fathers. As yet there are very few educated Catholic women in the north, but the Franciscan Missionaries of Mary and the White Sisters are making strenuous efforts to fill this gap. The nurses' training school at Jirapa is the most advanced in all the northern region, and the nurses even better equipped than those in Tamale, the capital city of the region.

We turned back, on the road again . . . the stretches of dry savannah grasslands, the red soil shimmering with heat . . . an occasional swoop of a bright blue-feathered bird, and the pad-pad-pad of the cows, herded in a cloud of dust and whipped along by small boys, faces glistening with sweat, and thin black bodies covered with dust. They waved and shouted, "Yani-yani-yani," and I waved back and was content and caught up and so surely part of it all, and fully aware of that human dimension of communication with one another.

Ghana is a nation on the move. Since 1957 it has struck out enthusiastically on its own. The Ghanaians take pride in their identity as Africans—the "African personality," as Nkrumah puts it, means much to them. The people seem driven by the vision of a transformed, industrialized, modern, educated Ghana. They have universal primary education, with some excellent secondary schools, a widespread system of adult education, and a pair of first-class higher institutions. African music, art and general culture are very much alive, and the people take pride in their cultural heritage.

The Republic of Ghana has been a sign and a symbol in Africa as the nation which set off the "Independence Parade." This continent caught up in turbulent change is pregnant with immense possibilities, as millions of men aspire to a new freedom and dignity, and struggle to achieve a synthesis between their African heritage and modern civilization.

PART III Showdown

Sharing news from home with some of the women at the Social Training Center in Mwanza. The students come from all over East Africa and will be responsible to introduce new ideas to their communities.

SHOWDOWN

"Thank God our times are now
when wrong comes up to face us everywhere,
Never to leave us
Until we take the longest stride of soul man ever took.
Affairs are now soul size.
The enterprise
Is exploration unto God."

—Christopher Fry

Chapter Twenty-Eight

Showdown

I HAVE a reason for writing this book, and it is this. During the past ten years I have had the chance to live and work across five continents, and now to be in the compact world community of the United Nations in New York. Because of this experience, I have come face to face with the needs of the family of man—both material and spiritual, and I am deeply troubled by what I have seen and heard. We Christians *are* faced with hard problems and they demand more than a half answer. They demand our full response.

The world has shrunk, the meeting of all men has become a reality. We are confronted with terrible contrasts, as we see fifteen percent of the world's people dispose of eighty-eight percent of the world's resources; as we watch the endless processions of deported, dispossessed, and brutalized human beings on the roads of the world. Our consciences are pricked as we become aware of the growing aspirations of the peoples of the world for education, for economic advancement, for equality and freedom. Into all this yearning and striving of the family of man, into all this chaos, comes international Communism—an idea in full expansion, bringing separation of man from man with its Iron Curtain in Europe and its Bamboo Curtain in Asia, and using the anguish of the human family to win for itself world domination. In West Africa in 1960 and in East Africa in 1961 I have been aware of many of the same things I saw happening in Asia ten years ago. The Communists seize every opportunity to offer technical assistance, to exploit nationalism, to heighten tensions.

We Christians have a key role to play in the growing world community, and we will not play this role without being involved in its problems, without being convulsed by its agonies and inspired by its aspirations. It is in order to challenge us with the needs of our time that I write this book.

Chapter Twenty-Nine

One Sky

THAT WE all live under the same sky on the same globe has not been news since the time of Vasco da Gama and Christopher Columbus; but today's global communications have telescoped time and distance into a smallness that makes us feel like Alice in Wonderland, as the whole earth shrinks into one tiny neighborhood.

A jet takes off from Idlewild in New York and swoops down in London six hours later; someone in Sydney twirls a knob on his radio and listens to a speech in Tokyo; a businessman picks up his telephone in Chicago and speaks to his partner in Amsterdam; a small refugee boy off the streets of Hong Kong sits beside his American classmates in a parochial school in Detroit. Physical interdependence has become a fact for a large part of humanity. What has not accompanied this sudden development is a corresponding enlargement of the sense of mankind's moral interdependence. The fact that through press and film, radio and TV, we know more about each other does not necessarily mean that we understand each other any better. The "I see" of the tourist or TV viewer does not always mean "I understand," let alone, "I appreciate." In other words, though the physical barriers to unity have been removed, the truth that all men are one-in-Christ is as shadowy and remote for most of us as before the great discoveries which brought the whole world onto a single map and into a single communications network.

We have to try to become aware of ourselves as members of one human family, intrinsically bound up with each other, in deep unity even in diversity. Our first cries may have broken the air in the high white peaks of the Himalayas or the Andes; in the sodden steaming jungles along the Limpopo or the Amazon; in the steel-ribbed cities of the world or in its fertile valleys and plains; under the harsh blue sky of the island continent, or in the mists and rains of the northern lands. The place does not matter —it is a human person who is born. The skin that covers us may be yellow, black, brown or white; and we speak as many tongues as there are sparrows chirping on telegraph poles. We plough the earth, we fish, we hunt, we provide shelter and food and clothing, we sing, we weep, we laugh, we love, we worship, we die.

But we are not two billion nine hundred and fifty million points on a chart; we are living breathing people who desire to love and to be loved. We are the family of man.

Chapter Thirty

And Most of Us Are Hungry

HAVE YOU ever had a nightmare? The kind that keeps on coming back: first when you were ten years old, and later when you were perhaps eighteen, and again and again at intervals as you grow to maturity. For me it is always the same theme, now from one angle, now from another, but always to do with hungry people.

If you are inclined to be flippant, you may retort: "That's easy. As a baby, your mother must have missed your feeding time." She didn't. Fact of the matter was, so my family tells me, there never was a baby who ate as I did! So it must be something else. I only know that I am acutely aware of the ever present economic crisis in the world. Years of reporting CRS-NCWC relief distribution, sitting on the UNICEF subcommittee at the United Nations now, only heighten this knowing of the struggle of the world's hungry people for food.

Every night two-thirds of us go to sleep with hunger cramps because we have no food to nourish us. There are famines and floods and wars and migrations, and we starve; while in other places the earth yields huge surpluses of food, which are ploughed back in, or stored at astronomical expense, or left to rot.

Try to imagine a line starting at your kitchen door made up

of the hungry people of the world. The line forms, and then goes on out of sight, over continent and ocean, around the world 25,000 miles and returns to your kitchen door. On and on it stretches, circling the earth not twice, not five times, but twenty-five times, and everyone in that line is a hungry person.

Or, if we drove ten hours a day, averaging fifty miles an hour, it would take us three and a half years to cover the present line of hungry people—and that line is expanding twenty miles a day. Undernourishment calls forth the most basic urge in man, the urge for survival. It is this which has made hunger one of the most fundamental and explosive forces in history and in the world today.

It is difficult to know what hunger is when we haven't experienced it at first hand, but let me describe one woman, who in a way can stand for all women, in this great mass of hungry people.

The place is Hong Kong, where 300,000 completely destitute refugees bed down on the sidewalk each night. Hundreds of thousands of people go hungry every day in Hong Kong, so when an announcement is made that there will be a distribution of food relief, it does not take long for a crowd to gather. Patient crowds, who move slowly and know how to wait.

It was a dark drizzly morning. My right shoulder was numb from carrying the heavy camera case. It had hung there for over three hours as I sloshed up and down the narrow alley taking pictures. I was tired and cold and sad. I sat on the edge of the gutter and began idly taking "pot-shots" of those gray, huddled figures squatted shoulder to shoulder against the dirty brick wall. I focussed on a woman with a wailing infant on her arm and two tiny girls curled between her legs to keep warm.

It was the anguish on the mother's face that held me. Deep lines of suffering etched around her mouth, her endless patience with the children, her own cramped position to shelter them. I took a few shots of the little group. Shortly after she caught my attention again. She was edging her way to her feet, slowly and painfully. Then I saw her rally all her resources, step out of place in the line and walk to the social welfare worker who was giving out the cold cooked rice.

The woman pointed to her flattened breasts and said in a low voice, "It is not food I want for myself, it is milk for my baby." And she began to weep. There was no milk. In desperation she took a handful of rice; she had no container to receive it, just her cupped hand. She stumbled back to her place opposite me. I saw her look at the little wizened scrap of humanity in the crook of her arm, then back at the rice, place it in her own mouth, chew it to make it soft and warm, then take it from her mouth and place it in that of her baby. This is hunger. This is destitution.

The modern meeting of men brings all humanity, and especially us Christians, face to face with hard problems. Is peace possible in our time if one-third of the world's population grows richer and richer while two-thirds gets poorer and poorer? Can we hope to Christianize people if we have not first helped them to stay alive at more than a starvation level?

Chapter Thirty-One

And Millions Are Uprooted

D.P.'S, EXPELLEES, deportees, evacuees, refugees—how many new words have become part of our daily vocabulary in this time, words which our grandmothers would not have understood, but all intended to describe the same thing, people who have lost their homes. Millions of people in our time—more than 16,000,000 in the last decade to be exact—have been taken from their cities and villages and towns in the greatest uprooting the world has ever known. Driven like leaves in a storm over the face of the earth, fleeing from oppression and horror or moved about like pawns in the political game, refugees from the homes of the rich as well as the poor, this throng of vulnerable strangers are forced to meet with strangers, being received sometimes in love, many times with indifference, sometimes with hostility.

Let us take a closer look. One day in Korea, I flew in a helicopter in the Chun-chon area near Panmunjon. We hovered low in order to get pictures of the refugees pouring south. I saw trains so filled with people that arms and legs and heads stuck out of the carriage windows and people clung to the bumper bars between the cars. The roads were a mêlée of frightened people: mothers pushing their bedding and cooking pots in wheelbarrows in front of them, burdened at the same time with two or more children clinging to their backs. Sometimes a truck limping south, already overcrowded, would stop as people reached out to be taken on top. Perhaps a mother and some children would struggle on, and the father with the rest of the family would be left behind, with only the remotest chance of ever being reunited.

And from the midst of these uprooted ones, a close-up of one refugee. I saw her, a young woman, standing apart from the crowd in the receiving post. She was standing alone, and her complete stillness isolated her from the others as they milled around, untying bundles and staking out small sections of the floor for their families.

The commanding officer told me that she was in a state of shock, having seen her husband and baby killed instantly when a truck overturned a few hours earlier. Her hands hung loose at her side, empty and open, those hands which had been forced to let go all the familiar things—her rice bowls and sleeping mats, the needles and thread and cloth from which she stitched her family's clothes, the warm living clasp of her husband, the child she had nurtured for so short a time.

For perhaps half an hour I could think of no way to approach her—those hands, empty and open—balked me. I had so much and she had nothing. Then I saw a cross on a chain round her neck, and I pulled mine out over my parka and went over and took her hands in mine, and she began to weep. We sat down on the floor together and later slept. I spoke no Korean and she spoke no English, but the next morning when we walked up the hill to Mass at the Seoul Cathedral I think she understood that she was not alone, but with Christ on His Cross.

This continuing tragedy of the driven men, women and children making their way along the roads of the world remains one of the major issues of our time.

In India about one person in forty-two is a refugee; in Vietnam one in twelve; in Pakistan one in eleven; in Korea one in four; and in Hong Kong one in three.

In the Middle East there are 1,350,000 refugees including the Arabs in Syria, Lebanon, Iraq, Jordan and the Gaza strip, some of whom have been waiting ten years in wretched camps for resettlement. A tragic factor, mentioned more than once in U.N. debates on the Arab refugee question, is the danger that this human misery will be exploited for political ends.

In Europe there are still 6,000,000 refugees, among them "the hard core"—the aged, the ill, the unemployable—for whom the nations refuse to open their doors. And from behind the Iron Curtain new refugees continue to pour into West Germany; over 250,000 arrived last year alone.

Refugees are not new in human history—always there have been men who left their homelands for political or religious reasons to find asylum elsewhere. But it is the mark of the twentieth century that it is almost impossible for the refugee to find a new home. In a world divided among sovereign nations, today's refugees taste the truth of that wry Russian proverb, "A man consists of a body, a soul and a passport." Facing almost insurmountable immigration barriers, shunted from place to place because they lack the all-important "papers," demoralized by prolonged periods in refugee camps, these millions of unfortunates make ours the "Century of the Homeless."

Chapter Thirty-Two

And Always There Is Sickness

BECAUSE of all the uprooting, because of hunger and malnutrition, because of ignorance and lack of sanitation and limited supplies of medicine, inevitably there is sickness. I remember some makeshift hospitals with three patients to a bed—two on top, and one underneath, with three different diseases. Thousands of swollen stomachs bulge out at me from photos I've taken of children made grotesque with beriberi; there are chests racked by coughing; eyes glazed by trachoma; lean brown bodies quivering with malaria; the gaping sores of yaws; limbs twisted in pain; lips parched with fever.

And once again I am confronted with the sickening contrasts of the haves and the have-nots. Mulling over statistics at the United Nations I found that there are 1,200,000 trained doctors in the world—925,000 of them in North America and Europe. In other words, three-quarters of the world's medicos confine their attention to one-quarter of the world's people. In Ghana there is only one doctor for every 23,000 people and in Pakistan one for every 35,000.

An American child at birth may expect to live seventy years; but life expectancy in Costa Rica is only fifty-six, in Egypt thirty-eight, and in India a mere thirty-two years. Then these figures merge into faces and I think about the people whom I have known who are not privileged white westerners; and I go back to a day in Korea when all I had was a camera.

Down along that alley in Pusan, hawkers cried stridently. Infants strapped to their mothers' backs wailed from pain and cold and hunger. Weary people huddled in an endless coiling queue that stopped at a sign on a wooden gate, "Maryknoll Sisters' Clinic."

All day I had worked there with my camera, getting pictures and human interest stories which could be used in America for CRS-NCWC. In the late afternoon, returning to the lane to see how many people were still waiting, I saw a woman huddled near a wall with a grey-blanketed bundle hugged to her breast.

She kept peering anxiously at her burden and I became curious to see why she was so concerned. I tugged at the blanket and she looked up at me with such a longing in her eyes that I tugged a little harder.

I saw a child of about three years covered with smallpox, not a sound spot on the whole body or face. A slit for the child's mouth breathed out hot gasps of breath over a black hard tongue like a sun-dried piece of wet leather, and all I had was a camera. It could not heal, it could only record this misery.

Then Sister Mercy came, but it was too late to do anything to help the child, and the supply of penicillin had run out. Water was brought to moisten the child's mouth and some rice was given to the mother.

Later I watched this refugee woman disappear into the dusk to her home on the curb with her precious bundle, baptized now, another Christ filling up in his tiny body what is wanting to the conversion of the world in our time.

I turned to look for my transportation back to the correspondent's billet. Sister Mercy walked with me to the gate. We heard a faint cry, and I saw her stoop and pick up a tiny baby abandoned in the corner of the lane. She looked worn and grey, this Maryknoll Sister-doctor, but when I saw her lift that child to her cheek, then gather him under her coat to make him warm, I saw in a little minute Christ's love, Christ's passion being lived out now, and I knew surely that all the suffering of the people in the alley and all the toil of the nurses and doctors with too much to do, are part of the redeeming Cross in our time.

Chapter Thirty-Three

New Aspirations Stirring

THE MOST deep-rooted, long-cherished hopes of man to find some measure of security and peace and freedom are compelling now as never before in history, as all nations and races are caught up in the modern communications network.

The Filipino worker threshing sugar cane around his barrio knows how his counterpart in Australia or America lives. He too wants a house that doesn't leak, and education for his children, and perhaps a bicycle and a radio when he is not at work in the canefields. The educated African in Accra, Ibadan or Kampala has a burning desire to have all the things his professional counterpart enjoys in Liverpool, Pittsburgh or Sydney.

The people of the newly emerging nations aspire not only to economic betterment and political freedom, but to a full development of themselves in education, social welfare and culture. Kwame Nkrumah, President of Ghana, voiced this aspiration at the First Conference of Independent African States in Accra in 1958: "I say that once Africa is free and independent, we shall see a flowering of the human spirit second to none. . . . Some of us, I think, need reminding that Africa is a continent on its own. It is not an extension of Europe or any other continent. We want therefore to develop our own community and an African personality." Among African intellectuals there is a passionate insistence on the need to form a synthesis of African character and Western civilization. "We want to be civilized Africans, not Europeans with black skins. While assimilating the values of Western civilization, we want to remain ourselves. We ask of the West an effort to understand our legitimate aspirations and to help us to achieve them." Archbishop Denis Hurley, O.M.I., of Durban, South Africa, has pointed out that the vigor of an awakened Africa, which has been manifested thus far mainly in the political sphere, may be expected to overflow into art, writing, philosophy. "Shall we see African Platos and Aristotles, Augustines and Aquinases, Dantes, da Vincis, Michelangelos and Shakespeares?" he asks. "The stage is set for such developments, with a people suddenly awakened to a vision beyond the wildest dreams of their fathers and roused to a terrible hunger for knowledge and accomplishment."

Basically, the Christian must sympathize with the tremendous aspirations astir among the newly emerging nations. The Church has always been concerned that men attain their full human dignity and realize their potentialities. Whatever contributes to the true development of the person prepares the way for grace.

"Freedom" is the rallying cry which sums up all the new aspirations, but there is a danger that men may fail to realize the work and responsibility that freedom entails. William Hessler, writing in the *Reporter,* makes this comment: "The typical African's notion of freedom has little or nothing to do with democratic self-government, or civil rights, or citizens' obligations—and certainly nothing to do with such distasteful things as taxes. For him, independence means catching up with the living standards of the white western world— at once. African leaders who know better are too preoccupied with freedom and its attainment to bother with telling uneducated followers about the long uphill road which lies ahead of them."

Freedom may be the end of the nationalist struggle, but it is only the beginning of a long agenda of new problems, dimly seen, if at all, by the rank and file. The leaders of Africa and

Asia know that in order to meet the ferment of longing, immense problems must be solved: roads, rail and waterways built; communications systems established; agriculture improved; hydroelectric and other sources of power developed; industry and commerce encouraged; modern forms of government introduced; hospitals and medical care provided. They also know that too few have the education to achieve these improvements.

The first time I took a straight look on a world level at the literacy figures I was staggered. It is hard to believe that in this time, when we are faced with astounding developments in science and technology, more than half the world can't read.

I have seen in Central Java, in Togoland, Ghana and Sierra Leone, village schools packed night after night with adults, as a fundamental education program got under way. For men and women struggling for survival, literacy can rarely be an end in itself. So the experts link the three "R's" to the needs of the illiterate adults—to health, sanitation, nutrition, farming methods. The new terms in our vocabulary—"basic education," "mass education," "community development,"—all indicate the consuming thirst for knowledge on the part of the common people.

But an education program must do more than teach the ABC's to the illiterate. It must prepare leaders, well-educated and capable of carrying top level responsibility, and technicians able to carry on the manifold services demanded by modern civilization. A modern nation needs machinists and merchant mariners, engineers, soil conservationists, statisticians, financiers, school teachers, journalists, legislators, executives—and on this level of administrative and technical personnel the numbers are dangerously thin.

Tanganyika, for example, which got its first African majority government in 1960, has around one thousand, five hundred key jobs in public service, administration and technology. Tanganyika needs this many civil servants in order to function as a state. Today there are about three hundred fifty Africans who qualify for these posts, with another one hundred fifty graduating from school this year. Nigeria is better off and has a larger educated group to draw on. It has a university at Ibadan with over a thousand students, and there are about eight thousand Nigerians studying in universities overseas.

It is worth noting that in most countries of Africa, and some of Asia, education has been largely the work of the missions with some government support in recent years. Without the work of the Christian missions during the past fifty years, education in most of Africa would be practically nonexistent today, and the new African nations would be starting out with an insurmountable handicap.

Expectations run high in the new nations. Leaders may have promised the moon to their constituents in order to get into power. Too often a tragic gap yawns between expectations and reality, and disillusion threatens. The rapid changes—industrialization, urbanization, detribalization—tend to produce social disorganization. The Communist idea thrives on this kind of chaos and discontent, and the Russians come to Africa with "clean hands" so far as colonialism is concerned. By and large, they are regarded as people from another underdeveloped area who have made good in an amazingly short time. Where the white Westerner is inevitably associated with the former colonial powers and hence regarded with some distrust, the Russians may make themselves acceptable.

And the Communist influence is there—I saw Communist news agencies in Ghana in all the major centers, in Togoland, in Sierra Leone, and more markedly in Guinea. There were very few American correspondents anywhere in tropical Africa, and news agencies are a two-way traffic. Embassies from the USSR and the satellite nations are much in evidence as well.

To meet the revolution of rising expectations is a gigantic task. Perhaps the first requirement is sympathy without condescension for peoples striving to span centuries of human development in years, if not in months. The second requirement is in terms of concrete aid, funds and expert assistance, through private and public means, through foundations, businesses, scholarships. In stirring the currents of sympathy and practical help, the members of the universal Church have a special responsibility. To quote a recent directive of the Holy See to the Catholic International Organizations: "Even at the price of great sacrifice on their part, Catholics must strive tirelessly after the human betterment and Christian development of the less-favored nations and peoples."

Chapter Thirty-Four

International Communism

BOUNCING along the rutted, twisted road from Panmunjon back to Seoul after the first exchange of the prisoners of war through Freedom Village, I tried to get my thoughts straight on what makes Communism tick. All day I had been sitting on a narrow wooden bench in the yellow tent following the exchange between the truce delegates, and I was tired of grappling with this thing which I only partly understood.

I knew the political commissar did not lie when to a group of Catholic Chinese prisoners of war headed by Melchior Liu he said: "Our popular democracy has two great enemies: materially, America; spiritually, the pope and the Catholic Church. We can't establish our regime over the whole world, for your Church and its head will always oppose us. You Catholics are even worse enemies of the people than the Americans."

Six years have gone by since that afternoon in Korea, and I have come to know a little more about international Communism from a variety of people. I met Douglas Hyde in Hong Kong, who was for twenty years a Communist Party member, and an active Marxist writer; and Father Francis Dufay, M.E.P., the French Marxist scholar, was one of the priests in our parish at Taikoolau. I have listened for hours on end at the United Nations to Andrei Fomin, who is the counsellor and senior advisor of the USSR to the Economic and Social Council; and to Arkady Aleksandrovich Sobolev, who for years has been permanent representative there; as well, I have followed the full debate on the Five Member Special Committee Report on Hungary in the General Assembly.

In order to understand Communism we have to try to put ourselves in the "other fellow's shoes." Any Communist who judged the Church on its external activities would be very wide of the mark of its real import and reason for being. In the same way, for us to grasp the full import of Communism, we have to try to examine it from within. I have talked with people who are Communists, people who have tried Communism and been disillusioned, people who have suffered under its system. From my experience and observations four major points have emerged: Communism is a fact; it is a philosophy; it is a historical, economic and social theory, and a political system; it is a mystique in action, based on primitive emotions and instincts.

Communism is a fact. For a long time ignored, its strength underestimated, its doctrines spurned, today it has become the foremost political problem in the world. Around Communism, for or against it, the statesmen and leaders of the world must take up their positions. International Communism is a movement of enormous dynamism. Before World War II, one man out of twelve lived under a Communist regime; today the proportion is one in three. Never before in human history has there been such a rapid spread of an ideology and a system of political control.

Communism is a philosophy, based on materialism and atheism, purporting to give a complete explanation of the world, the way it works, and its ultimate end. Engels states the Communist dogma: "The material, sensuously perceptible world to which we belong is the only reality." Hence, God does not exist, man is not immortal, the individual is a temporary phenomenon, totally subject to the perfection of society. "Religion is the opiate of the people," distracting man from the realities of his situation with promises of "pie in the sky."

As a philosophy, Communism is simple and complete—and this perhaps explains some of its attraction, for a true but complicated idea often has less chance of succeeding than one which is false but simple. Another element which makes Communism tick is its essentially practical outlook. "Hitherto," Marx wrote, "philosophers have only interpreted the world differently; the point is, to change it," and change it he has. As Douglas Hyde states: "Communism is a conscious attempt to recreate creation; to reconstruct the world in the image of matter. Man from a son of God becomes a slave of matter; his life changes from one of harmony born of love to one of discord born of hate." The objective is the new Marxist man, who is the exact opposite of the new man in Christ. If one triumphs, it can only be by the death of the other, or by the conversion of the Marxist world by God's grace.

Communism is a historical, economic and social theory, and a political system to apply the theory. For Marx, the decisive element in human history is the material situation under which men and women work for their living. Everything else—politics, philosophy, art, religion—is simply a reflection and result of the underlying economic arrangements—the way property is divided, the techniques of production, the methods of exchange. As Engels put it in a speech delivered at Marx's grave-side, "Marx discovered the law of evolution in human history . . . the degree of economic development attained by a given people forms the foundation upon which the state institutions, the legal conceptions, the art and even the religious ideas of the people concerned have been evolved and in the light of which these things must therefore be explained."

Thus, feudalism produced the bourgeoisie—the merchants, bankers, industrialists—who destroyed it and founded capitalism. From capitalism comes a class of propertyless workers, the proletariat, who are the antithesis of the bourgeoisie and who established socialism. So each new society is conceived in the womb of the society which preceded it. Each system produces the class which destroys it, but out of the conflict comes the new and higher order of society.

We must recognize, then, that deep in Communist consciousness is the notion that Communists are on the side of history, "the conscious instruments of the historic dialectic process," and that they are identified with the very laws which govern the entire universe. Therefore, they believe that they above all others have the right to mold minds; and they justify any course of action, however brutal, which advances the historic process towards the ultimate classless society.

In order to accelerate this process of change, Communism stimulates the conflicting interests between the haves and the have-nots, the rulers and the ruled. In fact, the Communist Party exists to aid in the class struggle and thereby speed up history. The Party must educate the workers to realize their oppression and the means of deliverance. It must take advantage of poverty, unemployment, exploitation, economic depressions and imperialist wars to promote class warfare. Communism follows the geography of human misery. Only by intensifying conflict between workers and capitalists, colonial subjects and colonizing powers, can the Communists help to destroy the existing system and contribute to the new order which must follow. Since the struggle is world wide, Communist organization must be international.

Once the "expropriators are expropriated," and the proletariat take over ownership of the means of production, the new millennium of the classless society will emerge, the state will "wither away," and society will function according to the ideal, "from each according to his abilities, to each according to his needs."

It has often been pointed out that the Marxist vision of the classless society—which is surely one of the great sources of Communism's appeal—is a kind of secularized version of the Messianic Kingdom. Not German materialistic philosophy so much as passionate Jewish idealism has winged the Communist message. And this brings me to the fourth point.

Communism is a mystique in action. What do I mean by a mystique? A mystique is a faith above rational criticism, charged with a dynamic conviction and directed to action. In a curious way, the Communist mystique is an inversion of the Church. I discussed this at some length with Father Joseph McGinn of Maryknoll after he was expelled from South China.

"You can see so many elements the same," he concluded, "dogma, hierarchy, discipline, intellectual and moral asceticism, sacrifice, driving force of action, and a doctrine of man's fate. The spiritual attitude of the Communist towards his ideology is similar in many ways to the attitude of the Christian towards his faith."

It is Communist re-education which gradually creates the new Marxist man. Minds are turned against the old order, the family, religion, the basic units of society. Evolution of thought helps along a change of institutions, the change in the institutions impresses the new ideas more deeply on the people's minds and causes the process to move another pace forward.

An example is the re-education of the Chinese masses regarding the institution of the family. For seven years indoctrination courses have gone on over the whole land of China, to undermine this strong traditional unit of Chinese society. Then came 1958, the year dedicated by Mao's government to the "great leap forward," and we find now ninety-nine percent of the peasants in people's communes set up in every province. The antlike life of the communes has been greeted abroad with horror in the West, by outspoken distaste in India. Crossing the border to Hong Kong, an Indian population expert who had just made a journey through continental China had this to say: "China is like a big zoo; in all my travels there I never saw any real sense of happiness on any face."

How often have I listened to Radio Canton broadcast the

mass re-education courses being given in South China. Everything is made to contribute to the process—the press, public speeches, festivals, the cinema, day and night, everywhere. In the army, in the schools and Marxist universities, the indoctrination goes on for years.

To press this point home, here is a verbatim report given me by an expelled missionary. He described an indoctrination center, one of many functioning in China today. To courses at this center come returned overseas students, young men and women who for the most part are being trained as village cadres.

People from the area are invited to take part in the public sessions, but the trainees live together and carry on intensified private sessions as well, for periods varying from weeks to months.

"Anyone who witnesses the big public sessions," this priest told me, "becomes conscious of an extraordinary perfection of method, an incomparable handling of crowds. Mass hysteria is deliberately created; it rises and grows, until the depersonalized crowd is no more than an unconscious plaything of the leaders. When the meeting picks on someone for denunciation, a great wave of hatred is released; it is infused, distilled to a degree which becomes appalling. I know nothing more calculated to bewilder than the nocturnal meetings which, literally translated, are called 'recital of the miseries of life.' In the semi-darkness, in strained silence, each member of the actor audience comes in turn to the middle of the circle and weeps at the recollection of his former existence, and the misery and oppression of which he was a victim.

"The sinister lamentation swells," the priest went on, "as the shrill voices of the women, and the cries of vengeance against those responsible for all the many evils of life, rise in intensity. The lowest and most frightening depths are reached when one of the accusers points to the father, mother, wife or child of one of those present. Then indeed one is conscious of the diabolical character of this thing.

"Each person must confess before the assembled company the number of times he has betrayed the Communist ideal and include even his most secret failings. In the course of such a public confession one can see the guilty man sob and even roll himself on the ground in despair."

The atmosphere of these assemblies cannot be described; one must have experienced it for oneself. The victims in the end arrive at the firm conviction that their leaders know all, that they read their very thoughts, and that there is nothing for it but to confess completely to absolutely everything.

Outside these public exercises, I have been told by one who went through them, total silence is enforced; nothing must disturb the time set apart for solitary meditation. After the last public exercises, and towards the end of the course, each one takes solemnly, before the assembled company, the pledge to dedicate his life and blood to the triumph of the Communist ideal throughout the world; each puts himself at the service of humanity.

What I have just described is an appeal to the emotions. The intellectual formation comes from the big Marxist lecture courses and the innumerable study circles. In these everything is dealt with—every sort of human activity, on every conceivable plane, is subjected to criticism under the searchlight of historical materialism.

It is not force as such that ensures the maintenance of the Communist regime, as so many people tend to think. It is rather the penetration into human souls of the Marxist materialistic philosophy. When the penetration is complete the Communist man has unshakable faith in his cause.

So many times I have been asked by Australian and American audiences why it is that the Communists are so fervent, and we Catholics so often mediocre.

I would say that we have not penetrated deeply enough the mysteries of our faith; we have not shown a radical readiness to change, a passionate will to give ourselves to Christ. We put limits on our answer to Christ's call, and our Christian dynamism is smothered.

What is the answer to all this? I will tell you a story, a true story, about a Chinese girl. Kwok Kwoon is just a little thing, quick and responsive, with a shy smile and a listening ear. On the outside there is nothing special about her, she can always pass in a crowd. She looks like millions of other Cantonese girls—that is one reason, I imagine, why she has become "seed" for tomorrow's harvest.

Kwok Kwoon was born into a Buddhist family in Hong Kong. During the war years she came in contact with the Church and was baptized just before the liberation of Hong Kong from the Japanese. She was one of the first girls in Hong Kong to join a lay apostolic group started by Father Nicholas Maestrini, who was then the Director of the Hong Kong Catholic Truth Society. At that time there were no facilities to train lay leaders in Hong Kong so Father Maestrini arranged for two other girls and Kwok Kwoon to come to Grailville in the U.S.A. After two years there, she returned to work with our team in Hong Kong. As a registered teacher she soon got a job on the staff of a large Catholic girls' high school. Shortly after this, word came through that the Bishop of Canton, the biggest city across the border, needed lay helpers to go and work with him, as all the foreign priests and sisters had either been imprisoned or expelled, and there was a great shortage of personnel.

Kwok Kwoon was approached by an expelled missioner from the area to see whether she might go back in. It wasn't something one could urge another to do—the need could be indicated, but the decision finally rested with Kwok Kwoon alone. She knew, as we all knew, it would mean ultimately almost certain imprisonment and possibly death. We prayed to know what God's will was in the matter.

Then Kwok Kwoon said quite simply: "I must go back in. I can do it, no one will notice me. I am a Cantonese; these are my people."

She went home for a few days to see her family. They were not Catholics and could not understand why she should leave a good job in Hong Kong to go to Canton.

We had agreed that we would meet at the Cathedral of the Immaculate Conception for our last Mass together, and to say goodbye. I remember that morning very well. I got there first and after some time, someone slipped in beside me. I didn't recognize Kwok Kwoon. She had been a sophisticated Chinese girl—she had traveled and studied in America—but kneeling beside me I saw a simple village woman. She wore the Cantonese traditional black saam-foo, trousers and short jacket, and held in her hand a little bundle containing all her worldly possessions.

The prayers from the Mass that morning are deep in my heart: "God uses the weak things of this world to confound the strong." Believe me, I felt like a gnat spiritually and a camel physically as I knelt beside my little Chinese colleague. After Mass we came outside. Kwok Kwoon gave me her Missal with the various holy cards, her spiritual reading—two books of Dom Marmion. She left behind her all those external signs of the faith that is in her, those things which we use to bring us nearer to God. Then I said, "Kwok Kwoon, I'll walk you down to the station," but she answered, "No, better not to be seen with a foreigner. It is better to say goodbye here."

I stood with her Missal and books and watched the small figure going down the narrow alley, through those people-packed sidewalks of Hong Kong, and then suddenly she was merged in the midst of the people and I could see her no longer. I was left in Hong Kong, in a city with a house to live in, and a place to eat and things to do, with friends and people whom I knew—and Kwok Kwoon went in alone behind the Bamboo Curtain.

That was 1951. From 1951 to 1954 we had communication with each other. From time to time a letter would come introducing some student who needed help. We had hoped that she would be able to return after a year to renew herself spiritually and physically, but the Communists would not give her an exit permit. She wrote she was raising rabbits for a living, and selling their blood for medicine. We knew her work was producing fruit as young people came across the border from her—her godchildren in Baptism, mine in Confirmation.

Then I heard she had tuberculosis and needed medicine. I sent in cod-liver oil and penicillin with someone, but I never heard that it reached her. Then news came that on the Saturday before Passion Sunday in 1957 she was imprisoned in Canton, along with several Chinese sisters with whom she had been staying since her sickness.

As far as I know, she is there today. For Kwok Kwoon there was no limit in her answer to Christ's call to the apostolate. She had grasped the full import of the Christian call and, without reserve, left everything behind.

Kwok Kwoon is one small "seed," but we can be sure she has counterparts in other areas of the Church of Silence: in Albania, Latvia, Lithuania, Poland, Russia, North Vietnam, North Korea, East Germany, Yugoslavia and the U.S.S.R. It is for us of the free world to bring these seeds to a radiant blossoming.

Chapter Thirty-Five

The Brilliant Game of Love

"URGENCY-URGENCY-URGENCY" ground out the wheels of the "Northern Zephyr" speeding along the Mississippi towards the Twin Cities; "urgency-urgency" clattered the electric train in the subways under the granite city of New York; "urgency" whispered back the moss-grown trees along the bayous of Louisiana. In Pennsylvania and Kentucky, Ohio and California, and a score of other places, I have been constrained a hundred times to begin a lecture with this word "urgency."

Urgency to commit ourselves in this time; to understand deeply the meaning of engagement, involvement, commitment; to focus our hearts and minds until we have the vision of the whole—a vision which means seeing the end in the beginning. The end which is the Redemption brought to all men, and the beginning which is our response in this time to the magnificent, mysterious fact that we Christians have a work to *do* in the fulfillment of God's plan for man.

And I do not mean a half-hearted response, a timid "yes" in vague goodwill, a fumbling inadequate answer to the magnitude of the world's suffering which cries out to be caught up in the redeeming act of love. I mean a daring response, which sees the apostolate as a great tactical adventure in the struggle for the soul of man.

What can we do? Where to begin in the face of the overwhelming problems of the world? People ask me this so often, after a lecture or meeting, that I've been moved to draw up a list of starting points, not exhaustive by any means, but suggestive and within the reach of most of us, personally and in whatever groups or organizations we may belong to. Let me make three concrete suggestions:

First, we can deepen our vision of the Church, of the world's needs, of our own role as adult Christians in these critical times. There is no quick way to this broader, deeper vision. We must take time out to pray and for good, hard, concentrated study of the doctrine of the Mystical Body of Christ with all its implications for our lives.

With this foundation, we can begin to delve into the Christian approach to such world problems as hunger, sickness, population explosions, social and racial justice, education for the millions. In the stories in this book I have tried to translate the abstract problems into concrete people. Thinking of the living men and women, it is not so difficult to know in oneself the sorrow of their plight, the anguish of the hungry and the sick, the privations of the homeless, the fear of the persecuted, the confusion of those subject to Communist indoctrination, the glowing, impractical hopes of the newly free. Growing in com-passion, literally "feeling with" these others and beginning to know their struggles as our own, brings us to a point of action.

For those of us who will remain at home base, there are all the opportunities to provide a current of better formed and informed public opinion. We can work through all the modern means of communication to rouse a universal concern among Catholics to strive for social justice and love the world over.

We can foster Christian attitudes and practices with regard to racial and cultural differences in our own environments.

We need not go far to meet some of the tensions caused by racial and cultural differences—they exist in our own neighborhoods and cities. Injustice, especially racial injustice, doesn't stay in our own back yard—it reverberates around the world, as Little Rock did, for instance. To be quite practical, we can witness to Christian ideals of unity and love by refusing to listen to defamatory remarks based on race or nation or religion; we can go out of our way to welcome people of different racial and national origins to our homes, parishes, social groups; we can employ men and women in our shops and offices without regard to racial or other prejudice; we can support Church and civic programs for better housing, fair employment, slum clearance, and so on.

A special opportunity is presented by the more than 50,000 international students from over two hundred countries of the world at present attending colleges and universities in the United States. Opening our homes to these young people, making friends, introducing them to American Catholic life can widen our horizons and build international understanding at a grass-roots level as well.

In this group working at home, I think of the millions of American Catholic families and their many organizations—the National Councils of Men and Women, the Retreat Movement, the Catholic Daughters, the Legion of Mary, the Catholic Family Movement, among others. In cross-country tours in the last few years I have spoken to thousands of American Catholics and I know their kindly responsiveness and warmth, and what they can accomplish if only they become more aware, more deeply involved in the problems which confront our world.

And finally, some of us belong overseas, in Asia this side of the bamboo curtain, in Africa, in Latin America, wherever we are needed to give our skills, our faith, ourselves. Effective service overseas requires preparation—serious study of the background, language, social structure and culture of the lands to which we go; understanding of the theology and methods of the apostolate; and that personal spiritual deepening which makes the work truly fruitful for the growth of Christ's Kingdom. Among the groups in the United States which offer training for the laity are: for women, the Grail Overseas Training Programs in Brooklyn, Grailville, and San Jose, California; and the International Catholic Auxiliaries in Chicago; for men and married couples, AID in New Jersey; for those wishing to work in Latin America, PAVLA, with an intercultural study center in Mexico.

It takes imagination as well as daring to realize the particular contribution the educated Catholic of today can make to the international work of the Church. Teachers, nurses, doctors, journalists, economists, engineers, artists, social workers, university professors, could take a leap into the unknown and be present in all levels and structures of the newly evolving societies of the young nations.

Take the field of communications, for example. How many strategic openings in this field are waiting for those who dare! Russian broadcasters are busy two-hundred and fifty-six hours a week sending their message to southeast Asia as against seventy-nine hours for the United States; in Africa, Russia broadcasts forty-two hours a week to the U.S.A.'s four hours. Why continue being a radio announcer using your hard-won professional skill to promote cornflakes or soft drinks, when your voice could be on the air-waves of Latin America, Asia, or Africa, speaking the Church's social teaching or exposing the Communist lie?

I have seen in Asia, in Africa, how a handful of trained people, acting in love, sharing the aspirations and struggles of the new nations, can have an influence all out of proportion to their numbers. The lay mission groups are ready with opportunities for training and placement. And we need not handfuls but boatloads to begin to meet the needs of our time.

There is still one other area I would like to point up: the Christian presence in the international structures which increasingly characterize our age, as governments and private agencies, secular and religious groups struggle to build a world community. Where are the Catholic intellectuals who should be present in the forefront of the dialogue at the United Nations, which is the sounding board of the peoples of the world? The Catholic in these international structures has a contribution of exceptional value to make to the building of a unified world. Can the dignity of man find a deeper, more genuine foundation than in our faith of common redemption and eternal destiny? Is there in the world a spiritual community comparable to the Christian community, which has such a truly human social doctrine adapted to the needs of the time, and capable in application of solving social and economic problems?

And where are the Catholics in other international organizations? The Holy Father has stressed the new duty of Catholics to be present, to collaborate, to penetrate international institutions with a Christian spirit. Catholics are not yet present in sufficient numbers at the international level, as civil servants, members of secretariats, governmental delegates, members of a mission of experts. Over and over again I have heard from people in ICA,* for example, that they are disappointed by the failure of Catholics to apply for international posts.

For Americans, the Peace Corps offers a special channel and challenge. The idea of using the force of youth as a force for peace has reached the hearts of millions across the world. "Magnificent," was the comment of the Vatican Radio when the program was announced. The American bishops have established a Peace Corps Desk at National Catholic Welfare Conference Headquarters in Washington, D.C., to facilitate the cooperation of Catholics in the projects.

For short term service, Operation Crossroads Africa, organized by the Director of Morningside Community Center in New York, has demonstrated a workable pattern. Since its beginnings in 1958, Operation Crossroads Africa has grown to a project of one-hundred eighty college students, who are chosen from seven hundred applicants and who pay an all-inclusive $900 for their summer in Africa. At Prampram, a fishing village on the Ghana coast, I saw a Crossroads project in action—fourteen Americans together with thirty Ghanaians to build a schoolhouse. They had

* International Cooperation Administration.

no modern amenities: they brought water by bucket from the village well, cooked their own meals, managed without electricity. But they had the satisfaction of doing a real job and building bonds of friendship in the doing.

And where are the Catholics ready to give competent service in the specifically Catholic international organizations, seeing the vast significance of their work? There is need for Catholic experts, especially in ethnology, demography, sociology and allied fields, to assist in surveying the vast social changes in the human family and to bring Christian values into social planning.

All along the line we need education for world community and vocational guidance with a world vision. Parents, teachers, priests can help by pointing out to young people the opportunities in international life, and by encouraging study and careers in the international sphere. If ever Catholics have had a chance to make an impact on the peoples of the world who cry out for brotherhood, then it is in our times.

Greater personal involvement in the world mission of the Church—this was the message of Cardinal Agagianian, head of Propagation of the Faith, when he visited the States in 1961. "Others may think of life in terms of color, or race, they may speak of backward countries and more advanced ones, of the civilized and the primitive, of Orient and Occident. For us these words have only superficial significance. . . . Though separated by miles of geography, by language and history and custom, though unknown to each other and without visible means of communication, every member of the Church is brother to every other and must bear realistically the responsibilities of this brotherhood."

Let us be realistic—we have come to a showdown in this second half of the twentieth century, everything must now be staked, on hatred, cowardice, or love.

I have tried to show what hatred in the heart of a man does to the human family; let us look at the other two possibilities, cowardice and love.

A coward is one who fears to risk himself, who saves his own skin in a dangerous situation. We all agree we are thrust into the dangerous situation, what about the choice? It is free. We can say either "yes" or "no." To remain inert, asleep in our safe Christian folds, ignoring the needs of our time, the letters of the Holy Father urging us to catch this moment in history in Asia, Africa and Latin America, to pull our weight in the struggle, is to say "no"—a "no" which could well boomerang on us, as history will continue to be made whether we influence it or not.

It was on the response of a woman that the whole of history hung, when Our Lady was asked to become the mother of the Redeemer. And her "yes" has continued through the centuries through the assents of other Christians, who have responded and become one in Christ's sacrifice to redeem the world of their time. But for us, now, what is needed is a thunderous response, a mighty "yes," not from one or two womanly hearts, but from hundreds of thousands who will pit themselves against the powers of hate by playing a brilliant game of love.

Index

This [illegible] ated by Stanley
Mor[illegible] signed for the
Lon[illegible] d be clear and
legib[illegible] r but not con-
dens[illegible] process, with
chara[illegible] he clear, open
chara[illegible] ar printing on
any [illegible] or the finest
coate[illegible] the Wicker-
sham [illegible] by Moore and
Comp[illegible] ard N. King.

266.2 46451
R 272

Reid, Elizabeth
I belong where I'm needed.

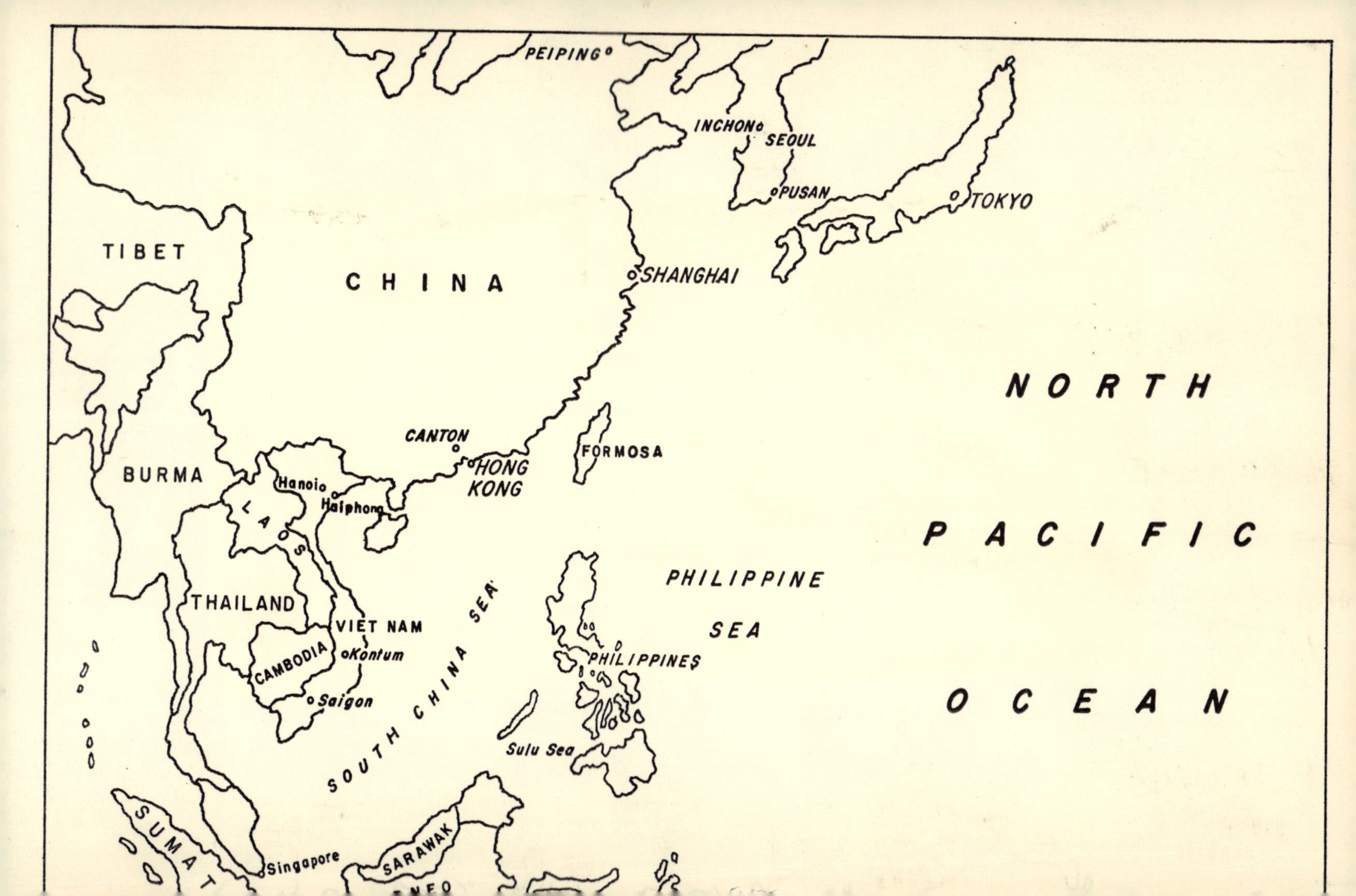
PEIPING
INCHON
SEOUL
PUSAN
TOKYO
TIBET
CHINA
SHANGHAI
NORTH PACIFIC OCEAN
CANTON
HONG KONG
FORMOSA
BURMA
Hanoi
Haiphong
LAOS
THAILAND
VIET NAM
Kontum
CAMBODIA
Saigon
SOUTH CHINA SEA
PHILIPPINE SEA
PHILIPPINES
Sulu Sea
SUMAT
Singapore
SARAWAK